INTERACTIVE FOR CROSS-CULTURAL PSYCHOLOGY

Interactive Exercises for Cross-Cultural Psychology provides material for interactive discussion of a range of topics in cross-cultural psychology, including regional and indigenous psychology; symbolic and expressive psychology; identity; social perception and cognition; interpersonal interaction; emotion, motivation, and health; development and family; government and law; economics and work; environmental psychology; animals and other species; and the psychology of recreation and sports. It will help students apply cultural psychology to social issues, and makes these issues relevant to students in health, forensic, organizational, sports and exercise, and other applied psychology fields. It offers suggestions for exposition, simulation, and confrontation of important cultural issues that matter to students, while allowing for maximum creativity in instructional design. Thoroughly and currently referenced, with connections to a wide range of accessible web-based and open-source materials, it is user-friendly across a spectrum of classroom and workshop applications, including online delivery.

DAVID C. DEVONIS is a veteran instructor of psychology across a wide range of areas, theoretical and applied. He is the author of the award-winning short history of psychology, *History of Psychology 101* (Springer Publishing Co., 2014).

INTERACTIVE EXERCISES FOR CROSS-CULTURAL PSYCHOLOGY

ENCOUNTERS WITH A COMPLEX WORLD

David C. Devonis

Routledge
Taylor & Francis Group

NEW YORK AND LONDON

First published 2018
by Routledge
711 Third Avenue, New York, NY 10017

and by Routledge
2 Park Square, Milton Park, Abingdon,
Oxon, OX14 4RN

*Routledge is an imprint of the Taylor & Francis Group,
an informa business*

Library of Congress Cataloging-in-Publication Data
A catalog record for this title has been requested

ISBN: 978-1-138-63284-4 (hbk)
ISBN: 978-1-138-63285-1 (pbk)
ISBN: 978-1-351-01371-0 (ebk)

Typeset in Minion Pro
by Apex CoVantage, LLC

CONTENTS

PHOTO CREDITS

Cover: "Food Pyramid" by Anne Simpkins. Reproduced by permission of the artist.

ACKNOWLEDGMENTS

This book would not have taken this form without the collective efforts of several Cross Cultural Psychology classes at Graceland University between 2015 and 2017. Their members believed in the project (and suspended belief when necessary), and suggested, piloted, and critiqued many of the VICIs and activities contained in it. Their names are listed here, giving the lie to those who claim that diversity is not our strength. In fact, it is not only our strength, but life itself.

PSYC 3370 Graceland University Spring 2015

Natalie Bender
Analyn Blake
Manuel Bompart
Kyle Brown
Joseph Canady
Clarence Counts
Julie Davis
Rony Diaz
Nikki Dilts
Chaddrick Ellis
Kristen Gilpatrick
Shane Grant
Brittany Gunn
Askia Harris
Hannah Henson

Shawn Hovlid
Jamall Hudson
Carols Jimenez Lopez
Roosevelt McNeil
Pinky Montalvo-Castillo
Katie Rincon
Diego Riverol
Natalia Robles
Savannah Ruby
SantaLucia, Chelsea
Mariah Santiago
Amber Sistoza
Colleen Smith
Emily Smith
Josiah Smith

Efrain Solis
Bre Suyeyoshi
Cody Thornton
Bryan Tidwell
Cordell Towers

Katelynn Tracy
Karrah Varner
Sean Walsh
Mallory Walters
Tyler Wise

PSYC 3370 Graceland University Spring 2016

Suzie Amador
Jeremy Barnes
Monique Barrera
Jessie Bennetts
Christa Caldwell
Nicholas Coca
Kody Crank
Shyanne DeVore
Melissa Dotson
Zachary Ferrara
Destiny Garcia
Katherine Gardner
Markel Garner
Antonio Godinez
Jacey Hanna
Megan Hartnett
Tyrell Hemingway
Dana Hosley
Gene Hurley
Cesar Meza-Prado
Gonzo Munoz
Alice Nelms

Jordan Newburg
Taylor O'Neal
Ethan Peacock
Galu Peapealalo
Sarah Peck
Ariel Pepe
Mike Pierre
Megan Poppa
Elizabeth Reynolds
Victoria Roberts
Christopher Robinson
Whitney Ronk
Zachary Salazar
Brandon Seward-Sherrod
Emily Sutt
Amber Takeda
Stanley Thomas
Mike Torres
Eli Wilson
Tyeesha Winston
Kate Ytell

PSYC 3370 Graceland University Spring 2017

Keishawna Bailey
Samantha Banner

Elana Beck
Deion Betts

Gabi Boling

Joy Bragg

Keone Coronado

Christacia Dawkins

Alexis Ebensberger

Hannah Farley

Breanna Fortune

Rayshawn Fuchs

Kaetlynn Gifford

Bre Griffin

Courtney Hackett

Becca Hoff

Zach Kraus

Shelby Leahy

Michael Lugo

Emily McLaughlin

Leon Medina

Paige Mitchell

Rachel Norling

Azra Pita

Hannah Reisinger

Shannon Reynolds

Devin Rose

Kiana Sai

Keslie Sickels

Megan Smith

Dylan Springer

Amanda Stephens

Zacary Stetzel

Paul Stewart

Deandre Thomas

Savannah Vinyard

Kyle West

Maddie White

Julia Wiedmier

Andrew Wintermote

John Zeiger

Thanks, also, to GU students Lucy Bergere for commentary on early drafts and Madeline Glodowski for indexing.

Introduction and User Guide

"We Must Maintain Our Core Values and Culture"

Before beginning to read this introduction, reflect on the phrase above and write down the precise place where and when you think that this motto was found hanging framed on a wall.

After doing that, turn the page.

If you guessed 'Costco in West Des Moines, Iowa in 2016' you would be exactly right, but you would also be right about hundreds of other corporations who have this phrase, or something similar, in their mission statements, corporate documents, or on their websites. When I first saw it in the Costco breakroom, out of the corner of my eye on the way to the restroom, it struck me as jarring and discordant. How could, I thought, a mega-retailer whose function is apparently (at least to me) delivering megadoses of consumer products to already bloated and sated Iowans represent *any* form of culture? (Not only to Iowans! Costco has warehouses in nine countries.)

My reaction was due to the persistence of my traditional perception of culture, in which what is 'cultured' connects with the accumulated intellectual products of humanity, best typified by 'high-cultural' productions such as opera, poetry, novels, and dance, and from which big-box retailers are excluded. Others, however, to whom I put this question about the motto's location suggest many other sources of organized culture: churches of all sorts, military or police organizations (the US Marine Corps got more than a few votes), and nonprofit organizations and schools were among the entities suggested.

This example reveals at once the ragged nature of the definition of culture. In 1952 the cultural anthropologists Ernest Kroeber and Clyde Kluckhohn identified over 150 different definitions (Kroeber & Kluckhohn, 1952). For present purposes, the basic defining feature of culture will be 'the communication of shared values and traditions'. This might well be the ultimate definition in Kroeber and Kluckhohn's survey since it is one of the last ones they mentioned, though I've chosen it because it was voted the best definition of those which my students, just setting out on the journey of a cross-cultural psychology course, provided at their first class meeting.

The source of this definition also reflects the spirit of development of this book, namely 'for students and by students'. It is intended for students of all ages and all levels of expertise who want to examine the relation of culture and psychology in all its diversity and complexity. Its premise is that this relationship will be best understood through discussion and questioning of the nature and multiple meanings of culturally significant ideas, objects, and practices. Students—in this case, typically aged college students from classes at a small, relatively diverse college in the US Midwest—have played a primary role in its development. Its hundred-odd subjects have been winnowed out of more than twice that number of suggested VICIs (Very Important Cultural Issues—VICIs for short) generated by students, and many of the interactive activities suggested here have emerged from short student presentations in classes.

The idea that cross-cultural psychology, more so perhaps than other areas of psychology, needs to be taught in an atmosphere of open discussion and speculation is not new. Indeed, this book is intended to update and expand the range of existing collections of interactive exercises, for instance the well-known Peace Corps training manual *Culture Matters* (Peace Corps, n.d.), the APA volume of *110 Exercises for Teaching Cross-Cultural Psychology* (Pedersen, 2004), and Susan Goldstein's *Cross-Cultural Explorations* (Goldstein, 2008). Some familiar subjects will be encountered (e.g., aging, back-translation) along with others that are rarely if ever found in any of the standard collections of interactive exercises (e.g., friendship, rights, police and law enforcement, loyalty, and sports, among others).

The core values of psychology represented in his book are, beyond openness to experience and reliance on evidence, a set of 'three F's' (well, at least they all *sound* like 'f') germane to cross-cultural study in psychology. These are: *familiarity* (becoming aware of the range and diversity of issues), *phenomenology* (focusing on the actual experiences and practices in various cultural settings), and *forgivingness* or tolerance of diverse points of view. No particular theoretical orientation is embodied or advanced. Rather, this set of topics and exercises should be understood as a framework in which any and all theoretical formulations may be brought to bear on the basic materials of sense and evidence.

THE CONTENTS

My interest in cross-cultural psychology stemmed first from experiences hosting international exchange students with my wife.

What had to that point been theoretical became actual, and I resolved to convey the positive nature of intercultural experience in my teaching. In my first attempts at teaching it, my classes and I would work through between 40 and 60 of the exercises in the aforementioned Goldstein book, doing as many of the activities interactively as possible. This proved to be an engaging method, though it became clear over time that no cultural text can be complete and that additions were always needed. After a five-year break from the course, I resumed teaching it three years ago and decided to start fresh by examining the places where the Goldstein interactive exercises needed expansion. I also resolved to look at the problem of teaching cultural psychology from the students' perspective, and to this end I began surveying classes to find out what they considered VICIs, and in three iterations of the course since 2015 they generated several raw lists of these. The students surveyed represent a sample of US college students, average age about 20, from a small Midwestern (Iowa, United States) school. Approximately 15 to 20 percent are from US African-American and Latinx cultures; about 5 to 10 percent from cultures outside the United States. From those lists we selected, by vote in each class, those that gathered the most interest, after which students developed interactive activities of our own based on them. The combined raw list of student VICIs voted most interesting from the past three years totaled 115 distinct topics: about a third of these were presented interactively in one or more classes. To this list of 115 I added a couple of dozen concepts from applied psychology in the areas of industrial/ organizational psychology, environmental psychology, sports psychology, and psychology and law. I also drew on the *Encyclopedia of Cross-cultural Psychology* and several textbooks and news sources to round out the list, which ultimately grew to more than 150 separate topics. This I distilled to the topics included here.

THE STRUCTURE OF THE ENTRIES

Each entry is an elaboration of the advice I would give to my students when they were planning to construct and carry out an interactive presentation.

It is a menu planner rather than a cookbook. While some structured activities are included, and in some instances (e.g., 'The Club') are the sole recommendation, for the most part each entry offers directions in which construction can proceed based on the inclinations and experience of the planners rather than specific 'can't miss' recipes (which usually have close to a 50 percent success rate, in my experience). This past summer I encountered, carved in granite along the Tampa Riverwalk, General George Patton's maxim for instruction: "Never tell people how to do things. Tell them what to do and they will surprise you with their ingenuity" (Patton, 1947, p. 357), which wholly reflects my attitude toward fostering creativity in instruction.

A SAMPLE ENTRY

Title ⟶

VEXILLOLOGY, THE SCIENCE OF FLAGS

Introduction ⟶

One snap definition of a country or culture might be 'having a flag'. The history of regions and territories can be seen in the progression of their multiple flags over time, for instance that of Texas, which in its comparatively short life as a region has been under six (at least). Flags are symbolically and metaphorically rich. They are memorials to territorial conquest and to ownership, both terrestrial, extra-terrestrial (Fincannon, 2012), and commercial. They are communicative devices for everything from weather danger to, in Tibetan Buddhist culture, prayer. They convey messages of national solidarity (Hanna, 2017) and also divisiveness. For example, the immediate replacement of the German national flag by the swastika banner overnight in 1933 was a symbol of menace and an alarm signaling the time to flee. Above all, for purposes of an introduction to cultural psychology and cultural studies focusing on the communication of values and traditions, flags express values in a graphic and often highly emotional form. Sometimes, flags are worth dying for (Marshall, 2017). Flags are omnipresent shorthand for all of the levels of culture represented in this book—not only nations, but also indigenous and ethnic groups (Donella, 2017), individual cities and towns, corporations, religions, and schools; social movements (e.g., the graphically effective Equality flag of the US Human Rights Campaign for LGBTQ rights) and even the North American Vexillogical Association (NAVA, n.d.) assemble under their respective banners.

Exposition,
Confrontation,
and Simulation

Exposition, Confrontation, and Simulation

Interactivity might be set up in the form of a contest to redesign an existing flag of a particular culture with known values. However, I've found it more interesting and entertaining to ask students to design a flag from scratch to represent the immediate culture of the class. This is an effective way of focusing the conversation, at the

outset, on shared or divergent values. The task of designing a flag is often delegated to amateurs (for instance, legislators) and often flags that become the official symbols of regions, especially cities and states, can be pretty frightful (or humorous) from a design perspective. Some existing flags have been termed 'hot messes' (Spicuzza, 2016) and some have been, due to the confusing nature of their design, inadvertently flown upside down for some time (Nohr, 2017). But if the products of amateurs are messy, they also reverberate with cultural pulses, and a banner—or in the case of courses I've taught, usually six banners at least—is a natural rallying point. Another possibility for interactivity might be to introduce some graphic style into what might clearly reflect the phrase 'designed by committee'. One suggestion for this would be to examine and imitate flags that effectively express cultural and historical traditions, for instance the Lebanese flag with its cedar, the Canadian maple leaf, or—my own favorite—the flag of Nunavut with its indigenous stele. A further variation can be, along with the cultural flag, to adopt or create a shared cultural song.

References and Suggested Readings ⟶

REFERENCES AND SUGGESTED READINGS

Donella, L. (2017, July 14). On Flag Day, remembering the Red, Black, and Green. *National Public*

Radio Code Switch (online broadcast transcript). Retrieved from www.npr.org/sections/codeswitch/2017/06/14/532667081/on-flag-day-remembering-the-red-black-and-green [Accessed October 14, 2017].

Fincannon, J. (2012). Six flags on the moon: What is their current condition? *Apollo Lunar Surface Journal* (US National Aeronautics and Space Administration) (online). Retrieved from www.hq.nasa.gov/alsj/ApolloFlags-Condition.html [Accessed October 14, 2017].

Hanna, B. (2017, August 18). After Charlottesville, only one flag flies over Six Flags theme park now. *Fort Worth Star-Telegram* (online newspaper). Retrieved from www.star-telegram.com/news/local/community/arlington/article167953237.html [Accessed October 14, 2017].

Marshall, T. (2017). *A flag worth dying for: The power and politics of national symbols.* New York: Scribner.

NAVA. (n.d.). North American vexillogical association website. (online). Retrieved from https://nava.org/ [Accessed October 14, 2017].

Nohr, E. (2017, January 31). Nebraska flag flew upside down at Capitol for 10 days and 'nobody noticed,' says senator who wants design change. *Omaha (NE) World-Herald* (online newspaper). Retrieved from www.omaha.com/news/legislature/nebraska-flag-flew-upside-down-at-capitol-for-days-and/article_1d3e0bf2-e6ff-11e6-a11e-6b5a251ccef1.html [Accessed October 14, 2017].

Spicuzza, M. (2016, May 11). Design contest hopes to improve city's 'hot mess' of a flag. *USA Today* (online newspaper). Retrieved from www.usatoday.com/story/news/local/milwaukee/2016/05/11/design-contest-hopes-to-improve-citys-hot-mess-of-a-flag/84983134/ [Accessed October 14, 2017].

Cross-references ⟶ Cross-references: Rights, Citizenship, and Voting; Language; Conscription and Volunteering; Corporate and Work Culture

The individual entries, of which this variation on a familiar theme is one (it is typically the first exercise for my cross-cultural class) are structured in the following way:

Title   ⟶

Introduction   ⟶

Exposition,   ⟶
Confrontation,
and Simulation

(1) **TITLE:** The title will usually be a single word. If the word is somewhat unfamiliar in the context of cross-cultural psychology, or if it reflects only an aspect of what is contained in the entry, then a brief explanatory phrase will follow it, as it does here. The word 'and' in the title indicates that the entry contains at least two separate but related areas of interest and interaction (e.g., Rights, Citizenship, and Voting). Entries with an 'and' will typically be at least twice as long as single-titled entries and will contain twice as many supporting references.

(2) **INTRODUCTION**: This section contains a definition and description of the topic area, along with its relation to both psychology and culture. References mentioned in this section will usually be to sources that treat the subject comprehensively.

(3) **Exposition, Confrontation, and Simulation**: This section follows each introduction and contains suggestions for ways that interactive exercises can be planned. There are many ways of

packaging and exploring the materials presented here. These may include (but are not limited to):

- taking inventories of current knowledge about the topic in the group or environment;
- constructing and conducting surveys (from scratch, or by borrowing ready-made survey instruments);
- completing existing psychometric tests that measure aspects of the topic;
- annotating and discussing articles about the topic;
- interaction around physical objects (graphics, artifacts, or specially constructed items, for instance a 'halo' worn to demonstrate variances in acceptable personal distance);
- TED talks and other short video or audio material that can augment a presentation;
- films and literature as applicable;
- simulations, dramatizations, and virtual reality;
- replication of parts of relevant research studies;
- and other strategies as applicable.

Interactions are envisioned as brief, but any of these suggestions may be extended ad lib to the taste of the group. Occasionally a specific activity is the focus of ECS (e.g., 'The Club') but this is typically not the case. Rather, there will be five or six suggestions such as I would provide to anyone planning an interactive instructional activity in each area. Some topics are more confrontational than others, as the titles and contents will show. I'm neither promoting nor denying confrontation as a method: when it occurs, and when it's controlled, it's among the best outcomes of the course.

References and Suggested Readings ⟶

(4) **References and Suggested Readings:** A set of entry-specific references follows the Introduction and ECS for each entry. These references have been chosen, for the most part, from the currently available material at the time of writing and are, as far as possible, based on reliable journalism or open-source scientific publications. Occasionally there are some references to books or articles that are available only through an academic or professional library or by subscription, but even without these, acceptable substitutes of similar material can usually be easily found, as long as internet access is available. As far as

Cross-references ⟶

> possible I've kept in mind especially the needs of online course designers and teachers, whose dependence on the web and open-source publications is heightened over that of those working in more traditional instructional settings. If I could find it in a blog, I included it.
>
> **(5) Cross-references**: This is a list of other entries that are related to or can be combined with the materials in the entry.

SUPPLEMENTARY MATERIALS AND METHODS OF USE

The topics here cover a generous portion of the cross-cultural literature and could be used by themselves to structure a comprehensive course. I often tell my classes to plan their interactive presentations as if they are going to be in a place without the internet and with only the most primitive means of illustrating a point (my expression for this is 'a stick in the sand'). But, like stone soup, this text will be even more useful if there is access to the internet and to sufficient library resources such that some or all of the following are in place, either as backup reference sources or required course materials:

1. **Encyclopedias and reference sources**: for example, the *Encyclopedia of Cross-cultural Psychology* (Keith, 2013). About half of the terms in this book are indexed in the ECCP.

2. **Textbooks**: likewise, depending on the ideas emphasized in a cross-cultural text, about half of the terms in this book will find fuller treatment in a text.

3. **Theoretical structuring**: Personally, I am less interested in theory than in observation and description. At introductory levels, I sense that theory may foreclose discussion as much as it structures and guides it. Nonetheless, I frequently refer to Geert Hofstede's 6-D Model (Hofstede, n.d.) here and in my classes, and I also utilize the venerable Peace Corps training manual mentioned earlier, *Culture Matters*. For suggestions on increasing the range of potential subjects of interest in cross-cultural psychology, examine *Culture Reexamined* (Cohen, 2014).

4. **Data sources:** for example, the *World Values Survey* and the *CIA World Factbook*.

5. **Media, news, and blogs** (a wide spectrum of which is reflected in the entries' references—but new sources are always coming online so be prepared for frequent updating here).

6. **Literature, art, and film.**

I've also found it useful to assemble a suite of simple integrative activities to use when starting the course before entering into a fully interactive series of presentations. Some of these can introduce students to aspects of the field (e.g., the Vexillology exercise earlier). Some can assist in showing how to set up simple interactive demonstrations. For instance, I've gotten good results by getting a box of old T-shirts and setting up a simulated assembly line with workers and managers for folding and shipping them as if they were membership premiums, varying 'managers' attitudes regarding time and power distance, and surveying perceptions of the activity afterward. Other possibilities for interactive activity can be often found in the news, and read and discussed to recognize the multiple dimensions of culture and psychology present: for example a relatively recent case in which a Muslim woman prevailed in the US Supreme Court against clothing retailers Abercrombie & Fitch, who denied her right to wear a headscarf at work (Liptak, 2015).

A note regarding online courses: at first glance it might seem that an interactive course in cross-cultural psychology would be a poor bet for online treatment. However, my experience leads me to think that, so long as students can utilize the various strategies available for peer interaction and critique that are embodied in well-structured online courses, the variety of net-accessible sources here should facilitate rather than impede discussion of the issues. I've even had good results one-on-one online with students using the Goldstein exercises and discussing them with me directly. The inherent interest of the material, I find, transcends the limitations of its means of transmission.

Having said something about what this book contains and about suggestions for its use, here would be a good spot to say some things about what it does not intend to do, and what is perhaps less prominent in it than in other cross-cultural texts. As mentioned earlier, it was designed to open up some new areas of interest in cross-cultural psychology across the psychology curriculum, especially in applied areas. It intends to provide maximum creative range and flexibility, and thus does not provide too many highly specific instructions for activity design. Regarding the scope of the contents, no student of cross-cultural psychology should expect that the cross-cultural course alone will provide everything that can be said about the subject. Everything in the world has a cultural aspect. It may support, but it will not and should not supplant courses in cultural anthropology, race and ethnicity, privilege, sociology of the family, international business, intercultural communication, cultural health and counseling psychology, women's studies, gender and queer studies, sexuality, political psychology, and immigration, a selection of which should also be in the serious culture student's transcript.

Some of the entries are envisioned as fulcrums for further exploration of related VICIs that are not specifically named in the entries' titles. For instance, military culture, absolutely a world unto itself, can be reached via interactions with law enforcement or physical toughness. Similarly, I've alluded to the 'two cultures' gulf between science and literature in the High and Low Culture entry. (Possibly any discussion generated there could also be extended to cover science vs. antiscience, a component of current cultural wars.) Likewise, the cultural importance of education and literacy, the effect of the lack of which is impossible to convey by simulation, can be approached indirectly. A good recent example of this occurs in a Pakistani context, where the English language is valued so much as an elite accomplishment that it is taught even though its teachers often cannot speak it (Naviwala, 2017).

Some topics receive less coverage here than possibly they deserve, given their central relation to culture. Less is said here about mental health and psychopathology than in typical textbook treatments of cultural psychological issues. One reason for this is, frankly, personal resistance to the collapsing of psychology into psychiatry and the casting of psychology as primarily a health-care profession. Another is that discussions of psychopathology in cross-cultural psychology tend to emphasize differences between cultures' particular expressions of psychological distress, focusing on 'culture specific syndromes' and masking the universality of mental illness in its most virulent forms (e.g., Nock et al., 2008). Another large area that I specifically excluded is substance abuse. Alcohol and drugs of abuse may be—after earth, wind, water, and fire—the fifth element, and they are always an attractant for classroom discussion. Students in a recent class enacted one particularly effective demonstration of the relation between integrity and alcohol abuse. They showed, graphically in a simple skit, that alcohol use increases the likelihood of acts that impair individual moral decision-making and also promotes behavior that damages society and culture as a whole (i.e., increasing the potential for petty theft and assault). Beyond this suggestion, however, I can't offer any other good simulations of drug abuse, of psychopathology, or of antisocial and criminal behavior generally. Self-expression via the body is only partially addressed here in connection with fashion and dance: tattooing and cross-cultural/cross-ethnic concepts of attractiveness come naturally to mind and are likely to arise spontaneously as interactive discussion topics (good cultural narratives come up repeatedly in connection with tattoos). Body shaming and other forms of prejudice are also difficult to simulate: given liberty, students have proved effective in devising illustrations. Skillful excerpting from and discussion of accounts of discrimination can be an alternate route to examination of this and other forms of prejudice, for instance Gabrielle Deydier's memoir of her experience of being fat in France (Rubin, 2017). Art and music—though they get brief nods, and literature gets a little more—are underrepresented here, as they are in other textbooks of psychology, not because they are of peripheral importance but because, here as elsewhere, exposition and simulation are best left to the professional educators in those areas. Recommended reading in cultural aspects of the arts might include Walter Benjamin and other similar critics (Ross, 2014) for 20th century historical cultural context, and Anthony Heilbut (2013) for the current context. Pop culture, media culture, and the cultures of celebrity and fame are not specifically addressed. Currently in the United States, we gleefully or ruefully survey the extent to which reality show hosts have their fingers near nuclear triggers. This bears mentioning but beggars exposition, confrontation, or simulation. Sometimes simply pointing to reality and saying 'look there' is enough for a cultural lesson.

I hope to have provided ample material for constructing new thoughts and thoughtful cultural lessons. In light of the apparent impossibility of assimilating all culture, might I remind the users of this text, and myself, that the attempt is valuable and the returns, though incomplete and imperfect, are great. For those like myself, American citizens, mainly monolingual and of multiple European ancestry, I can only say, with Emily Dickinson, that regarding culture

> I never saw a moor,
> I never saw the sea;
> Yet know I now the heather looks,
> And what a wave must be.

> I never spoke with God,
> Nor visited in heaven;
> Yet certain am I of the spot
> As if the chart were given.

REFERENCES AND SUGGESTED READINGS

Cohen, A. (Ed.) (2014). *Culture reexamined: Broadening our understanding of social and evolutionary influences.* Washington, DC: American Psychological Association.

Goldstein, S. (2008). *Cross-cultural explorations: Activities in culture and psychology.* Boston, MA: Allyn & Bacon.

Heilbut, A. (2013). *The fan who knew too much: The secret closets of American culture.* Berkeley, CA: Soft Skull Press.

Hofstede, G. (n.d.). *The 6-D model of national culture. Geert Hofstede (official website)* (online). Retrieved from http://geerthofstede.com/culture-geert-hofstede-gert-jan-hofstede/6d-model-of-national-culture/ [Accessed October 21, 2017].

Keith, K. (Ed.) (2013). *The encyclopedia of cross-cultural psychology* (3 vols.). New York: Wiley-Blackwell.

Kroeber, A., & Kluckhohn, C. (1952). *Culture: A critical review of concepts and definitions.* Chicago, IL: University of Chicago Press.

Liptak, A. (2015, June 1). Muslim woman denied job over head scarf wins in Supreme Court. *The New York Times.* Accessed March 4, 2018 at https://www.nytimes.com/2015/06/02/us/supreme-court-rules-in-samantha-elauf-abercrombie-fitch-case.html

Naviwala, N. (2017, October 18). What's really keeping Pakistan's children out of school? *The New York Times* (online newspaper). Retrieved from www.nytimes.com/2017/10/18/opinion/pakistan-education-schools.html [Accessed October 21, 2017].

Nock, M. K., Borges, G., Bromet, E. J., Alonson, J., Angermeyer, M., Beautrais, A., Bruffaerts, R., . . . Williams, D. R. (2008). Cross-national prevalence and risk factors for suicidal ideation, plans, and attempts. *British Journal of Psychiatry, 192,* 98–105.

Patton Jr., G. S. (1947). *War as I knew it.* Boston, MA: Houghton Mifflin Company.

Peace Corps. (n.d.). *Culture matters: The peace corps cross-cultural workbook.* Washington, DC: US Government Printing Office (online). Retrieved from http://files.peacecorps.gov/multimedia/pdf/library/T0087_culturematters.pdf [Accessed November 4, 2017].

Pedersen, P. B. (2004). *110 experiences for multicultural learning.* Washington, DC: American Psychological Association.

Ross, A. (2014, September 15). The naysayers: Walter Benjamin, Theodor Adorno, and the critique of pop culture. *The New Yorker* (online magazine). Retrieved from www.newyorker.com/magazine/2014/09/15/naysayers [Accessed October 16, 2017].

Rubin, A. J. (2017, October 21). Memoir of growing up fat forces France to look in the mirror. *The New York Times* (online newspaper). Retrieved from www.nytimes.com/2017/10/21/world/europe/gabrielle-deydier-france-obesity-on-ne-nait-pas-grosse.html [Accessed October 21, 2017].

Regional

BOUNDARIES AND MAPS

Immigration and the desire for refuge depend on boundaries: the concept of boundaries also has interpersonal, intergenerational, and social connotations as well. Boundaries are sites for playing out the dynamics of cultural exchange and cultural friction. An example of only a small sliver of the territory covered by psychological studies investigating boundaries is the literature on sexual behavior. Recent psychological literature records dozens of articles dealing with sexual and gender boundaries, for example between individuals in consensual sexual communities (Holt, 2016), between clients and therapist in contested sexual territory with the added complication of social media thrown in (Brown, 2011), and between gender-nonconformists and religious communities (Kashubeck-West, Whiteley, Vossenkemper, Robinson, & Deitz, 2017). In the United States, the arbitrary drawing of boundaries in election districts results in sharpened contrasts between antithetical political subcultures and leads to differential participation in elections by specific cultural groups (Amos, Smith, & Ste. Claire, 2017). This pattern of psychic exclusion of groups by the erection of socially policed symbolic boundaries is a feature of contested cultural spaces internationally as well. A recent study in Israel (Guetzkow, 2016) contrasts the immigrant-specific prejudices and attitudes that are directed against immigrant Ethiopian Jews with the entrenched, chronic discriminatory behaviors contributing to the perception on the part of Arab Palestinians that it is hopeless to expect changes in their status relative to the dominant culture.

Exposition, Confrontation, and Simulation

Boundary concepts can be integrated with discussions of immigration, sexuality, or any other area where ingroup and outgroup are foregrounded. Following on Guetzkow's 2016 work cited earlier, an inventory might be constructed of the symbolic ways in which individuals are made to feel unwelcome in their immediate environment. Preliminary exploration might be directed in more objective ways toward an examination of the geography of boundaries and the physical constructions that establish and maintain them. Cartographic exploration can be a starting point: London-based cartographic connoisseur Frank Jacobs's blog contributions to *BigThink* are provocative (e.g., Jacobs, 2017) and suggest ways to conceptually examine the physical status of cultural differences. Programs exist to draw maps and one might be employed to chart, for instance, the fluid boundaries of local social groups. An excellent set of basic exercises in understanding boundaries at the physical level is the *New York Times*'s set of simple lesson plans for geography (Marshall & Gonchar, 2012). Students with a biological or neuropsychological sensibility may want to examine in detail both the blood-brain barrier and the immune system.

REFERENCES AND SUGGESTED READINGS

Amos, B., Smith, D. A., & Ste. Claire, C. (2017). Reprecincting and voting behavior. *Political Behavior, 39*(1), 133–156.

Brown, L. (2011). Everyone I know knows everyone I know: Boundary overlap in the life of one lesbian psychotherapist. In W. B. Johnson & J. P. Koocher (Eds.), *Ethical conundrums, quandaries, and predicaments in mental health practice: A casebook from the files of experts* (pp. 17–23). New York: Oxford University Press.

Guetzkow, J. (2016). How symbolic boundaries shape the experience of social exclusion: A case comparison of Arab Palestinian citizens and Ethiopian Jews in Israel. *American Behavioral Scientist, 60*(2), 150–171.

Holt, K. (2016). Blacklisted: Boundaries, violations, and retaliatory behavior in the BDSM community. *Deviant Behavior, 37*(8), 917–930.

Jacobs, F. (2017, May 31). *The world's data holes, quantified: BigThink* (Online blog resource) (online). Retrieved from http://bigthink.com/strange-maps/the-worlds-data-holes-quantified [Accessed July 20, 2017].

Kashubeck-West, S., Whiteley, A. M., Vossenkemper, T., Robinson, C., & Deitz, C. (2017). In K. A. DeBord, A. R. Fischer, Bieschke, K. J., & Perez, R. M. (Eds.), Conflicting identities: sexual minority, transgender, and gender nonconforming individuals navigating between religion and gender-sexual orientation identity. In *Handbook of sexual orientation and gender diversity in counseling and psychotherapy* (pp. 213–238). Washington, DC: American Psychological Association.

Marshall, T., & Gonchar, M. (2012, December 4). All over the map: 10 ways to teach about geography. *The Learning Network: Teaching and Learning with the New York Times.* Blog in *The New York Times* (Online resource). Retrieved from https://learning.blogs. nytimes.com/2012/12/04/all-over-the-map-10-ways-to-teach-about-geography/ [Accessed July 20, 2017].

Cross-references: Immigration and Refugees; Sexuality

IMMIGRATION AND REFUGEES

At its roots, migration is a biological phenomenon: the movement of populations of living beings, from birds to fish to plants, is ubiquitous in nature. Animal migrations are usually cyclic and often based on seasonal changes: hummingbirds return and leave on schedule every year. However, colonization occurs across all species as well (Onofri, 2008). Migration accompanied by conquest and colonization set the pattern worldwide for the current arrangement of nation states. Viewed from a current vantage point in a mostly post-colonial world, the distinction between 'immigrant' and 'refugee' is not that large. Both groups cross borders and can be ranged on a sliding scale of freedom of choice of their status. Immigrants are relatively voluntary refugees; refugees are involuntary or coerced immigrants. The political and social forces that impel movements of people to seek other places either for increased opportunity or for safe refuge are essentially the same throughout history: relatively rarely is the immigrant or refugee journey taken as a caprice. Science and psychology have some famous refugees in their history: both Albert Einstein's and Sigmund Freud's flights, like thousands of others' during the 1930s, were contingent on their imminent execution had they stayed in Hitler's Europe. Persons of wealth and influence protected Einstein and Freud, as did their own perceived value to the cultures to which they migrated. Often, however, both the refugee and the immigrant alike are relatively powerless and poor. Their journeys are often perilous and deadly. Established groups within nations and cultures resist, sometimes violently, those who they perceive as foreign or as enemies: the willingness of individuals to risk their lives to emigrate, as many from Africa do today in trying to reach Europe, is a testament to courage. Those immigrants and refugees who do succeed in their new cultures often have a history of victimization and trauma that is hard to share publicly. The American Psychological Association acknowledges the severe psychological consequences to refugees, which now number more than 60 million worldwide, and it has developed an extensive network of resources for psychological professionals concerned with immigrants and refugees (APA, 2017).

Exposition, Confrontation, and Simulation

At the very least the subject of immigration and refugees can and should prompt consideration of the virtue of courage, which is often hidden in psychological discourse but which is central to the preservation of culture (Lear, 2008). Some insight into the situation of forced emigration can be gained from participation in one of several dramatizations of the scenario entitled 'Five Minutes to Pack,' which simulates the actual conditions under which many otherwise established persons suddenly become refugees. These simulations are part of many educational programs designed for preadolescents (and thus very accessible and easy to demonstrate) available on the web for learning about refugees (e.g., PBS, 2011; Pessoa, 2016). The basic premise is that there are five minutes to pack and, either from a prearranged list or from memory, bags or suitcases are stuffed with things that are perceived to be important. This exercise can differ in its suddenness: compare a rationally composed list of necessaries and one that is assembled on the spot and under duress. Voluntary immigration can be explored by visiting the websites of various countries' immigration services. Working through all aspects of an application for naturalization will be instructive and depressing at the same time (for instance, when discovering the length of residence necessary to be considered as a permanent resident or naturalized citizen). Note that, for instance, becoming a Japanese citizen by naturalization would involve being able to read and write Japanese at the level of an 8-year-old schoolchild, proving an income and tax payments, and also renouncing any other citizenships. How likely is it that a US citizen will comply with the latter? A challenging exercise would be to discover the reasons why the relative handful of US citizens renounce their citizenship yearly (Wood, 2017).

Pragmatic approaches to the successful cultural integration of immigrants and refugees might start with readings drawn from psychologists who empathize with this area of experience, for instance Mary Pipher's book—now out of print but widely available in libraries and used—*The Middle of Everywhere: Helping Refugees Enter the American Community*

(Pipher, 2003). This reading would be particularly instructive since its narrative centers around the refugee experience in the United States in a time when borders and public attitudes were more open a generation ago. Reading should extend to stories by and about acculturative experiences (e.g., Nguyen, 2017); find and listen to the podcasts of Maeve Higgins (2017). Finally, seek out contrasting news stories of successful accomplishment of immigration or refuge. For example, just at the time of composing this set of recommendations, the following two accounts were published. The first describes an Egyptian man, Hatem el-Gamasy, who delivers a well-respected TV commentary on US politics for Egyptian TV out of the back room of the New York bodega and sandwich shop he's managed for more than 15 years. In America, he says, "the sky's the limit!" (Nir, 2017). The second is the story of Sudanese women, possessionless refugees arriving in Uganda (the country that in 2017 receives the most refugees in the world), reassembling their homes with their own hands on grants of bush land (Alexander, 2017).

REFERENCES AND SUGGESTED READINGS

Alexander, R. (2017, September 15). Starting from scratch in Uganda. *BBC News Magazine* (online). Retrieved from www.bbc.com/news/magazine-41255233 [Accessed September 16, 2017].

APA. (2017, July–August). APA's refugee mental health resource network. *APA Monitor* (online magazine). Retrieved from www.apa.org/monitor/2017/07-08/sanctuary-sidebar.aspx [Accessed September 16, 2017].

Higgins, M. (2017, Ongoing). *Maeve in America* (online podcast). Retrieved from www.maeveinamerica.com/ [Accessed September 3, 2017].

Lear, J. (2008). *Radical hope: Ethics in the face of cultural devastation.* Cambridge, MA: Harvard University Press.

Nguyen, V. T. (2017). *The refugees.* New York: Grove Press.

Nir, S. M. (2017, September 16). Hold the egg sandwich: Egyptian TV is calling. *The New York Times Magazine* (online). Retrieved from www.nytimes.com/2017/09/16/nyregion/hatem-el-gamasy-bodega-television-egypt-pundit.html?mcubz=3&_r=0 [Accessed September 16, 2017].

Onofri, S. (2008). Colonization (Biological). In M. Gargaud et al. (Eds.), *Encyclopedia of astrobiology* (pp. 326–328). Berlin (DE): Springer.

PBS. (2011, June 24). Virtual education: Learning about refugees. *PBS NewsHour Extra* (online news source). Retrieved from www.pbs.org/newshour/extra/daily_videos/virtual-education-learning-about-refugees/ [Accessed September 16, 2017].

Pessoa, C. (2016, March 28). Talking to your kids about the refugee crisis: 8 activities for families. *Redefining Welcome* (a blog by Linda Hartke): *LIRS (Lutheran Immigration and Refugee Service) website* (online). Retrieved from http://blog.lirs.org/talking-to-your-kids-about-the-refugee-crisis-8-activities-for-families/ [Accessed September 16, 2017].

Pipher, M. (2003). *The middle of everywhere: Helping refugees enter the American community.* New York: Mariner Books.

Wood, R. W. (2017, June 12). More Americans renounce citizenship: New list released. *Forbes* (online magazine). Retrieved from www.forbes.com/sites/robertwood/2017/06/12/more-americans-renounce-citizenship-new-list-released/#76a1654c6fe9 [Accessed September 16, 2017].

Cross-references: Rights, Citizenship, and Voting; Forms of Government; Boundaries and Maps

REGIONAL AND INDIGENOUS PSYCHOLOGY

Briefly put, 'regional' delimits a geographic area; 'indigenous' refers to the native people of that area and also to the conceptual framework of culture developed by those people (Pickren, 2015). Each of these terms, *regional psychology* and *indigenous psychology*, can be a subject of study in its own right. A recent essay in the APA volume *Culture Reexamined* (Vandello, Hettinger, & Michniewicz, 2014) presents regional psychology as a specific and independent area of cross-cultural study. Indigenous psychology likewise has a separate presence in cross-cultural psychological research. But rather than two separate and autonomous areas, there is instead a spectrum of mixtures of the two. At one extreme there is pure regionality, that is, regions entirely void of peoples or cultures. Its very farthest extreme would be the moon or the planets, or on earth, Antarctica. Next, on the terrestrial globe, are places (regions) where indigenous tribes or groups have lived for many centuries. These places are of very high interest for anthropologists especially since there are now comparatively few of them due to the displacements contingent on expanding megacultures. Examples could be the grazing range of the reindeer of Lapps, the Himalayan regions populated by Tibetan natives, the remote regions where some Native American tribal groups in Canada and the Americas live, and the rainforests and plains of Amazonian and African hunter-gatherer cultures. Even these, however, are hardly untouched by global expansion and technological change. Except for those that are farthest remote, most of the original indigenous cultures of most global regions survive as remnants outside of their historic ones, within regions which have taken on the primary cultural characteristics of their colonizers or settlers. 'Indigenous' may sometimes be equated with 'static' or 'unchanging,' and some indigenous cultures are so. But as Pickren (2015) notes, indigenization appears to be an ongoing, evolutionary process in which cultures that were formerly native to a region or area are infused with the practices and ideas of newcomers. As the boundaries of the world shrink, the pressure to create new hybridizations of culture grows. Little has been said here about specific psychological beliefs of indigenous groups: in the United States, psychology as a field has recognized that all cultures have evolved particular sets of ideas and attitudes about human behavior and the mind, such that all psychologies are in a real sense indigenous (Marsella, 2013). Recently there have been attempts to collect these: an example is the *Handbook of Arab American Psychology* (Amer & Awad, 2016).

Exposition, Confrontation, and Simulation

As can be seen from the preceding short sketch, it can be difficult to tell when a culture is indigenous, and preexisting templates do not capture the fluidity of cultural interchange and adaptation. The United States is a good example of the kind of patchwork of indigenousness and ongoing indigenizations that occur within geographically distinct regions. Perhaps a good starting point would be to contrast the range, scope, and focus of the organizational presentations of a conceptually regional group, for example the Center for the Study of Southern Culture based at the University of Mississippi (CSSC, 2017) and a group that emphasizes its specific indigenousness, for instance Indigenous Iowa (II, 2017). Indigenous identity is maintained in the face of ongoing incursions from surrounding or intruding cultures by demands for recognition, equality, and—sometimes—apologies or restitution. One example of this is the recent apology and request for forgiveness addressed by Amish groups living in Ohio to the descendants of Native American groups in the region for the way that their ancestors deprived the tribes of land (Brubaker, 2016). This is remarkable in the context of regionality and indigenousness, as the Amish themselves can be taken as representative of a kind of indigenousness transplanted whole and maintained intact in a new region. An exercise that might prove very useful in revealing the many interwoven strands of regionality and indigenousness could be to sketch out how many apologies might be delivered in such a meeting of groups in any region of a previously colonized area. A bonus would be if such an activity were, after such a plan were made, carried out.

REFERENCES AND SUGGESTED READINGS

Amer, M. M., & Awad, G. H. (Eds.) (2016). *Handbook of Arab American psychology*. New York: Routledge.

Brubaker, J. (2016, August 1). The Scribbler: Amish ask for forgiveness from Native Americans. *Lancaster Online* (online newspaper). Retrieved from http://lancasteronline.com/opinion/the_scribbler/the-scribbler-amish-ask-for-forgiveness-from-native-americans/article_4c4f8b02-54d1-11e6-a2ef-7b51a8d22c78.html [Accessed September 1, 2017].

CSSC. (2017). *Center for the study of Southern culture: University of Mississippi* (organizational website). Retrieved from http://southernstudies.olemiss.edu/ [Accessed September 2, 2017].

II. (2017). *Indigenous Iowa* (organizational website). Retrieved from www.indigenousiowa.org/ [Accessed September 1, 2017].

Marsella, A. (2013). All psychologies are indigenous psychologies: Reflections on psychology in a global era. *Psychology International* (online magazine, American Psychological Association Division 52). Retrieved from www.apa.org/international/pi/2013/12/reflections.aspx [Accessed September 1, 2017].

Pickren, W. (2015). Indigenization. In K. Keith (Ed.), *The encyclopedia of cross-cultural psychology* (pp. 698–699). New York: Wiley-Blackwell.

Vandello, J. A., Hettinger, V. E., & Michniewicz, K. (2014). Regional culture. In A. Cohen (Ed.), *Culture reexamined: Broadening our understanding of social and evolutionary influences*. Washington, DC: American Psychological Association.

Cross-references: Immigration and Refugees; Boundaries and Maps

Symbolic and Expressive Culture

CULTURAL APPROPRIATION

Cultural appropriation is currently construed either as a violation of property law and rights (Baker, 2012; Nittle, 2017) or a form of oppression by a dominant group (Johnson, 2015). Typical quick-and-dirty examples of appropriation, not watertight by any means, are the name of the Cleveland (Ohio, United States) baseball franchise (the 'Indians'), the common Anglo practice of picking up a sombrero as a souvenir of a trip to Mexico, or a faux-geisha or faux-African costume worn by a popular US singer. Sometimes it is difficult to trace the true source of appropriation: the sombrero brought back from Mexico by a US tourist was likely to have been manufactured, along with appropriated symbols of other cultures large and small, in China (Holcombe, 2016). Searching the subject heading of 'cultural appropriation' in the psychological research literature uncovers a quite substantial amount of research consideration of the topic, ranging from consideration of appropriation as a means of developing cultural diversity via music (e.g., Schneider & Sippola, 2017) to description of the long-term harmful psychological effects of colonization (e.g., BigFoot & England-Aytes, 2016).

Exposition, Confrontation, and Simulation

Discussion could start by consideration of all the points raised by Johnson (2015) and others about instances of cultural appropriation: an inventory of experiences, by both appropriators and their exploitees, would be appropriate. The subject lends itself well to case studies. For example, recently (July 2017) in Des Moines, Iowa, a local restaurateur wished to open an Asian-fusion restaurant incorporating Vietnamese and other Asian cuisines in a casual, friendly setting. The name suggested for this enterprise was 'Me So Hungry.' This is a play on words based on a phrase used in *Full Metal Jacket*, a 1987 film about American soldiers in the Vietnam war. Actually, in this case, it was a play on words from a rap song (and on stereotyped accents) from the 1990s by the group 2 Live Crew which was based on the same movie scene. It caused enough automatically negative reactions that plans for using this name were quickly squelched. I would recommend looking up the event and re-creating it for discussion (see e.g., Brennan, 2017; McGowan, 2017). Another instance that could be converted to a case study would be the continuing history of the King Biscuit Blues Festival in Helena, Arkansas: Scafidi (2005) provides the backstory up until 2005. The Delta itself is a good place to start for examination of the unstable equilibrium of cultures within the United States.

REFERENCES AND SUGGESTED READINGS

Baker, K. J. M. (2012, November 13). A much-needed primer on cultural appropriation. *Jezebel* (Web magazine). Retrieved from https://jezebel.com/5959698/a-much-needed-primer-on-cultural-appropriation [Accessed August 6, 2017].

BigFoot, D. S., & England-Aytes, P. J. (2016). Application: Cultural trauma in American Indian populations. In R. W. Summers (Ed.), *Social psychology: How other people influence our thoughts and actions*. Santa Barbara, CA: ABC-CLIO/Greenwood.

Brennan, P. (2017, July 19). West Des Moines café drops its racist-sounding name after online pushback. *Little Village/Iowa City-Cedar Rapids* (online magazine). Retrieved from http://littlevillagemag.com/me-so-hungry/ [Accessed August 6, 2017].

Holcombe, C. (2016, October 24). Balancing cultural appropriation with good business: The fine line between a fashion statement and political correctness. *South China Morning Post* (online newspaper). Retrieved from www.scmp.com/business/article/2039486/balancing-cultural-appropriation-good-business [Accessed August 6, 2017].

Johnson, M. Z. (2015, June 14). What's wrong with cultural appropriation? These 9 answers reveal its harm. *Everyday Feminism* (online magazine). Retrieved from http://everydayfeminism.com/2015/06/cultural-appropriation-wrong/ [Accessed August 6, 2017].

McGowan, K. (2017, July 19). Me so hungry to change name after online backlash. *Des Moines Register* (online newspaper). Retrieved from www.desmoinesregister.com/story/news/2017/07/19/dong-post-calls-me-so-hungry-name-tasteless/489953001/ [Accessed August 6, 2017].

Nittle, N. K. (2017). What is cultural appropriation and why is it wrong? *ThoughtCo.* (Web magazine). Retrieved from www.thoughtco.com/cultural-appropriation-and-why-iits-wrong-2834561 [Accessed August 6, 2017].

Scafidi, S. (2005). *Who owns culture appropriation and authenticity in American law*. New Brunswick, NJ: Rutgers University Press.

Schneider, B., & Sippola, E. (2017). Introduction: Language ideologies in music. *Language and Communication, 52*, 1–6.

Cross-references: Regional and Indigenous Psychology; Cannibalism and Culture Jams (Enemy Images); Dance

DANCE

Dance has been a focus of interest in varied ways in psychology since the early beginnings of the field. Kate Gordon (later Kate Gordon Moore, 1878–1963), preeminent in the establishment of principles of gender equity in the field (Young, 2010), viewed dance in an evolutionary context, as an elaboration of movements involved in fighting and other forms of social interaction (Gordon, 1908). In the 1950s, Marian Chace and others began to engage with patients in mental institutions through dance (Chace, 1953) and grounded what is now dance therapy. Within the last 10 years dance has been linked to the basic perceptual systems underlying language and also to social entrainment, the ability to form social bonds through imitative motion (Singer, 2017). Also in that time, dance has emerged as a factor in developing identity, individual and cultural. Hill, Sandford, and Enright (2016) challenge standard body images in the context of established ballet forms. Lee's dissertation (2015), which traces the development of queer Asianness in artistic opposition to mainstream Canadian culture, is particularly interesting for its examination of the many layers of cross-cutting identities in play in a world in which comfortable established cultural stereotypes are dissolving.

Exposition, Confrontation, and Simulation

One way of entering the subject theoretically could be to pursue the many metaphorical uses of the term 'dance,' for example in the title of Gary Zukav's now quite old but recently reprinted book *The Dancing Wu Li Masters* (Zukav, 1979/2009), which trades on Zukav's interpretation via tai chi of the Chinese term for physics (*WuLi*) as 'patterns of organic energy.' Building on this, a more directly interactive engagement with the subject could involve various forms of movement-based meditative activity, tai chi and yoga for instance, contingent on the availability of local practitioners and experts. Further, there are nearly infinite possibilities for individual, partnered, and group dance across multiple cultures, and many internet sites and instructional videos for the same. Ideally the result would be an entire classroom engaging in organized (or disorganized) dance. Caution should be exercised with the *Hopak* (dial this up on YouTube). Speculative experimentation might be carried out to determine whether, for example, people otherwise randomly assorted into groups might feel better both about themselves and the group after dancing.

REFERENCES AND SUGGESTED READINGS

Chace, M. (1953). Dance as an adjunctive therapy with hospitalized mental patients. *Bulletin of the Menninger Clinic, 17,* 219–225.

Gordon, K. (1908). Pragmatism in aesthetics. In E. L. Thorndike (Ed.), *Essays philosophical and psychological in honor of William James by his colleagues at Columbia University.* New York: Longmans, Green. Available online at A Mead Project (Brock University, Canada). Retrieved from https://brocku.ca/MeadProject/sup/Gordon_1908.html [Accessed July 21, 2017].

Hill, J., Sandford, R., & Enright, E. (2016). 'It has really amazed me what my body can now do': Boundary work and the construction of a body-positive dance community. *Sport in Society, 19*(5), 667–679.

Lee, A. W. L. (2015). *Performing ManChyna: Unmapping promissory exaltation, multicultural eugenics, and the new whiteness (or, 'call me Dr. ManChyna').* PhD Dissertation, Queen's University (Canada) (online). Retrieved from https://qspace.library.queensu.ca/bitstream/handle/1974/13741/Lee_Andrew_W_201509_PhD.pdf?sequence=1&isAllowed=y [Accessed July 21, 2017].

Lee, E. (2013, June 24). Asian Americans break stereotypes through urban dance. *Voice of America News* (online resource). Retrieved from www.voanews.com/a/asian-american-break-steriotypes-through-urban-dance/1687837.html [Accessed July 21, 2017].

Singer, T. (2017). Does dancing just feel good, or did it help early humans survive? *Scientific American, 317*(1), 67–71.

Young, J. L. (2010). Profile of Kate Gordon Moore. In A. Rutherford (Eds.), *Psychology's feminist voices multimedia internet archive* (online resource). Retrieved from www.feministvoices.com/kate-gordon-moore/ [Accessed July 21, 2017].

Zukav, G. (1979/2009). *The dancing Wu Li masters: An overview of the new physics.* New York: HarperOne.

Cross-references: Food and Art; High and Low Culture; Language and Accents

FASHION AND DRESS

Clothing is one of the most immediate and tangible ways to encounter culture. Behind couture fashion, a huge international economic driver which sometimes descends into cultural appropriation, lie the multiple significances of dress. Dress is an indicator of economic position and social status; it serves as a cultural advertisement, signal, or flag; it commands authority; it is integral to ritual; it is specialized for occupations, sports, and leisure. Both anthropology (Dudley, 2011) and psychology (Pine, 2014) offer multiple contemporary perspectives on dress and the ways in which it interacts with human behavior. There are also numerous recent cross-cultural studies and episodes specifically connected to aspects of fashion. For instance, Natascha Radclyffe-Thomas, teaching in the London College of Fashion at the University of Arts in London (UK), observes that students from diverse cultures are attracted to the centers of creative fashion production located in major world cities, yet find their particular cultural forms of creativity marginalized there (Radclyffe-Thomas, 2015). And some African countries, in order to develop their home clothing industries and support indigenous designers, have proposed bans on importing secondhand clothing from the United States, the major source of affordable apparel there (Peralta, 2017).

Exposition, Confrontation, and Simulation

There's no end to web images of clothing: search the web for candid street scenes to prove that denim is really the choice of half the population anywhere on any given day (Hegarty, 2012). A fashion show would be awesome, though it would probably take as much time to set up as a negotiation simulation. It's worth examining the many guides for avoiding looking like a tourist (pretty much one per country). Regarding clothing as a symbol of authority, beyond 'dressing for success,' examine—regardless of home country—the range of public opinion about Commanders-in-Chief wearing military uniforms. Some cultures want to keep the distinction between civilian and military explicitly distinct and assign the duty of chief military director to a civilian in mufti. Clothing marks off cultural distinctions not only in the present but also in the past. Examination of films set in historical periods often can uncover not only inaccuracies in dress but also in cultural representation as well (Lipsitz, 2001). 'Native' or traditional clothing is often exaggerated for effect in caricatures and in the popular imagination, but it is worth attempting to replicate the observation of Talha that members of some cultures—in her case, Pakistan—feel more secure and less anxious dressing in culturally traditional modes (Talha, 2012).

REFERENCES AND SUGGESTED READINGS

Dudley, S. H. (2011). Material visions: Dress and textiles. In M. Banks & J. Ruby (Eds.), *Made to be seen: Perspectives on the history of visual anthropology* (pp. 45–73). Chicago, IL: University of Chicago Press.

Hegarty, S. (2012, February 28). How jeans conquered the world. *BBC World Service News Magazine* (Transcript of radio broadcast) (online). Retrieved from www.bbc.com/news/magazine-17101768 [Accessed August 13, 2017].

Lipsitz, G. (2001). *Time passages: Collective memory and American popular culture.* Minneapolis, MN: University of Minnesota Press. (Originally published 1990).

Peralta, E. (2017, July 21). Rwanda works to ban sale of secondhand clothes within 2 years. *NPR All Things Considered* (Transcript of radio broadcast) (online). Retrieved from www.npr.org/2017/07/21/538608486/rwanda-works-to-ban-sale-of-second-hand-clothes-within-2-years [Accessed August 13, 2017].

Pine, K. (2014). *Mind what you wear.* E-Book: Amazon Digital Services LLC. Retrieved from http://karenpine.com/research/fashion-psychology/

Radclyffe-Thomas, N. (2015). Fashioning cross-cultural creativity: Investigating the situated pedagogy of creativity. *Psychology of Aesthetics, Creativity, and the Arts, 9*(2), 152–160.

Talha, S. (2012). *Cross-cultural influences on female apparel selection: A comparison of Norway and Pakistan.* M.A. Thesis, Business Administration, University of Agder. Retrieved from https://brage.bibsys.no/xmlui/bitstream/handle/11250/135843/Oppgave%20Sanaa%20Talha.pdf?sequence=1&isAllowed=y

Cross-references: Cartoons; Cannibalism and Culture Jams (Enemy Images)

FOOD AND ART

A mashup of food and art—aside from being a bad pun—may seem almost impossible to achieve, given the size and scope of each. Remarkably, these immense subjects are only weakly in evidence in cross-cultural psychology texts and reference works. Art, to many ways of thinking, is synonymous with culture, and food culture surely extends beyond yogurt. And while no one mistakes the Palace of Culture for the Chinese Palace Restaurant, every major art museum comes equipped with at least a café, if not a full-scale fine dining establishment. (Whether its food is equal to the cultural diversity of the art is a matter for the critics to decide.) On the art side, basic background reading might start with the Khan Academy's introduction to its contribution to AP Art History (Harris & Zucker, n.d.) which asserts the direct connection between history and visual culture and which contains the usual basic iconographic prompts. The only limitation to assembling culture-related art materials for review and discussion is the degree of art historical sophistication of the instructor and students. In academic environments, artists and art historians are usually only too happy to oblige the psychologist with their collateral expertise. On the food side, comprehensive histories of cuisine like Civitello's (2011) along with Leon Rappoport's (2003) treatment of the psychological dimensions of eating are essential, and yet not absolutely necessary, given the infinite amount of web-based material available. Raw ingredients abound.

Exposition, Confrontation, and Simulation

The idea of a multicultural potluck might seem trite or in some way an instance of cultural appropriation, but most assuredly it is not—these are invariably delicious. Amateur outsiders should be encouraged to create specific cultural dishes with no more guidance than internet recipes. Arrange beforehand for critiques by knowledgeable experts. Depending on the environment, food is a natural impetus for field tripping—to markets or, if lucky, to intercultural festivals. Asian and African markets are particularly good sources for unusual vegetables: possibly insects could also be on the menu (Le Cam, 2017). Menus are available worldwide on the web, as are, likewise, restaurant reviews—the more scathing, the more enjoyable, in some mysterious *Schadenfreudliche* way (e.g., Rayner, 2017). Alongside this culinary tour, take time to read and discuss accounts of the move of the largest Kosher slaughterhouse from New York City to Postville, Iowa (Bloom, 2000; Grey, Devlin, & Goldsmith, 2009). Up until 2008, Postville was considered by many a remarkably successful example of intercultural integration in the United States. Eventually the town, previously heading for rural impoverishment, became home to not only strict Orthodox Jews but also to Mexicans and Russians as well as to Iowans—immigrants only slightly further removed—who had lived there for generations. In 2008 a major immigration enforcement raid occurred, and at the same time extensive corruption and fraud were uncovered in the management of the slaughterhouse, which resulted in convictions and extensive jail time for those involved. The saga is still ongoing (Tapper, 2016), and lays bare the whole anatomy of US cultural relations as they have evolved to date.

It was B. F. Skinner (1970) who observed many times that primitive humans' first forays into art were depictions of what they ate, or at least what they aimed at to eat. (You art what you eat!) Food and iconography have an intimate, multifaceted relationship. Start with still lifes. Barr (2015) observes that, for example, the eggplant has an advantage over the model because it smokes only when placed in oil. Collect, compose, create, and compare. Examine food photography: this occurs worldwide and is a specialized photographic craft. Many websites offer coaching in the basics (e.g., Achitoff-Grey, Wasik, & Lopez-Alt, n.d.). After gathering some examples, experiment—cellphones will do in lieu of more complicated equipment—and then compare with expert results. Also compare the content of food photography carried out in luxury vs. subsistence conditions, for example, Hong Kong vs. west-central Africa. A simpler and fun way to begin thinking about food iconography is to distribute blank paper plates and markers or crayons, and set the group the task of designing a plate for a restaurant in a specific culture. Commonalities emerge that are partly stereotypical, to be sure, but which also show significant awareness of the typical folk art of many cultures which is residually available in memory and only waiting for a prompt. If the group is lucky enough to live near an art museum that will certainly be on the to-do list.

REFERENCES AND SUGGESTED READINGS

Achitoff-Grey, N., Wasik, V., & Lopez-Alt, J. K. (n.d.). The *Serious Eats* guide to food photography. *Serious Eats* (online blog). Retrieved from www.seriouseats.com/2015/03/beginners-guide-to-food-photography.html [Accessed September 17, 2017].

Barr, L. B. (2015). Still life: Theory and practice. *Cream City Review, 39*(1), 84–91.

Bloom, S. (2000). *Postville: A clash of cultures in heartland America.* New York: Mariner Books.

Civitello, L. (2011). *Cuisine and culture* (3rd ed.). New York: Wiley-Blackwell.

Grey, M. A., Devlin, M., & Goldsmith, A. (2009). *Postville, U.S. A.: Surviving diversity in small-town America.* Boston, MA: Gemma Media.

Harris, B., & Zucker, S. (n.d.). A brief history of Western culture. *Khan Academy website* (online). Retrieved from www.khanacademy.org/humanities/ap-art-history/cultures-religions-ap-arthistory/a/a-brief-history-of-western-culture [Accessed September 17, 2017].

Le Cam, M. (2017, February 17). Can crunchy caterpillars help tackle malnutrition in Burkina Faso? *The Guardian* (online newspaper). Retrieved from www.theguardian.com/global-development/2017/feb/17/can-crunchy-caterpillars-help-tackle-malnutrition-in-burkina-faso [Accessed September 17, 2017].

Rappoport, L. (2003). *How we eat: Culture, appetite, and the psychology of food.* Toronto, CA: ECW Press.

Rayner, J. (2017, April 9). Le Cinq, Paris: Restaurant review. *The Guardian* (online newspaper). Retrieved from www.theguardian.com/lifeandstyle/2017/apr/09/le-cinq-paris-restaurant-review-jay-rayner [Accessed September 17, 2017].

Skinner, B. F. (1970). Creating the creative artist. In A. Toynbee et al. (Eds.), *On the future of art.* New York: Viking Press.

Tapper, J. (2016, February 2). Years after raid, Postville, Iowa's Jewish community is smaller, more self-reliant. *Jewish Telegraphic Agency* (online newspaper). Retrieved from www.jta.org/2016/02/02/news-opinion/united-states/years-after-raid-postville-iowas-jewish-community-is-smaller-more-self-reliant [Accessed September 17, 2017].

Cross-references: Immigrants and Refugees; Hunger; Corruption; Cultural Appropriation; Museum Culture

HIGH AND LOW CULTURE

The distinction between high culture and low culture has a long history. Part of the distinction turns on questions of taste. In a famous statement, the English philosopher Jeremy Bentham asserted that a trivial game was, all things equal, no better or worse than art and poetry, a claim that has animated philosophic discussions of good and bad taste since that time (Kivy, 2015). Distinctions are also drawn between culture that is owned by, and distinguishes, individuals of high caste, class, or rank (high culture) and culture that is shared by those who are poor and marginalized (low culture). An example in music is the contrast that is drawn between 'classical music' and 'popular music.' Viewed through the lens of a theorist such as Pierre Bourdieu (1987), distinctions such as this one accrue through the processes of establishing class boundaries and are reinforced by economic and political rules. Under pressure from population, economics, and competition for access to resources worldwide, along with the vast increase in accessibility to all forms of artistic representation via digitization, the boundary between 'high' and 'low' has been steadily eroding. Halifu Osumare, a specialist in both culture and dance, has examined the penetration of hip-hop and rap music worldwide and sees the underlying dynamic of culture change as a process of developing "connective marginalities" (Osumare, 2001, 2012). Elements of an art form associated with cultural marginalization and oppression find an echo worldwide in populations experiencing similar strivings and obstacles. This process, 'bottom up' in terms of the direction of artistic change, is complemented by 'top down' movements within high culture to, for example, bring opera to the streets. For example, Yuval Sharon's staging of *Hopscotch: An Opera for 24 Cars* in Los Angeles in 2015 transposed the restrictive fixed setting of the opera house to a series of cabs and limos proceeding from one scene to the next on the street in real time (Allen, 2017). The focus here on art forms should not preclude investigation and discussion of other cultural dualisms, for instance castes (Parth, 2014) or purely intellectual distinctions, such as the 'two cultures' hypothesis of C. P. Snow in which science excludes art and vice versa (Krauss, 2009).

Exposition, Confrontation, and Simulation

Googling 'high and low culture' will lead to discussions of 'high vs. low context cultures' which is not the subject of discussion here. Entry into this area might start with playing a recording of the US country singer Garth Brooks's 'I've Got Friends In Low Places' and go from there to examining perceptions of what constitutes 'high' and 'low,' artistically and culturally. Much hip-hop is overtly confrontational and should be confronted. The recent award of a Nobel Prize for Literature to the US singer/songwriter Bob Dylan could also be another jumping-off place. Within visual and plastic arts specifically, some suggestions for creating an inventory or questionnaire about what constitutes 'high' vs. 'popular' art could be guided by reference to Barragán (2014). Also, the concept of 'slumming,' in its general historic meaning of dipping into forbidden lower depths of culture, or in the specific meaning of engaging in voyeuristic slum tourism (Frenzel, 2016) might be introduced and discussed.

REFERENCES AND SUGGESTED READINGS

Allen, D. (2017, July 20). Opera's disrupter in residence, heading to Bayreuth. *The New York Times* (online). Retrieved from www.nytimes.com/2017/07/20/arts/music/operas-disrupter-in-residence-heading-to-bayreuth.html?_r=0 [Accessed July 22, 2017].

Barragán, P. (2014). High art vs. pop culture now: An international survey. *Artpulse* (online magazine, Vol 5, No. 20). Retrieved from http://artpulsemagazine.com/high-art-versus-pop-culture-now-an-international-survey [Accessed July 22, 2017].

Bourdieu, P. (1987). *Distinction: A social critique of the judgment of taste* (Tr. Richard Nice). Cambridge, MA: Harvard University Press. (Originally published in France, 1979).

Frenzel, F. (2016). *Slumming it: The tourist valorization of urban poverty*. London: Zed Books.

Kivy, P. (2015). *De Gustibus: Arguing about taste and why we do it*. Oxford: Oxford University Press.

Krauss, L. M. (2009, September 1). An update on C. P. Snow's "two cultures". *Scientific American* (online magazine). Retrieved from www.scientificamerican.com/article/an-update-on-cp-snows-two-cultures/ [Accessed October 29, 2017].

Osumare, H. (2001). Beat streets in the global hood: Connective marginalities of the hip hop globe. *The Journal of American Culture, 24*(1–2), 171–181.

Osumare, H. (2012). *The hiplife in Ghana: West African indigenization of hip-hop.* Basingstoke: Palgrave Macmillan.

Parth, N. (2014, July 4). India's sewer cleaners keep working despite ban on job. *The Los Angeles Times* (online newspaper). Retrieved from www.latimes.com/world/asia/la-fg-india-sewers-20140704-story.html [Accessed October 29, 2017].

Cross-references: Regional and Indigenous Psychology; Tourism

MUSEUM CULTURE

Museums are one of the primary sites for contacting culture and are sometimes the only available means of learning about and understanding other cultures. While transmission of cultural information is the explicit function of museums, other implicit aspects are equally important, including the experiences and training of their curators, the purposes behind museums' creation, the sources of their funding, and the degree of embeddedness of the museum within its surrounding cultures. Museums take various forms, from small and haphazard collections to well-organized permanent exhibitions. Museums cover the cultural spectrum. There are museums for food (the Kimchikan Museum in Korea devoted to kimchi; the Cup Noodle Museum in Yokohama devoted to ramen; the SPAM Museum in Austin, Minnesota, United States devoted to SPAM®). There are museums for cultural artifacts (the Strong Museum of Play in Rochester, New York; the National Handicrafts and Handlooms Museum in New Delhi, India). And there are museums for entire cultures (The National Hispanic Cultural Center in Albuquerque, New Mexico, United States; the Delta Blues Museum in Clarksdale, Mississippi, United States). Psychologists have been involved as consultants on museum design for a long time: Edward S. Robinson wrote many articles on the subject in the 1930s (e.g., Robinson, 1933) and comprehensive psychological interest in all aspects of museum design, cognitive, emotional, and behavioral, continues today (Bitgood, 2010). Museums are also points at which cultural appropriation occurs: for a starting background on this, consult Pearce's edited collection of papers on the subject (Pearce, 2001).

Exposition, Confrontation, and Simulation

Visits to museums and post-visit comparisons are a prime requisite for interaction and background on this subject. Within a classroom, designing a museum seems a logical response. After deciding on a culture for curation, consult Stephen Bitgood's review of the environmental psychological factors involved in successful museum preparations (Bitgood, 2002) and Matassa (2011) for curatorial nuts and bolts. Next, decide whether the focus of this cultural museum will be on artifacts or on interpersonal relations. How to accomplish the demonstration of aspects of power distance, implicit vs. explicit cultural rules, and similar basic principles would be worthy tasks for developing future psychological exploratorium designers.

REFERENCES AND SUGGESTED READINGS

Bitgood, S. (2002). Environmental psychology in museums, zoos, and other exhibition centers. In R. Bechtel & A. Churchman (Eds.), *Handbook of environmental psychology* (pp. 461–480). New York: Wiley-Blackwell.

Bitgood, S. (2010). An attention-value model of museum visitors. *CAISE (Center for the Advancement of Informal Science Education, National Science Foundation) website* (online). Retrieved from www.informalscience.org/attention-value-model-museum-visitors [Accessed August 26, 2017].

Matassa, F. (2011). *Museum collections management: A handbook*. London: Facet Publishing.

Pearce, S. (Ed.) (2001). *Museums and the appropriation of culture*. London: Bloomsbury.

Robinson, E. S. (1933). The psychology of public education. *American Journal of Public Health, 23*(2), 123–128.

Cross-references: Cultural Appropriation; Food and Art

SACRED SPACES AND HOLY PLACES

Sacred spaces and holy places anchor cultures to their surroundings, physical and social, and to family and ancestry besides. Sacredness and holiness are brain-deep and fuse emotion and reason, earthiness and heavenliness (Beck, 2012). Sacred sites are usually associated with religion: cathedrals, temples, pagodas, roadside shrines, and mosques are always high on the list of places to visit for new arrivals to a culture—at least for those who have the liberty and leisure to appreciate them. The experience of sacredness and holiness connects to a range of self-transcendent experiences (Yaden, Haidt, Hood, Vago, & Newberg, 2017) which include awe and mystical experiences. Awesomeness is experienced in connection with physical vastness, not only in human-made spaces such as cathedrals but in the sanctuaries of nature, which themselves often connote mystical or religious elements (e.g., 'The Garden of the Gods'). Cemeteries and other memorials may be designed to create specific self-transcendent emotions (Petersson & Wingren, 2011). Conversely, mystical experience occurs even in the most mundane places apart from specific religious connections. Arriving refugees who are simply grateful to have escaped the place where they previously were might kiss the earth itself, rendering even the architecture of an anonymous airport sacred (Soeffer, 1997). One instance of this is the spontaneous emergence of reverent commemorative behavior among 'modern nomads' even in supermarkets in Britain (Walter, 2001), in spontaneous candlelight vigils for mass shootings, or the appearance of bundles of flowers, crosses, and other tributes at the sites of fatal motor accidents or other significant deaths (Santino, 2006). It is entirely possible that, if sacredness may emerge in any deep emotional connection anywhere, that wherever one currently stands may be someone's sacred space or place.

Exposition, Confrontation, and Simulation

It should not be difficult to find out the range of places sacred to individuals in any group: prompts might be to think of the place where a significant other was first met; where an important personal event occurred; or where family gathers for remembrance. Usually, too, there is some kind of public sacred space within walking distance of any classroom or meeting place, and this can be explored. This is lucky for anyone within walking distance of an actual cathedral! But graveyards can also be worthwhile to visit as well. The discussion might lead further toward consideration of personal experiences of awe or self-transcendence: the simple survey technique described by Jules Evans (2016) can be easily adapted and extended to reflect conceptions of spirituality across a range of cultures (e.g., Borislavova White, 2017).

REFERENCES AND SUGGESTED READINGS

Beck, R. (2012, April 2). The holiness of the F-word. *Experimental Theology* (author blog, Richard Beck, Abilene Christian University) (online). Retrieved from http://experimentaltheology.blogspot.com/2012/04/holiness-of-f-word.html [Accessed September 4, 2017].

Borislavova White, D. (2017). *Being and beholding: A comparative analysis of joy and awe in four cultures.* Doctoral dissertation, James Madison University. Proquest Dissertations Publishing (online). Retrieved from https://search.proquest.com/openview/f13b65c 26590ec2cb5dc7c6a765a1807/1?pq-origsite=gscholar&cbl=18750&diss=y [Accessed September 4, 2017].

Evans, J. (2016, February 5). The spiritual experiences survey: *Philosophy for life* (author blog of Jules Evans) (online). Retrieved from www.philosophyforlife.org/the-spiritual-experiences-survey/ [Accessed September 4, 2017].

Petersson, A., & Wingren, C. (2011). Designing a memorial place: Continuing care, passage landscapes and future memories. *Mortality, 16*(1), 54–69.

Santino, J. (Ed.) (2006). *Spontaneous shrines and the public memorialization of death.* New York: Palgrave Macmillan.

Soeffer, H. G. (1997). *The order of rituals: The interpretation of everyday life* (pp. 88–89). Piscataway, NJ: Transaction Publishers.

Walter, T. (2001). From cathedral to supermarket: Mourning, silence, and solidarity. *The Sociological Review, 49*(4), 494–511.

Yaden, D. B., Haidt, J., Hood Jr., R. W., Vago, D. R., & Newberg, A. B. (2017). The varieties of self-transcendent experience. *Review of General Psychology, 21*(2), 143–160.

Cross-reference: Silences

Language and Literature

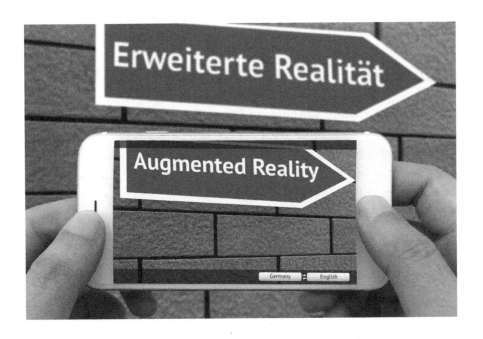

DYSTOPIAS AND UTOPIAS

In the same way that war is more interesting than peace, dystopias are often more arresting and attractive than accounts of cultures working well. Classic literary dystopias, for instance *Brave New World* (Huxley, 1932) vie with films old (*Metropolis*, Lang, 1927/2002) and new (*The Hunger Games*, Ross et al., 2012) to reveal the seamy side of cultures. Dissecting any dystopia will reveal the cultural bones of its model. Dystopias exist in all literary and filmic cultures and are valuable and underutilized probes for gaining a syntopic view of societies everywhere. I confess that as an observer of US culture my all-time favorite is *Idiocracy* (Judge, 2006), though it is only of middling tomato rank on the Rotten Tomatoes film rating website (there's no accounting for bad taste). There's a shortage of humor generally in cross-cultural studies: this less serious film can be a springboard for entering into the world of cross-cultural comedy and humor as well.

Exposition, Confrontation, and Simulation

Dystopias are preeminently filmic and many lists are available online (e.g., Santoni, 2014). Another line of approach could be to access some of the many dystopian novels not well known in the United States and read them in conjunction with some of the classic ones. Dystopias are often centered in cities: culturally contrastive readings in this venue might be selected from Prakash's (2010) collection of essays connected to contemporary city life; also consider reading Boo (2012). Googling 'games' can lead to simulations of dystopic societies or eras, for instance, a choose-your-adventure game involving the terrorization of escaping slaves in the antebellum period in US history (Maryland Public Television, 2017). In conjunction with this, contrast historian Roxane Gay's opinion on why re-creations of slavery do not live up the current dystopic state of race relations in the United States (Gay, 2017). Finally, all is not lost. After a showing of your favorite dystopic film, design an utopian antidote, using the template in Bufe and Hubbard's *Design Your Own Utopia* (Bufe & Hubbard, n.d.).

REFERENCES AND SUGGESTED READINGS

Boo, K. (2012). *Behind the beautiful forevers: Life, death, and hope in a Mumbai undercity.* New York: Random House.

Bufe, C., & Hubbard, L. (n.d.). Design your own utopia. Pamphlet posted on *See Sharp Press website* (online resource of See Sharp Press, Tucson, AZ). Retrieved from www.seesharppress.com/textsonline.html [Accessed July 20, 2017].

Gay, R. (2017, July 25). I don't want to watch slavery fan fiction. *The New York Times* (online). Retrieved from www.nytimes.com/2017/07/25/opinion/hbo-confederate-slavery-civil-war.html [Accessed July 25, 2017].

Gendler, A. (2016). How to recognize a dystopia. *TedEd* (online video resource). Retrieved from https://ed.ted.com/lessons/how-to-recognize-a-dystopia-alex-gendler#review [Accessed July 20, 2017].

Huxley, A. (1932). *Brave new world.* London (UK): Chatto & Windus.

Judge, M. (Director and screenplay) (2006). *Idiocracy* (film). 20th Century Fox/Ternion Pictures.

Lang, F., (Director) & Von Harbou (screenplay) (2002). *Metropolis* (film). New York: Kino on Video. (Originally a UFA production, 1927).

Maryland Public Television. (2017). Pathways to freedom: Maryland and the Underground Railroad. *Thinkport/Maryland Public Television* (instructional flash video) (online). Retrieved from http://pathways.thinkport.org/flash_home.cfm [Accessed July 25, 2017].

Prakash, G. (Ed.) (2010). *Noir urbanisms: Dystopic images of the modern city.* Princeton, NJ: Princeton University Press.

Ross, G., Tucci, S., Bentley, W., Banks, E., Lawrence, J., Hemsworth, L., Collins, S., . . . Alliance Films. (2012). *The hunger games.* United States: Alliance Film.

Santoni, E. (2014, October 14). 20 great dystopian films that are worth your time. *Taste of Cinema* (digital film magazine) (online). Retrieved from www.tasteofcinema.com/2014/20-great-dystopian-films-that-are-worth-your-time/ [Accessed July 25, 2017].

Cross-references: Literature and Translation; Cultural Appropriation

EUPHEMISMS

A distinction should be drawn between euphemisms, that is, expressions used to make painful truths less painful, and a number of related linguistic forms. Among those are 'minced oaths' (reduced-strength cursing), dysphemisms (intentional use of a stronger or more abusive expression, for example 'stiff' for 'dead body'), and other forms of indirect expression or irony. Euphemisms have been considered cross-culturally from the perspectives of linguistic theory and translation (Pour, 2010), communications theory (Al-Mulla, 1988), and politeness theory (Bargiela-Chiappini & Kadar, 2011). Fontes (2009) provides several examples of ways that euphemism enters into communications between psychological professionals and clients from different cultures.

Exposition, Confrontation, and Simulation

All cultures euphemize: a search will easily uncover these along with examples of ways in which euphemisms' valence changes based on culture. For instance, euphemisms for aging differ between the United States and China: since agedness is more highly respected in China, euphemisms for aging are less derogatory and more sympathetic (Guo, 2010). Euphemisms in the United States are usually viewed negatively. Some recent examples in the literature are euphemism impeding clear perception of proper ethical behavior in business settings (Rittenberg, Gladney, & Stephenson, 2016) and the phrase 'special needs' increasing negative perceptions of disability when contrasted with descriptions of precise disability conditions (Gernsbacher, Raimond, Balinghasay, & Boston, 2016). Discussion might center around whether euphemisms can ever have positive effects, for instance in the way that Sarawak Malay death euphemisms promote social solidarity and comfort (Wahab, Abdullah, Mis, & Salehuddin, 2016). If, as easily might occur, the discussion extends to cursing, there is recent evidence that the use of strong language has emotional effects and may increase pain tolerance (Wong, 2017).

REFERENCES AND SUGGESTED READINGS

Al-Mulla, M. A. A. (1988). *Cross-cultural misunderstanding in the language of international diplomacy*. Ph.D. Dissertation, Bangor University, Wales, UK. (online). Retrieved from http://e.bangor.ac.uk/4283/ [Accessed August 22, 2017].

Bargiela-Chiappini, F., & Kadar, D. Z. (add diacriticals) (Eds.) (2011). *Politeness across cultures*. Basel: Springer.

Fontes, L. A. (2009). *Interviewing clients across cultures: A practitioner's guide*. New York: Guilford Press.

Gernsbacher, M. A., Raimond, A. R., Balinghasay, M. T., & Boston, J. S. (2016). "Special needs" is an ineffective euphemism. *Cognitive Research: Principles and Implications, 1*, 29 (online). Retrieved from https://doi.org/10.1186/s41235-016-0025-4

Guo, Q. (2010). Cultural differences in Chinese and English euphemisms. *Cross-Cultural Communication, 6*(4), 135–141.

Pour, B. S. (2010, October). A study of euphemisms from the perspectives of cultural translation and linguistics. *Translation Journal 14*(4), (online). Retrieved from August 20, 2017 from http://translationjournal.net/journal/54euphemisms.htm

Rittenberg, T., Gladney, G. A., & Stephenson, T. (2016). The effects of euphemism usage in business contexts. *Journal of Business Ethics, 137*, 315–320.

Wahab, H. A., Abdullah, I. H., Mis, M. A., & Salehuddin, K. (2016). An analysis of death euphemisms in sarawak malay community from the perspective of cognitive semantics. *GEMA Online Journal of Language Studies, 16*(2). (online). Retrieved from https://ukm.pure.elsevier.com/en/publications/an-analysis-of-death-euphemisms-in-sarawak-malay-community-from-t [Accessed August 20, 2017].

Wong, K. (2017, July 27). The case for cursing. *The New York Times* (online newspaper). Retrieved from www.nytimes.com/2017/07/27/smarter-living/the-case-for-cursing.html?mcubz=3&_r=0 [Accessed August 22, 2017].

Cross-reference: Language and Accents

LANGUAGE AND ACCENTS

Conceptions of the role that language plays in psychological theorizing date well before the time of Charles Darwin, who himself explored similarities between diverse languages at the beginning of his quest for a comprehensive theory of evolution (Darwin Correspondence Project, 2017). Darwin himself did not draw a firm distinction between the language of humans and the communication he observed in other species, nor did behavioristically oriented psychologists in the early 20th century, who subscribed by and large to the idea that thought was internalized speech (Levelt, 2014). A modernized version of this theory attributes the origin of consciousness, and much more of human cultural heritage besides, to the internalization of external speech in connection with the perception of ongoing tasks (Kuijsten, 2016). Current theories of language development suggest that there are species-typical roots of language that can be intuited from the prelinguistic behavior of infants, for instance, common behaviors of pointing (Liszkowski, Brown, Callaghan, Takada, & de Vos, 2012). Another level of cultural universality is indicated by research that suggests that infants acquire culturally universal musical and prosodic elements of language first (Brandt, Gebrian, & Slevc, 2012). It is certain that infants acquire, and embed neurologically, culturally specific features of language before their first year in a process termed "neural commitment" (Kuhl, 2010). Before this time, achieving multilinguality is relatively easy: after this, without specific attention to language learning and immersion, second-language learning becomes more arduous and accents become more permanent. Accents, as a specific feature of language, reveal important dimensions of the role of language in culture. They are another factor in early language development, influencing the rate of language acquisition, and are also one of the most prominent ways in which cultures encounter each other in everyday interaction. Accents, like languages themselves, are an alternative form of cultural boundary, fluid rather than geographically fixed, and reflect another way that cultures cohere internally while at the same time repelling outside influences. The ability to gauge cultural membership from accents is acquired soon after speech: from the age of

4 or 5, cultural members can recognize each other as well as isolate and discriminate against outsiders automatically by accent (Chakraborty, 2007; Weatherhead, White, & Friedman, 2015). Alternative accents may be adopted as camouflage by those who otherwise would experience this form of linguistic discrimination (Nath, 2011). Nor is this form of discrimination limited only to national origin. Sexual orientation may also be detected and attacked on the basis of perceived speech, as vividly expressed in the documentary film *Do I Sound Gay?* (Thorpe, 2015).

Exposition, Confrontation, and Simulation

Discussion might begin with surveying the number of languages in the world, and then finding out how many are in use in the immediate area: for example, there are 145 languages spoken in Houston, Texas, in the United States (Kriel, 2015). The UNESCO Atlas of the World's Languages in Danger (UNESCO, 2017) shows how vulnerable many languages are to extinction. Interaction might occur around the question "Suppose you are the last speaker of _____. What would you most want to preserve about this language and how would you go about doing it?" As an entry into prelinguistics, try to set up and perform a complex task (for example, the simulated work task involving folding T-shirts described in this book's introduction) entirely without using spoken language. A most effective interactive experience of the immigrant experience and also of the problems inherent in second language acquisition after the critical period for multilinguality can be set up by enlisting native speakers of another language to interact suddenly with a class (or individually via recording online) using their own language—unfamiliar to the group and spoken rapidly—to command a response to tasks to be performed in an intake area. Question members of the group during and after the experience regarding the meaning of what was said as well as their emotional reactions. Accents are often encountered on the phone as many service workers are immigrants or members of different subcultures. A simulation of a call center can be set up with both native speakers and accented ones (and possibly, following Nath (2011), ones that are simulating a native accent!), and reactions to different voices may be surveyed. Discrimination based on accent is illegal in many places and a search for and survey of the laws surrounding accents will be instructive. Finally, though the function of language and accents as a tool for discrimination and exclusion has been focused on in this entry, accents can be interesting and even beautiful in their own right. The Speech Accent Archive at George Mason University (Weinberger, 2015)—which offers a bountiful collection of speakers of dozens of languages, representing all ages and genders, saying the same paragraph-length phrase in English—might be explored to see which accents are most readily perceived and also which are judged pleasant (very likely all of them!).

REFERENCES AND SUGGESTED READINGS

Brandt, A., Gebrian, M., & Slevc, L. R. (2012, September 11). Music and early language acquisition. *Frontiers in Psychology, 3*, 327 (online open access). Retrieved from http://journal.frontiersin.org/article/10.3389/fpsyg.2012.00327/full; https://doi.org/10.3389/fpsyg.2012.00327 [Accessed September 6, 2017].

Chakraborty, R. (2007). A short note on accent-bias, social identity, and ethnocentrism. *Advances in Language and Literary Studies, 8*(4), 57–64.

Darwin Correspondence Project. (2017). The origin of language. *University of Cambridge, Darwin Correspondence Project* (online website for the Darwin Correspondence Project). Retrieved from www.darwinproject.ac.uk/commentary/human-nature/origin-language [Accessed September 6, 2017].

Kriel, L. (2015, November 5). Just how diverse is Houston? 145 languages spoken here. *Houston Chronicle* (online newspaper). Retrieved from www.houstonchronicle.com/news/houston-texas/article/Houstonians-speak-at-least-145-languages-at-home-6613182.php [Accessed September 6, 2017].

Kuhl, P. K. (2010). Brain mechanisms in early language acquisition. *Neuron, 67*(5), 713–727.

Kuijsten, M. (Ed.) (2016). *Gods, voices, and the bicameral mind: the theories of Julian Jaynes.* Henderson, NV: The Julian Jaynes Society. Retrieved from www.julianjaynes.org/contact.php

Levelt, W. (2014). *A history of psycholinguistics: the Pre-Chomskyan era.* New York: Oxford University Press.

Liszkowski, U., Brown, P., Callaghan, T., Takada, A., & de Vos, C. (2012). A prelinguistic gestural universal of human communication. *Cognitive Science, 36*(4), 698–713.

Nath, V. (2011). Aesthetic and emotional labor through stigma: National identity management and racial abuse in offshored Indian call centres. *Work, Employment, and Society, 25*(4), 709–725.

Thorpe, D. (Dir.) (2015). *Do I sound gay?* (film). Impact Partners/Little Punk/Think Thorpe.

UNESCO. (2017). *UNESCO atlas of the world's languages in danger* (online atlas, United Nations Educational, Scientific, and Cultural Organization). Retrieved from www.unesco.org/languages-atlas/index.php [Accessed September 6, 2017].

Weatherhead, D., White, K. S., & Friedman, O. (2015). Where are you from? Preschoolers infer background from accent. *Journal of Experimental Child Psychology, 143*, 171–178.

Weinberger, S. (2015). *Speech accent archive* (online open-source archive). Retrieved from http://accent.gmu.edu [Accessed September 6, 2017].

Cross-references: Boundaries and Maps; Immigration and Refugees

LITERATURE AND TRANSLATION

Social science has long observed a lack of attention to the role of imaginative literature and its cognates, drama and screenplay, in the understanding of culture (Albrecht, 1954), and it is true that theory and the experimental attitude dominate. But this is a great paradox, since the intimate relation of literature and culture in all their varieties is attested to both theoretically (Rieber & Kelly, 2014) and in practice in psychology and its cognate fields. Practically speaking it is impossible to fully convey the wealth of material available. Simple googling 'sources for teaching cultural psychology through literature' or similar phrases will uncover many compilations, not all of which are current but all of which are rich. For one example, CARLA (the Center for Advanced Research on Language Acquisition at the University of Minnesota, a US Department of Education Title VI National Language Resource Center, has amassed a large network of links to literature, teaching resources and activities, and films connected to intercultural understanding (CARLA, 2017). Searching for specific types of literature or film will lead to reservoirs of attractive material. Ethnographic films, for instance, are available and underutilized (Lemelson, 2014): some of these, for instance *Babies,*' cited in the Parenting entry in this book, have a great popular following. Websites, for instance the aforementioned CARLA, collate accessible popular feature films along with specialized documentaries and educational materials. Many other sites gather '10 best' examples of imaginative literature from countries and regions (e.g., Telegraph, 2014). More attention has been given to translation within cross-cultural psychology. This occurs most often in connection with the process of 'back-translation,' a process designed to enable, as far as possible, English-language materials and the concepts they embody to be utilized in non-English speaking countries (WHO, 2017). However, the question of translation extends well beyond the exporting of Western science. From a historical perspective, many of the founding documents of psychology were written in languages other than English and persuasive cases can be made for their having been mistranslated or culturally misconstrued (Kermode, 1983). The deep intertwining of culture and translation (Cutler, 2017) and the persistent idea that some texts and ideas are untranslatable should suggest caution to anyone venturing into literature as a way of understanding culture. Nonetheless, much vividness will be missed by not doing so.

Exposition, Confrontation, and Simulation

More specific exercises can be sketched for practice in translation and back-translation than for the introduction of literature into the cross-cultural curriculum. Short measurement instruments with a cultural purpose can be readily translated if there are some bilingual members in the class or group to translate and explain their translations. Some attention can be given to the idea of untranslatability: suggestions can be solicited of words, ideas, or experiences that are hard to describe and then matched up with various lists of untranslatable words readily available on the internet and also in a recent *Scientific American* article (Lomas, 2016). Turning to literature, enlistment of experts in literary studies would be essential in seeking suggestions for how to get psychologists to engage with imaginative texts. Design of a regional reading list will lead to better understanding of the region as well as the reading. But the first choice of text will sometimes obviate the need for specific motivators for engagement. Just yesterday I searched for information on Max Graf, the Austrian musicologist who was a friend of both Freud and Gustav Mahler. While I was searching, the indefatigable Google provided, through the medium of Google Books, two captivating chapters of the autobiography of Lotfi Mansouri (1929–2013) co-authored with Donald Arthur, *Lotfi Mansouri: An Operatic Journey* (Mansouri & Arthur, 2010). Mansouri was an ebullient opera impresario who was born in Iran and eventually made himself at home in cultures worldwide. His storytelling—for instance of his trip back to Iran in 1970 after an absence of 23 years, including the episode of having to run through jammed traffic to rescue his two passports from a traffic jam pickpocket (!)—is hilarious. His poignant and accurate account of the psychic terrors he experienced in not having a home culture, even as a widely successful man, and the therapy that pulled him through those, give insight into the level at which culture and the psyche interact that can't be understood except in the near-face-to-face encounter that narrative provides. Of course, I'm an opera fan: I would gravitate to this serendipitous find. But other finds await regardless of taste: see for example Norman Van Aken's account of his chef's career and its intersections with the polyglot cultures of the US food scene (Van Aken, 2013). All you need to do is reach down your hand to scoop the cultural waters and you will have a meal.

REFERENCES AND SUGGESTED READINGS

Albrecht, M. C. (1954). The relationship of literature and society. *American Journal of Sociology, 59*, 425–436.

CARLA. (2017). *The Center for Advanced Research on Language Acquisition (CARLA)* (organization website) (online). Retrieved from http://carla.umn.edu/index.html [Accessed September 8, 2017].

Cutler, S. (2017, March 9). What the act of translation reveals. *Brigham Young University Humanities Department website* (online). Retrieved from https://humanities.byu.edu/ what-the-act-of-translation-reveals/ [Accessed September 8, 2017].

Kermode, F. (1983, February 6). Freud is better in German. *The New York Times* (online newspaper). Retrieved from www.nytimes.com/books/00/06/25/specials/kermode-betterlheim.html?mcubz=3 [Accessed September 8, 2017].

Lemelson, R. (2014, February 12). 20 ethnographic and documentary films psychological anthropologists should be teaching. *Psychocultural Cinema* (online resource). Retrieved from http://psychoculturalcinema.com/20-ethnographic-and-documentary-films-psychological-anthropologists-should-be-teaching/ [Accessed September 8, 2017].

Lomas, T. (2016, July 12). The magic of "untranslatable" words. *Scientific American* (online magazine). Retrieved from www.scientificamerican.com/article/the-magic-of-untranslatable-words/ [Accessed September 8, 2017].

Mansouri, L., & Arthur, D. (2010). *Lotfi Mansouri: An operatic journey*. Boston, MA: Northeastern University Press.

Rieber, R. W., & Kelly, R. J. (2014). *Film, television, and the psychology of the social dream*. New York: Springer-Verlag.

Telegraph. (2014, April 17). 10 best novels about Africa. *Telegraph Bookshop* (online newspaper section). Retrieved from www.telegraph.co.uk/culture/books/10631274/10-best-novels-about-Africa.html [Accessed September 8, 2017].

Van Aken, N. (2013). *No experience necessary: The culinary Odyssey of Norman Van Aken.* New York: Taylor Trade.

WHO. (2017). Process of translation and adaptation of instruments. *Management of substance abuse programme, World Health Organization* (official website, United Nations agency). Retrieved from www.who.int/substance_abuse/research_tools/translation/en/ [Accessed September 8, 2017].

Cross-references: Regional and Indigenous Psychology; Food and Art

SILENCES

"Whereof one cannot speak, thereof one must be silent."

—Ludwig Wittgenstein,
Tractatus Logico-Philosophicus 7.1 (trans. Caws, 2006)

Exposition, Confrontation, and Simulation

See references.

REFERENCES AND SUGGESTED READINGS

Caws, P. (2006, November–December). Tractatus 7.1: Translation and silence. *Philosophy Now: A Magazine of Ideas, 58* (online magazine). Retrieved from https://philosophynow.org/issues/58/Tractatus_71_Translation_and_Silence [Accessed November 4, 2017].

Daniels, D. (2016). Silence and void: Aesthetics of absence in space and time. In Y. Kaduri (Ed.), *The Oxford handbook of sound and image in Western art* (online reference). doi:10.1093/oxfordhb/9780199841547.013.11 [Accessed November 4, 2017].

Finkel, D. (2000). *Teaching with your mouth shut.* Portsmouth, NH: Heinemann.

Kolb, R. (2017, November 3). Sensations of sound: On deafness and music. *The New York Times* (online newspaper). Retrieved from www.nytimes.com/2017/11/03/opinion/cochlear-implant-sound-music.html?_r=0 [Accessed November 4, 2017].

Mannion, R., & Davies, H. T. (2015). Cultures of silence and cultures of voice: The role of whistleblowing in healthcare organisations. *International Journal of Health Policy and Management, 4*(8), 503–505.

Noelle-Neumann, E. (1991). The theory of public opinion: The concept of the Spiral of Silence. In J. A. Anderson (Ed.), *Communication yearbook, 14,* 256–287. Newbury Park, CA: Sage.

Shakespeare, W. (1609). *Sonnet 30.*

Spaeth, D. (2014, September 25). Silence, shunning, and shying away: Destroying personhood and connection through preserving the peace. *New Existentialists Posts, Saybrook University* (online). Retrieved from www.saybrook.edu/blog/2014/09/25/09-25-14/ [Accessed November 4, 2017].

US Department of State. (n.d.). Test your knowledge of cultural taboos. In *So you're an American? A guide to answering difficult questions abroad.* US Department of State (online cultural quizlets). Retrieved from www.state.gov/m/fsi/tc/answeringdifficult questions/html/app.htm?p=practice_p3.htm [Accessed November 4, 2017].

(note: highly interactive :)

Cross-references: Language and Accents; Dance; Literature and Translation

Identity

GLOBALITY, MULTICULTURALITY, AND BICULTURALITY

Often, cross-cultural psychology emphasizes differences between cultures and also preservation of cultural identity, for instance the identity and practices of indigenous peoples. The concepts identified in this entry's title challenge the idea of separate and preservable cultures (to say nothing of permanent social or racial differences) and suggest that—perhaps not at present but soon—there will be more de-differentiation, intermingling, and cultural blending. An approach to this set of concepts from a specifically cross-cultural psychological direction can begin with consulting the work of Angela-Minh Tu D. Nguyen, who has written extensively on the conceptual foundations of biculturalism (including the entry in the *Encyclopedia of Cross-Cultural Psychology*, Nguyen, 2013) and also on the relation between bilingualism, socialization practices, and biculturality (Nguyen & Ahmadpanah, 2014).

Exposition, Confrontation, and Simulation

This can be a naturally confrontational topic, since it directly opposes strident monoculturalism and monolingualism. The bigotry associated with these positions can be contextualized historically in psychology by consulting and directly discussing accounts of it, personal and professional (e.g., Sue, 2001). A less direct way of addressing specifically monocultural and often racist undertones to ordinary everyday reference to other people can be unpacked by designing a revised 'identity' question for the demographic section of research or census questionnaires. This survey of the myriad of cultures each individual carries with them—gender, ancestry, tastes, activities, occupations, and also national identity/ies— would also be desirable as an opening exercise in any course. Alongside this, use of the overtly racist term 'Caucasian' as a indicator of—whatever it indicates—can be challenged and hopefully demolished (Khan, 2011).

From a psychological measurement perspective, several biculturality scales from the wide variety of these developed over the past several decades (e.g., Basilio et al., 2015; Mezzich, Ruiperez, Yoon, Liu, & Zapata-Vega, 2009; Tropp, Erkut, Coll, Alarcon, & Vazquez-Garcia, 1999) can be searched, obtained, abstracted, and discussed after completion. Many relevant scales that accumulated through 2010 are collected and their contents available in Davis and Engel (2011).

REFERENCES AND SUGGESTED READINGS

Basilio, C. D., Knight, G. P., O'Donnell, M., Roosa, M. W., Umaña-Taylor, A. J., & Torres, M. (2015). The Mexican American Biculturalism Scale: Bicultural comfort, facility, and advantages for adolescents and adults. *Psychological Assessment, 26*(2), 539–554.

Davis, L. E., & Engel, R. (2011). *Measuring race and ethnicity*. New York: Springer-Verlag.

Khan, R. (2011, January 22). Stop using the word "Caucasian" to mean white. *Discover Magazine (Gene Expression* blog) (online). Retrieved from http://blogs. discovermagazine.com/gnxp/2011/01/stop-using-the-word-caucasian-to-mean-white/#.Wc_oYORhjIU [Accessed September 30, 2017].

Mezzich, J. E., Ruiperez, M. A., Yoon, G., Liu, J., & Zapata-Vega, M. I. (2009). Measuring cultural identity: Validation of a modified Cortes, Rogler, and Malgady Bicultural Scale in three ethnic groups in New York. *Culture, Medicine, and Psychiatry, 33*(3), 451–472.

Nguyen, A-M. D. (2013). Biculturalism. In K. Keith (Ed.), *Encyclopedia of cross-cultural psychology* (pp. 132–134). New York: Wiley-Blackwell.

Nguyen, A-M. D., & Ahmadpanah, S. S. (2014). The interplay between bicultural blending and dual language acquisition. *Journal of Cross-Cultural Psychology, 45*, 1215–1220.

Sue, D. W. (2001). Surviving monoculturalism and racism: A personal and professional journey. In J. G. Ponterotto, J. M. Casas, L. A. Suzuki, & C. M. Alexander (Eds.), *Handbook of multicultural counseling* (2nd ed., pp. 45–54). Thousand Oaks, CA: Sage.

Tropp, L. R., Erkut, S., Coll, C. G., Alarcon, O., & Vazquez-Garcia, H. A. (1999). Psychosocial acculturation: Development of a new measure for Puerto Ricans on the U.S. mainland. *Educational and Psychological Measurement, 59*, 351–357.

Cross-references: Regional and Indigenous Psychology; Disaster and War; Separateness and Secession; Color and Skin Color; Language and Accents

NAMES AND NAMING

Names have profound connections to the roots of all cultures. Some names are sacred, so much so that they are surrounded by mystery and secrecy and are not to be pronounced. Many names have origins in religious traditions, connecting to figures less secret but no less honored. Some names confer power, for instance titles attached to names. At the most mundane level, names can be pointers, not necessarily absolute, to at least the following important information: family membership; nationality; linguistic community; conformity or nonconformity to social norms; religious affiliation; subgroup or subculture membership (e.g., Amish names); age cohort; gender; criminality (e.g., mob nicknames); and geographical position within a region (e.g., Varnum & Kitayama, 2011). In cultural studies naming and cultural linguistics are linked. In psychology, naming leads mainly to studies of neurocognitive performance or deficit, but a little digging can uncover interesting cross-cultural connections (e.g., Watzlawick, Guimarães, Han, & Jung, 2016).

Exposition, Confrontation, and Simulation

Many interactive demonstrations of the cultural power and complexity of naming are possible. Luckily the materials for these are portable and easily accessible—individuals' names! Tracing the origin of names can lead to genealogy and immigration history. Distribution of names can be viewed with an eye to understanding how rapidly populations are merging worldwide, for instance via Forebears.io (Hopkins, 2017; Nguyen, 2015) or other websites that provide world maps of surnames. The question of whether a name can be changed, and how, can also be investigated. Ask individuals to suggest a name that they would choose if they had to 'pass' in another culture and describe the reasons for the choice of that particular name. Examine the gender-specificity of names in the immediate environment and extend this to cultures worldwide (Oyewumi, 1998). The power of elevating as well shaming by naming can also be examined, in local contexts as well as in the larger world political environment

(Pizano, 2014), with examples given of both honoring politically and socially significant individuals as well as dismissing them. Discussion of whether and how to use a first name instead of a formal title can be an interesting exercise in tracing power relationships and levels of respect (Lawrence-Lightfoot, 2000). Who in your immediate environment would you never call by a first name? The discussion of naming need not be focused only on humans and human cultures: pets, countries, behavioral practices, and products need names too. Experiment with naming new sandwiches, businesses, or furniture that will be distributed worldwide— trying to choose names that will be culturally universal and also culturally nonoffensive (Gabler, 2015; Quito, 2017).

REFERENCES AND SUGGESTED READINGS

Gabler, N. (2015, January 15). The weird science of naming new products. *The New York Times* (online). Retrieved from www.nytimes.com/2015/01/18/magazine/the-weird-science-of-naming-new-products.html?_r=0 [Accessed August 3, 2017].

Hopkins, D. et al. (2017). *Forebears website* (genealogical source) (online). Retrieved from http://forebears.io/surnames [Accessed August 3, 2017].

Lawrence-Lightfoot, S. (2000). *Respect: An exploration.* Cambridge, MA: Perseus Books.

Nguyen, C. (2015, November 2). Here's a global heatmap of people with your last name. *Vice Motherboard* (online magazine). Retrieved from https://motherboard.vice.com/en_us/article/mg7qwb/heres-a-global-heatmap-of-people-with-your-last-name [Accessed August 3, 2017].

Oyewumi, O. (1998). Making history, creating gender: Some methodological and interpretive questions in the writing of Oyo oral traditions. *African History, 25*, 263–305.

Pizano, P. (2014, August 5). The power of naming and shaming. *Foreign Policy* (online magazine). Retrieved from http://foreignpolicy.com/2014/08/05/the-power-of-naming-and-shaming/ [Accessed August 3, 2017].

Quito, A. (2017, January 30). The secret taxonomy behind IKEA's product names, from Billy to Poang. *Quartz* (online magazine). Retrieved from https://qz.com/896146/how-ikea-names-its-products-the-curious-taxonomy-behind-billy-poang-malm-kallax-and-rens/ [Accessed August 3, 2017].

Varnum, M. E. W., & Kitayama, S. (2011). What's in a name? Popular names are less common on frontiers. *Psychological Science, 22*(2), 176–183.

Watzlawick, M., Guimarães, D. S., Han, M., & Jung, A. J. (2016). First names as signs of personal identity: An intercultural comparison. *Psychology & Society, 8*(1), 1–21.

Cross-references: Euphemisms; Respect; Cannibalism and Culture Jams (Enemy Images); Sacred Spaces and Holy Places

SEXUALITY

S ex and sexuality can be daunting in terms of the sheer bulk of references to them in both general psychology (114 separate terms refer to sex or sexuality in the *APA Dictionary of Psychology*) and also in cross-cultural psychology (there 14 separate index headings and 8 separate entries for sex-related material in the *Encyclopedia of Cross-cultural Psychology*, or ECCP). For comparison, aggression (probably at least as important in terms of interpersonal relations) has only a single ECCP entry. Sexuality intersects with aggression (sexual assault, rape) and also with feeling (ranging from pain and pleasure during sex activity to the absence of sexual feeling or sexual anesthesia). On the sociocultural side sexuality connects to social roles and individual identity, positive and negative attitudes toward sex (Gregerson, 2013), and sexual value systems. On the biopsychological side, sexuality connects to cognitive processing differences, genetically linked behaviors across species including specific courtship rituals, and evolutionarily determined mating strategies (Buss, 2006). Some overtones of the older Freudian psychology still hover around the topic as well. Probably the most pressing issue in sexuality within culture currently is the conflict between thinking of sex and sexuality as expressions of an underlying mutually exclusive gender dichotomy between 'male' and 'female,' and thinking in terms of gender fluidity within a proliferating range of intermediate forms of both gender membership and sexual expression. Some psychologists and psychiatrists consider this class of 'nonbinary' or 'genderqueer' individuals as a group subject worldwide to marginalization and repression (Richards et al., 2016), as indeed it is. While discrimination against sexual orientation is officially prohibited in several African countries, for instance, persecution of gender-nonconforming behavior is frequent and often cruel, and can be a cause for flight and applications for asylum (Ghelli, 2014).

Exposition, Confrontation, and Simulation

Obviously, real interactive education in the physical dimensions of sexuality would be difficult to specify in a series of lesson plans. However, theoretical attention might be directed to any of the many areas to which sexuality connects, for instance the question of the relation of sexual aggression to cultural characteristics in the perception of sexual harassment. Rebecca Merkin (2008) has a brief, adaptable questionnaire that could be used for exploration of this. More positively, the concept of intimacy may be a good place to start a discussion that indirectly contacts the more physical dimensions of sexuality. William Jankowiak's (2008) edited volume on intimacy traces multiple aspects of universal romantic love (and its violations) across a wide spectrum of cultures. Included in it are, among many others, studies of infidelity in Papua New Guinea, intimacy and masculinity in Nigeria, and Indonesian wedding night stories, all of which should prove to be interesting departure points for conversation about personal experiences with intimacy and other aspects of sexuality.

REFERENCES AND SUGGESTED READINGS

Buss, D. (2006). Strategies of human mating. *Psychological Topics*, *15*(2), 239–260.

Ghelli, T. (2014, December 16). UNHCR helps gay Congolese rejected by his mother find a new home. *UNHCR* (The United Nations Refugee Agency) *website* (online). Retrieved from www.unhcr.org/en-us/news/makingdifference/2014/12/54905cf39/unhcr-helps-gay-congolese-rejected-mother-find-new-home.html [Accessed August 28, 2017].

Gregerson, M. (2013). Sex: Cultural context. In K. Keith (Ed.), *Encyclopedia of cross-cultural psychology* (pp. 1157–1161). New York: Wiley-Blackwell.

Jankowiak, W. R. (Ed.) (2008). *Intimacies: Love and sex across cultures*. New York: Columbia University Press.

Merkin, R. S. (2008). Cross-cultural differences in perceiving sexual harassment: Demographic incidence rates of sexual harassment/sexual aggression in Latin America. *North American Journal of Psychology*, *10*(2), 277–290.

Richards, C., Bouman, W. P., Seal, L., Barker, M. J., Nieder, T. O., & T'Sjoen, G. (2016). Non-binary or genderqueer genders. *International Review of Psychiatry*, *28*(1), 95–102. doi:10.3109/09540261.2015.1106446

Cross-references: Family; Pregnancy and Childbirth; Women's Roles and Rights

WOMEN'S ROLES AND RIGHTS

Neither of the two terms in the title of this entry are indexed in the most recent *APA Dictionary of Psychology*. It seems a reasonable starting point to assert that rights are rights, irrespective of gender or sex, and have been seen so ever since Olympe de Gouges, who should be read at the start, and Mary Wollstonecraft. Cultural theorists, however, reinforce ideas of specific, and often derogatory, inequality between women and others (e.g., by emphasizing the universality of relatively greater frequency of involvement in direct child care by women, or by describing cultures in terms of 'masculine' and 'feminine' values—drive for success, for example, for the former; nurturance for the latter). These asymmetries—which easily become inequalities in popular as well as academic discourse—are in themselves worth discussing. More to the point for this particular topic would be discussion about why the fundamental right to vote was awarded to women in the United States nearly 150 years after the country was founded, and why proposed constitutional amendments guaranteeing equal rights for women and men have foundered since that time at both the state and national levels. A discussion of this history would be in keeping with the feminism of current psychology (Isanski, 2009; Rutherford & Pettit, 2015).

Exposition, Confrontation, and Simulation

Mostly confrontation is recommended here. Spirited discussion can be had, the more so if the surrounding culture is high in power distance (i.e., inequality) and high masculine in the Hofstede system. The following two suggestions are offered to start:

1. In all countries, work is necessary and a primary form of self-definition and self-regard. Regarding compensated work only, it is also a worldwide phenomenon that women's work is compensated, on average, at about 65–70 percent of men's. Leaving aside for

the moment the question of how to define 'woman' and 'man' (which can itself be the basis of another spirited discussion, and very necessary if there is no parallel course in women's studies, psychology of gender, or the like), the issue can be raised for explanation and theorizing. The results may be predicted to be no less superstitious and preposterous as any others explaining and defending inequality. For a start, consult the World Bank's 2012 report entitled *Gender Equality and Development* (World Bank, 2012).

2. Should the discussion prompted by Option 1 prove too tame, shift to a more macroscopic view and compare the status of women in the immediate ambient culture with that of women in Ghor, Afghanistan (Mashal & Nader, 2017). Examples this strong may shock, but what else is a cross-cultural course for?

REFERENCES AND SUGGESTED READINGS

Isanski, B. (2009, July–August). The history of women in psychology. *APS (American Psychological Society) Observer* (online newsletter). Retrieved from www. psychologicalscience.org/observer/the-history-of-women-in-psychology [Accessed November 2, 2017].

Mashal, M., & Nader, Z. (2017, July 8). No justice, "no value" for women in a lawless Afghan province. *The New York Times* (online).Retrieved from www.nytimes.com/2017/07/08/ world/asia/afghanistan-women-honor-killings.html?_r=0 [Accessed July 9, 2017].

Rutherford, A., & Pettit, M. (2015). Feminism and/in/as psychology: The public sciences of sex and gender. *History of Psychology, 18*(3), 223–237. Retrieved from http://dx.doi. org/10.1037/a0039533

World Bank. (2012). *World development report 2012: Gender equality and development* (Chapter 5; Gender Differences in Employment and Why They Matter) (Online report). Retrieved from http://econ.worldbank.org/WBSITE/EXTERNAL/ EXTDEC/EXTRESEARCH/EXTWDRS/EXTWDR2012/0,contentMDK:22999750~ menuPK:8154981~pagePK:64167689~piPK:64167673~theSitePK:7778063,00.html [Accessed November 2, 2017].

Cross-references: Corporate and Work Culture; Pregnancy and Childbirth; Family

Social Perception and Cognition

BROOMS (ANIMISM, ANTHROPOMORPHISM, AND DEHUMANIZATION)

Animism and anthropomorphism are conceptually close: both imply the presence of life-like or human-like characteristics in nonhuman or inanimate objects. One benign psychological interpretation of animism is to see it as related to pantheism, panentheism, or pan-spiritualism. Some see religion as an outgrowth of the fusion, by distant early ancestors, of animistic or anthropomorphic traits to the idea of a single creator god (Peoples, Duda, & Marlowe, 2016). A more mundane interpretation is reflected in purchasers' imparting lifelike qualities to consumer products, for instance perceiving a certain car as an embodiment of love (Avis, 2011). Other somewhat more negative views of animism connect it, via the theories of Piaget and other developmentalists, to cognitive immaturity (Drescher, 2013). Recently, Lasana Harris and Susan Fiske (Harris & Fiske, 2008; Harris & Fiske, 2011) have drawn attention to the role that animism plays in dehumanization. Animism, they claim, referring as an example to the transmutation of the animated brooms in the early Walt Disney film *Fantasia* from willing helpers to conspiring killers, is a visible embodiment of cognitive processes related to making dispositional attributions about other humans. These ease the process of divesting groups of humans— including entire cultures—of their human characteristics, while also activating the amygdala, making them easier to hate and kill.

Exposition, Confrontation, and Simulation

Collect examples of characters and objects that reflect animism in both children and adults. These could range from Hello Kitty through Transformers to 'cute' products in the IKEA catalog. Likewise, collect, from as many cultural sources as possible, animations that embody the characteristics that make killing acceptable (these could be entirely innocent: my wife suggests Bugs Bunny). A search for violent animation across cultures should be an interesting voyage. Discuss common features of animism and attempt to draw the line between benign and dehumanizing varieties. As many will recall, sunglasses worn by the randomly assigned 'guards' were a memorable prop in the well-known Stanford Prison Experiment (Haney, Banks, & Zimbardo, 1973). A replication of Zhong et al.'s study (2010) in which wearing sunglasses decreased prosocial behavior should be easy to do and effective in conveying the essential features of the concept of dehumanization. Further, expand outward from Harris and Fiske to examine concepts of depersonalization, dehumanization, and distancing from moral responsibility as expressed in other comprehensive psychological theories, for example Albert Bandura's (2016) work on moral disengagement.

REFERENCES AND SUGGESTED READINGS

Avis, M. (2011). Anthropomorphism and animism theory in branding. In Z. Yi, J. J. Xiao, J. J. Cotte, & L. Price (Eds.), *AP-Asia Pacific advances in consumer research* (Vol. 9, pp. 313–319). Duluth, MN: Association for Consumer Research.

Bandura, A. (2016). *Moral disengagement: How people do harm and live with themselves*. New York: Worth Publishers.

Drescher, C. F. (2013). Animism. In K. Keith (Ed.), *Encyclopedia of cross-cultural psychology* (pp. 66–69). New York: Wiley-Blackwell.

Haney, C., Banks, C., & Zimbardo, P. (1973, September). A study of prisoners and guards in a simulated prison. *Naval Research Reviews*, 1–17.

Harris, L. T., & Fiske, S. T. (2008). The brooms in *Fantasia*: Neural correlates of anthropomorphizing objects. *Social Cognition*, *26*(2), 210–223.

Harris, L. T., & Fiske, S. T. (2011). Dehumanized perception: A psychological means to facilitate atrocities, torture, and genocide? *Zeitschrift für Psychologie*, *219*(3), 175–181.

Peoples, H. C., Duda, P., & Marlowe, F. W. (2016). Hunter-gatherers and the origins of religion. *Human Nature*, *27*(3), 261–282.

Zhong, C-B., Bohns, V. K., & Gino, F. (2010). Good lamps are the best police: Darkness increases dishonesty and self-interested behavior. *Psychological Science*, *21*, 311–314.

Cross-references: Cartoons; Cannibalism and Culture Jams (Enemy Images); Materialism and Consumer Culture

CANNIBALISM AND CULTURE JAMS (ENEMY IMAGES)

The visual representation of enemies flowered in the Renaissance: few modern artists can compete with Luca Signorelli (one of Freud's favorites) or Hieronymus Bosch in conjuring images of the Devil and his minions. Currently the whole of North Korea is a living enemy-images museum, faithfully reproducing—with some added traditional Asian luridness (and complete inaccuracy with regard to its subject matter)—the full aesthetic panoply of 1940s Soviet propaganda art. In psychological literature the Middle Ages brought forth the Malleus Maleficarum or 'Witches' Hammer,' which, at least in some psychiatrists' views (e.g. Menninger, 1968) presaged current psychiatric diagnostic manuals. Later evolutions led to the Freudian cabinet of the uncanny (Freud, 1919/1999) with its trenchant portraits of our oldest enemy, death. A peculiarly enticing image that encompasses all enemies, especially those from strange lands (read, other cultures) is the cannibal, as intellectual histories as well as poetry attest (Avramescu, 2011; Sinclair, 2016). Kelly Watson (2015) makes a persuasive case for the metaphoric transmutation of both women and indigenous cultures into the image of the cannibal, attacked and subdued by European colonizing masculinity. Turning from these classic literary and artistic images of the enemy to logos, which may be more familiar to cross-culturalists with a corporate bent, *culture jammers* deface and subvert the public corporate face of business and politics (Madrigal, 2012), not always to the disadvantage of the subverted (at least on the principle that 'any press is good press').

Exposition, Confrontation, and Simulation

Allowing that actual anthropophagy will probably not be countenanced, a good start can be had by doing the 'enemy images' exercise in Goldstein's *Cross-cultural Explorations* (mentioned already as a background text in the introduction to this book). This involves collecting images, and these are not hard to find in archives (e.g., National Archives, n.d.) or in more vernacular places, such as cartoons. Extension from images to verbal and gestural insults is natural and there are numerous web sources that will offer examples of these. An entertaining early historical psychological source is the collection of ethnophaulisms (cross-national, ethnic, and other group-related slurs) by Roback (1944): Rappoport (2005) and Hughes (2015) further extend this line of inquiry. Search for common features or apply theory ad lib. For a more activist culture jamming activity, appropriate political or corporate images and practice creative defacement, taking cues from Marcel Duchamp (L. H. O. O. Q.). Be careful, though, to do this where it does not violate local regulations as in some places interference with political speech is a misdemeanor offense.

REFERENCES AND SUGGESTED READINGS

Avramescu, C. (2011). *An intellectual history of cannibalism*. New Brunswick, NJ: Princeton University Press.

Freud, S. (1999). The "uncanny". In S. Freud (Ed.), *The standard edition of the psychological works of Sigmund Freud, Vol. XVII (1917–1919): An infantile neurosis and other works* (pp. 217–256). London: Vintage. (Originally published 1919).

Hughes, G. (2015). *An encyclopedia of swearing: The social history of oaths, profanity, foul language and ethnic slurs in the English-speaking world*. New York: Routledge.

Madrigal, A. C. (2012, May 15). The new culture jamming: How activists will respond to online advertising. *The Atlantic* (online magazine). Retrieved from www.theatlantic.com/technology/archive/2012/05/the-new-culture-jamming-how-activists-will-respond-to-online-advertising/257176/ [Accessed October 6, 2017].

Menninger, K. (1968). *The crime of punishment*. New York: The Viking Press.

National Archives (UK). (n.d.). The art of war: Propaganda. *The National Archives (UK) website* (online). Retrieved from www.nationalarchives.gov.uk/theartofwar/prop/ [Accessed October 6, 2017].

Rappoport, L. (2005). *Punchlines: The case for racial, ethnic, and gender humor*. New York: Greenwood Publishing Group.

Roback, A. A. (1944). *A dictionary of international slurs (ethnophaulisms): With a supplementary essay on aspects of ethnic prejudice*. Cambridge, MA: Sci-Art Publishers.

Sinclair, S. (2016). *Cannibal*. Lincoln, NE: University of Nebraska Press.

Watson, K. (2015). *Insatiable appetites: Imperial encounters with cannibals in the North Atlantic world*. New York: New York University Press.

Cross-references: Cartoons; Brooms (Animism, Anthropomorphism, and Dehumanization); Rights, Citizenship, and Voting; Petty Crime

CARTOONS

Cartooning occurs across the world: considered here will be only cartoons that are accessible via print or online news sources. The analysis of graffiti, whether raw or cooked, would itself be a great cross-cultural entry point. Cartooning has recently been a stimulant for eruptions of the greatest current world fear, terrorism, in connection with the depiction of religious figures in profane iconography, in Denmark and most recently in France, where the offices of a popular weekly were attacked in retaliation for depictions of Islam (Nugier & Guimond, 2016). The role of cartooning and caricature in cultural friction is beginning to be discussed by psychologists (e.g., Lading, 2008). Christine Davies's review of two recent books about Australian cartooning provides a framework for understanding cartooning as both humor and cultural commentary (Davies, 2014).

Exposition, Confrontation, and Simulation

Editorial or political cartoons are easy to get by googling. For instance, just now I googled 'political cartoons in Senegal.' My selection on the first page of images included some US cartoons referring to contagion and the Ebola virus in connection with Senegal, but most were actually from Senegal or other nearby regions. The third interesting image that I clicked led in two directions. It contained a wordless political cartoon from Africa depicting two Islamist extremists arguing over a bar of music, and an insightful short essay on the power of cartooning to change African politics and society (Omolayo, 2015), both of which could certainly serve as a reading and focus of discussion of cartooning's role across cultures. Both the imagery and the captions of cartoons can be foci of analysis and discussion. Most often cartoon captions are in the language common to the region: Pakistani and Indian cartoons sometimes cross this barrier for English. The Senegal cartoons I just saw contained phrases in both French (in which I'm only very weakly fluent after three college semesters) and Arabic (about which

I have little to no idea). This in itself should be a stimulus to research, if only to find a translator! Captions, as Mark Twain observed in *Life on the Mississippi*, are essential: a cartoon, like the paintings of celebrated US Civil War generals he was describing, "means nothing without its label" (Clemens, 1883, p. 448). Full analysis of any quotation may uncover, as I did when I traced the reference to Beatrice Cenci (do this!) in this passage from Mark Twain, instances of cultural "ghosting" (Fryd, 2006) of underlying motives for the actions in the cartoon.

REFERENCES AND SUGGESTED READINGS

Clemens, S. L. ("Mark Twain") (1883). *Life on the Mississippi*. Boston, MA: James Osgood and Company. Available via Project Gutenberg online www.gutenberg.org/files/245/245-h/245-h.htm and on Archive.org, paginated. Retrieved from https://archive.org/stream/lifeonmississipptwai#page/448/mode/2up/search/Jackson

Davies, C. (2014). Reviews of comic commentators: Contemporary political cartooning in Australia and The Ernies book: 1000 terrible things Australian men have said about women. *Humor: International Journal of Humor Research, 25*(4), 515–518.

Fryd, V. G. (2006). The "ghosting" of incest and female relations in Harriet Hosmer's "Beatrice Cenci". *The Art Bulletin, 88*(2), 292–309.

Lading, A. (2008). Kulturelle spejlinger af profeten Muhammad (Cultural reflections of the prophet Muhammad). *Matrix: Nordisk Tidsskrift for Psykoterapi, 25*(2), 177–191.

Nugier, A., & Guimond, S. (2016). "Je suis Charlie": New findings on the social and political psychology of terrorism. *International Review of Social Psychology, 29*(1), 45–49.

Omolayo, O. (2015). These cartoonists have helped to change the face of politics in Africa. *VentureAfrica* (web magazine) (online). Retrieved from http://venturesafrica.com/these-cartoonists-have-helped-to-change-the-face-of-politics-in-africa/ [Accessed August 6, 2017].

Cross-references: Cannibalism and Culture Jams (Enemy Images); Religion and Law; Language and Accents

COLOR AND SKIN COLOR

Psychologists address the question of whether people perceive or understand color differently due to their culture mostly from the perspective of language. Languages differ in the number of basic color categorizations, so some languages have only a few—as few as two (light and dark)—and some have upwards of 10. Evidence exists to support both the view that humans all see color in the same way due to the identity of eye and brain structures, as well as the view that language acquisition and learning create different color experiences across and within cultures. Until some more reliable method of telling whether one person's phenomenal experience (or hears, or feels, or tastes, or smells) emerges, this uncertainty will persist. Color symbolism differs across cultures and relates to language and learning as well as well as to the capability of humans to create arbitrary color categories, that is, colors that are purely symbolic, for instance, a particular shade of green used to identify a political party. Color's connection to emotion is likewise quite variable (Adams & Osgood, 1973; Hupka, Zaleski, Otto, Reidl, & Tarabina, 1997). Skin color is without doubt the most divisive concept in all of society all across the world, productive of hot and defensive emotions. For a recent example, observe the case of the too-light Beyoncé (Fortin, 2017). Skin color is a factor in computer face recognition, a complex problem which has not yet been fully solved. A decision is still pending on the optimal color space system for skin color discrimination (Shaik, Ganesan, Kalist, Sathish, & Jenitha, 2015) as well as on the optimal methods for doing so (Pujol, Pujol, Jimeno-Morenilla, & Pujol, 2017). At least one group of vision scientists has speculated on the possibility of brown being as elemental a color primary as yellow or red (Fuld, Werner, & Wooten, 1983). And, most recently, genetic research has uncovered genetic instructions for skin color that are shared worldwide, suggesting, again, that skin color is a relative and graded series rather than a set of discrete categories (Zimmer, 2017). But that does not stop humans from wielding skin color as a blunt discriminatory instrument unconnected to actual color theory and vision science, computer science, or science of any sort. See the recommended demonstration which follows.

Exposition, Confrontation, and Simulation

At least have fun with some of the color issues that this area of cross-cultural psychology uncovers. For theory's sake, review hue, brightness, lightness, and saturation; review the difference between light and pigment primaries (additive and subtractive mixtures); and get used to ranges within hues. Mix pigments to create an unusual color (e.g., rust), and show how it varies along a continuum of lightness by adding pure white (tinting) or pure black (shading). Be as creative when making colors as you can be—my favorite is chrome, and you might like colors with mixed glitter—but do include rust (and if so inclined to extra effort, produce a rust-colored light using mixed lights rather than pigments). Discuss emotionality regarding color: inventory everyone's favorite and least favorite colors in terms of the emotions that they evoke, collate these, and seek commonalities. Using Hupka et al.'s list of emotions, compare the local results. Discuss arbitrary color categories: would the 'red, white, and blue' of the US or French flags (among many others) be as meaningful if they had originally been the copper, eggshell, and licorice? Could they be changed, now, at will? Investigate the reasoning behind the blue of the Blue Man Group; compare this with the approach of Glenn Ligon to Blackness (Cotter, 2017). Compare and discuss colors of the human body that have little variance among people, for instance, the color of blood or the color of the liver. After doing that, do the following: Cut squares of white copier paper about 50 mm square, with an aperture about 20 mm square in the middle. Lay these squares on two human forearms or other places where skin is exposed and where a photograph (a cellphone is satisfactory) can be made of both surfaces together. Next, compare the colors showing in the apertures with each other, and with the surrounding paper square. Only one of these items will be *white*—ever. Establish the hue name for the colors in the apertures: someone who is adept at manipulating computer images should, if available, collect all the images and cut and arrange the aperture colors in a sequence from lightest to darkest. Compare this with the many iterations of skin color scales available online. There is a science of the variation in lightness, and it's worth discussing and reading the elementary education materials available (e.g., Smithsonian Institution, n.d.), but only after it's established with physical and theoretical certainty that the variance is one of degree, not kind.

REFERENCES AND SUGGESTED READINGS

Adams, F. M., & Osgood, C. E. (1973). A cross-cultural study of the affective meanings of color. *Journal of Cross-Cultural Psychology*, *4*(2), 135–156.

Cotter, H. (2017, August 10). Glenn Ligon rethinks the color line in the show "Blue Black." *The New York Times* (online newspaper). Retrieved from https://mobile.nytimes.com/2017/08/10/arts/design/glenn-ligon-rethinks-the-color-line-in-the-show-blue-black.html [Accessed September 17, 2017].

Fortin, J. (2017, July 21). Beyoncé statue at Madame Tussaud's is 'adjusted' after criticism. *The New York Times* (online newspaper). Retrieved from www.nytimes.com/2017/07/21/arts/music/beyonce-madame-tussauds-wax-statue.html?mcubz=3&_r=0 [Accessed September 17, 2017].

Fuld, K., Werner, J. S., & Wooten, B. R. (1983). The possible elemental nature of brown. *Vision Research*, *23*(6), 631–637.

Hupka, R. B., Zaleski, Z., Otto, J., Reidl, L., & Tarabina, N. V. (1997). The colors of anger, envy, fear, and jealousy. *Journal of Cross-cultural Psychology*, *28*(2),

Pujol, F., Pujol, M., Jimeno-Morenilla, A., & Pujol, M. J. (2017). Face detection based on skin color segmentation using fuzzy entropy. *Entropy*, *19*, 26. (MDPI).

Shaik, K. B., Ganesan, P., Kalist, V., Sathish, B. S., & Jenitha, J. M. M. (2015). Comparative study of skin color detection and segmentation in HSV and YcbCr color space. *Procedia Computer Science*, *57*, 41–48.

Smithsonian Institution. (n.d.). Human skin color variation. *On: What Does It Mean to Be Human?* (website page, Smithsonian Museum of Natural History). Retrieved from http://humanorigins.si.edu/evidence/genetics/human-skin-color-variation [Accessed September 17, 2017].

Zimmer, C. (2017). Genes for skin color rebut dated notions of race, researchers say. *The New York Times* (online newspaper). Retrieved from www.nytimes.com/2017/10/12/science/skin-color-race.html?_r=0 [Accessed November 1, 2017].

Cross-references: The Club (Privilege and Exclusion)

EYE CONTACT

Traditionally, cultures venerate the gaze: adages like 'the eyes are the windows of the soul' or the refrain "Drink to me only with thine eyes" from Ben Jonson's 'Song: To Celia' testify to the pervasiveness of the idea that sight projects power. Add to this the tradition in many cultures of the belief in the evil eye. Blue and white glass bulls-eye amulets themselves called 'evil eyes,' said to have power to avert malevolent rays of gaze and often interwoven with the hand-like symbol of the Hamsa, are readily available in shops and online from vendors catering to clientele from the Middle East and Africa. I received my first one from a Turkish friend, and I have anecdotal evidence for its effectiveness. Not everyone agrees about the positive importance or the value of gaze. The conceptual artist Robert Smithson, writing to his wife about an exhibit of his paintings in 1961, said that he was distressed by the public exposure of his art. "But what can I do?" he said.

> This is the 20th century and the whole world is on a tour inspecting the rotting remains of a vanished age. . . . People want to stare with aggressive eagerness or they feel they must stare in order to grant approval. There is something indecent about such staring.
>
> (Tsai, 2004, p. 41)

The neuropsychology of gaze reveals a widely distributed collection of brain regions that cooperate in social perception (Itier & Batty, 2009). Gaze may be at least unconsciously aimed at objects of affection, and individuals who are asked to gaze into each other's eyes report feeling heightened feelings of desire after the experience (Bolmont, Cacioppo, & Cacioppo, 2014; Epstein, 2010). Frequently gaze is cited as a primary physical and social marker of cultural membership and cultural difference. For example, an averted or indirect gaze in the United States may be interpreted as evasive or dishonest, while a similar downcast or avoidant gaze may be understood as a sign of respect in Asian and Middle Eastern cultures.

Exposition, Confrontation, and Simulation

Discussion may emerge from tabulation of gaze experiences or by listing places where staring is expected, and where it is not at all acceptable (e.g., New Jersey: "Whaddya lookin' at?"). The 'power of gaze' demonstration is simple to replicate (Catron, 2015). Cross-cultural examples of eye contact are embedded in the multitudinous sites offering cultural travel advice. Likewise, many examples of watching and being watched can be discovered in literature, art, and film.

REFERENCES AND SUGGESTED READINGS

Bolmont, M., Cacioppo, J. T., & Cacioppo, S. (2014). Love is in the gaze: An eye-tracking study of love and sexual desire. *Psychological Science, 25*, 1748–1756.

Catron, M. L. (2015, January 9). To fall in love with anyone, do this (Updated with podcast). *The New York Times (Modern Love Blog)* (online). Retrieved from www.nytimes.com/2015/01/11/fashion/modern-love-to-fall-in-love-with-anyone-do-this.html [Accessed July 13, 2017].

Epstein, R. (2010, March 3) Keeping love alive: *Scientific American* does its part. *Scientific American Mind Matters* (Blog). Retrieved from www.scientificamerican.com/article/science-of-love/ [Accessed July 18, 2015].

Itier, R. J., & Batty, M. (2009). Neural bases of eye and gaze processing: The core of social cognition. *Neuroscience and Biobehavioral Review, 33*(6), 843–863.

Tsai, E. (Ed.) (2004). *Robert Smithson*. Berkeley, CA: University of California Press.

Cross-references: Color and Skin Color; Food and Art; Surveillance and Eyewitnessing

PRIVACY

Privacy is a nexus term in psychology and culture: the concept intersects directly with ideas of boundaries, openness, secrecy, and rights. Within the United States, from an economic perspective it ties into the question of public vs. private services, a politically fraught border politically in virtually all areas of government and commerce (e.g., the question of private vs. public hospitals, or proposals to 'privatize' essential services such as air traffic control or the funding of road infrastructure construction). Privacy has been at the center of psychology's self-definition as a science. Questions of whether private events, whether thought or even speech, are ultimately private, inward, and therefore not directly observable have fueled debates about whether psychology can be a science based on publicly observable and replicable data. Cognitively and socially, privacy turns on questions of expectations. Exclusion and segregation link to the idea of a place which is personally inviolate and to self-defense. Ultimately there are deep connections between privacy and shame (Schneider, 1977). From a cultural perspective there are also interesting variations as well. Cultures that are more demonstrative and open may have less expectation and demand for privacy. Some remarkably well-regulated and sober cultures allow public nudity, for example, or periods of time when regulations are relaxed (e.g., Carnival times) and the private becomes momentarily publicly accessible for enjoyment. Irwin Altman (1977) and Newell (1998) together provide a panoramic view of the cultural differences in perceptions of privacy: recent research tends to focus on privacy vs. exposure across social media. Karniel and Lavie-Dinur (2015) examine how concepts of privacy are affected in Israel by the shift toward a more open, communicative, and individualistic society.

Exposition, Confrontation, and Simulation

List actions that can and cannot be done in public; list and discuss laws and areas of regulation specifically directed at ensuring privacy, for instance, expectations of privacy on the internet. Read Nathaniel Simmons's account of his big blue health secret (Simmons, 2014) for an idea of how different the experience of privacy can be in another culture. Historically, trace the evolution of modern privy councils from the groups of retainers who served and controlled access to medieval kings in their private rooms. Survey to find experiences of privacy violations in earlier educational and family environments: grade and junior-high teachers in the United States are sometimes quite intrusive in their management of electronic communications, and parents' transgressions into personal space increase during adolescence. Rather than engaging in any direct violations of personal privacy or space, take a more design-oriented approach. For example, sketch out how privacy would be managed and maintained in various situations (hospital, climbing expedition, traveling). Form groups and, after discussing the relative need for privacy among each, have each group design a living space that would accommodate both socialization and privacy.

REFERENCES AND SUGGESTED READINGS

Altman, I. (1977). Privacy regulation: Culturally universal or culturally specific? *Journal of Social Issues, 33*, 66–84.

Karniel, Y., & Lavie-Dinur, A. (2015). *Privacy and fame: How we expose ourselves across media platforms.* Lanham, MD: Lexington Books.

Newell, P. B. (1998). A cross-cultural comparison of privacy definitions and functions: A systems approach. *Journal of Environmental Psychology, 18*(4), 357–371.

Schneider, C. D. (1977). *Shame, exposure, and privacy.* New York: W. W. Norton & Company.

Simmons, N. (2014). My "big" blue health secret: My experience with privacy, or lack thereof, in Japan. *Health Communication, 29*, 634–636.

Cross-references: Housing, Personal Space, and Segregation; Rights, Citizenship, and Voting; Boundaries

SAFETY AND DANGER

Maslow's motivational framework slots safety, next to basic survival needs, as essential. The two main divisions of psychological theories of safety and danger are environmental and interpersonal. At the beginning of the 20th century, accidents were mostly explained, psychologically, with reference to the habits or personality of the unlucky victim (Burnham, 2010), summarized in the idea that some individuals were genetically more likely to be 'accident prone'. Over the past hundred years the development of a science of human-machine systems has removed the stigma of 'accident proneness' and replaced it with systems engineered to guide and reinforce safe operation of vehicles and machinery. But as vehicles have become more predictable, humans worldwide have remained prone to unsafe behavior. Partly this is due to environmental and economic factors. Rapid increases in car ownership in China and India, where roads are often unimproved and are crowded with pedestrians and motorized small craft, lead to fatality rates tens of times higher than in Europe. Unsafe behaviors are also determined by individual and cultural patterns of risk approach and avoidance. For instance, Chinese, Japanese, and US accident rates vary: Japanese accident rates are lower because the culture is more risk-averse than the others (Atchley, Shi, & Yamamoto, 2014). Also, cultures vary in the amount of safety devices they deploy and maintain. Guardrails, for instance, are placed along roads in both Denmark and Uganda. In Denmark they are a permanent part of the roadscape, but in Uganda they rapidly fall victim to economic necessity and are regularly stolen and turned into saucepans or privy supports. Cultural attitudes and behaviors toward alcohol also play a role in motor safety.

Exposition, Confrontation, and Simulation

Motor safety is only one small area in which safety behaviors are culturally modulated. Building outward from this, discussion could turn on the ways in which highly regimented safety cultures—air travel has many examples—can be defeated by cultural factors. Instructions to pilots may be misunderstood due to linguistic errors: disruption of flights by passengers claiming entitlements based on their place in a social hierarchy may occur (Borowiec, 2015). Development of a checklist that includes all potential sources of danger in air travel could be generated and compared with official protocols, for instance those of the US Transportation Safety Authority or the safety agencies in other countries (TSA, 2017). It should not be ignored that individuals are perceived as 'unsafe' based on specific appearance or mode of dress: this form of rapid cognitive typing could also be extended to other factors that may incite suspicion (Kane, Jacobs, & Hawkins, 2015). There are many lists of relatively safe vs. unsafe countries and these can also be launching points for discussion of practical ways to keep safe as well as of the metrics used to arrive at the definitions of countries or regions as 'safe'. One of the most successful classroom demonstrations I experienced was given by a student from Venezuela who used a combination of personal experience as well as YouTube videos incorporating surveillance footage of armed robbery and kidnapping to demonstrate the environment in which street smarts would need to be quickly learned (see e.g., Casey, 2016). If students are intending to travel abroad on internships or for enrichment, some cautionary tales could be told about the relative amounts of supervision and safeguards in remote locations. Finally, interpersonal and emotional safety can be discussed and dramatized in the contexts of cultural safety (Richardson & Williams, 2007) and 'safe spaces' for discourse.

REFERENCES AND SUGGESTED READINGS

Atchley, P., Shi, J., & Yamamoto, T. (2014, September). Cultural foundations of safety culture: A comparison of traffic safety culture in China, Japan, and the United States. *Transportation Research, Part F: Traffic Psychology and Behavior, 26*, Part B, 317–325.

Borowiec, S. (2015, February 12). Ex-Korean air executive sentenced to prison in 'nut rage' case. *Los Angeles Times* (online). Retrieved from www.latimes.com/world/asia/la-fg-south-korea-nut-rage-case-20150212-story.html [Accessed July 22, 2015].

Burnham, J. (2010). *Accident prone: A history of technology, psychology, and misfits in the machine age.* Chicago, IL: University of Chicago Press.

Casey, N. (2016, January 21). Q & A: Is it safe to visit Venezuela? In Moving to Venezuela, a land in turmoil. *The New York Times (World: Reporter's Notebook)*, January 21 through February 9, 2016 (online). Retrieved from www.nytimes.com/interactive/projects/cp/ reporters-notebook/moving-to-venezuela [Accessed July 22, 2017].

Kane, M. N., Jacobs, R. J., & Hawkins, W. E. (2015). Beliefs about safety and religious and cultural diversity. *Journal of Social Service Research, 41*(5), 622–641.

Richardson, S., & Williams, T. (2007). Why is cultural safety essential in health care? *Medicine and Law, 26*(4), 699–707.

TSA (Transportation Security Administration). (2017). Security screening. *TSA website* (online). Retrieved from www.tsa.gov/travel/security-screening [Accessed July 22, 2017].

Cross-references: Health and Sanitation; Insurance: Risk and Future Time Orientation

SURVEILLANCE AND EYEWITNESSING

Historically all cultures have had systems of surveillance and eyewitnessing. Watchtowers were built for observation and signaling; armies have always posted sentries. Seafarers, faced with the necessity for constant surveillance, evolved a complex system of watches designed to balance out hours on deck and night work (Lindsay, 1874). All legal systems rely on eyewitness testimony, which has a complex history itself. In the 17th century English law broke with traditions of Continental law that apportioned weights to witnesses based on their number and reliability (Wigmore, 1901); today there is still significant cultural variation in who can count as an eyewitness. For instance, in Yemen, a woman's testimony counts half as much as a man's (Basha, Ghanem, & Abdulhafid, 2005; Hoffman, 2016). Eyewitnessing also includes historic prophetic and cultural narrative traditions and extends to current queer-theoretical accounts of surveillance and control of gender and sexuality across cultures (McCormack, 2014).

Exposition, Confrontation, and Simulation

From a practical and current standpoint, surveillance and eyewitnessing come together in a US as well as a cross-cultural context around surveillance technology. In instructional settings, the following pathways are starting points for discussion:

1. Examine differential acceptance of surveillance across cultures *plus* acceptance of surveillance based on social connection to place. Various questionnaires can be created on-the-spot to evaluate group opinions about surveillance. Specifically, discussion could center around situations in which surveillance would be rated as acceptable (e.g., in the aftermath of terroristic events, e.g., Landler & Sussman, 2013). O'Donnell, Jetten, and Ryan (2010) suggest that identification with a group under threat will lead to

surveillance being perceived as more acceptable: this would be an easy result to replicate and test. Further discussion could extend ideas in the Privacy entry in this book. A survey of the areas in which surveillance cameras would be acceptable or not could be done in conjunction with a survey of situations rated as least to most private. Internet and social media privacy, very prominent in social science research recently as well as a focus of many legislative interventions (NCSL, 2017), would be an area in which many individuals would have had direct experience.

2. Examine eyewitness testimony research. Body cameras for police are being implemented worldwide (e.g., Correspondent Staff, 2017). These devices can be obtained fairly cheaply and getting one would be good investment. Simulation of a pursuit and arrest could be done and comparisons between eyewitness accounts and the body camera input could be made, extending the exercises provided by Gary Wells on his website (Wells, 2017).

3. In conjunction with Item 2, extend eyewitness testimony issues to the cross-*ethnicity* effect (Stepanova, 2013). Set up cross-ethnic/cross-gender simulations, film with the body camera, and discuss. In the absence of a body camera, photo decks for comparing faces can be easily assembled from published photos in news magazines or other sources online. A method for training the technique suggested by the studies of McDonnell, Bornstein, Laub, Mills, and Doddet al. (2014) of focusing more on the lower parts of the face in recognition tasks can be designed.

REFERENCES AND SUGGESTED READINGS

Basha, A., Ghanem, R., & Abdulhafid, N. (2005, October 14). Women's rights in the Middle East and North Africa—Yemen. *Freedom House* (online). Retrieved from www.refworld.org/docid/47387b712f.html [Accessed August 5, 2017].

Correspondent Staff. (2017, May 8). China: Body cameras on "chengguan" officers to boost public image. *Asian Correspondent* (online magazine). Retrieved from https://asiancorrespondent.com/2017/05/china-body-cameras-chengguan-officers-boost-public-image/#IOLjDLWImCHP4ldz.97 [Accessed August 11, 2017].

Hoffman, C. (2016, March 14). Yemen. *Women Around the World* (Weblog, Penn State University). Retrieved from https://sites.psu.edu/chloehoffmanciblog/2016/03/14/yemen/ [Accessed August 5, 2017].

Landler, M., & Sussman, D. (2013, April 30). Poll finds strong acceptance for public surveillance. *The New York Times* (online). Retrieved from www.nytimes.com/2013/05/01/us/poll-finds-strong-acceptance-for-public-surveillance.html [Accessed August 11, 2017].

Lindsay, W. S. (1874). *History of merchant shipping and ancient commerce.* London: S. Low.

McCormack, D. (2014). *Queer postcolonial narratives and the ethics of witnessing.* New York: Bloomsbury.

McDonnell, G. P., Bornstein, B. H., Laub, C. E., Mills, M., & Dodd, M. D. (2014). Perceptual processes in the cross-race effect: Evidence from eyetracking. *Basic and Applied Social Psychology, 36*(6), 478–493.

NCSL. (2017). State laws related to internet privacy. *National Conference of State Legislatures (NCSL) website* (online). Retrieved from www.ncsl.org/research/telecommunications-and-information-technology/state-laws-related-to-internet-privacy.aspx [accessed August 11, 2017].

O'Donnell, A. T., Jetten, J., & Ryan, M. K. (2010). Who is watching over you? The role of shared identity in perceptions of surveillance. *European Journal of Social Psychology, 40*(1), 135–147.

Stepanova, E. V. (2013). Cross-ethnicity effect (Face recognition). In K. D. Keith (Ed.), *Encyclopedia of cross cultural psychology* (pp. 286–288). New York: Wiley-Blackwell.

Wells, G. (2017). *Personal website, Iowa State University* (online). Retrieved from https://public.psych.iastate.edu/glwells/ [Accessed August 11, 2017].

Wigmore, J. H. (1901). Required numbers of witnesses: A brief history of the numerical system in England. *Harvard Law Review, 15*(2), 83–108.

Cross-references: Color and Skin Color; Women's Roles and Rights; Privacy; Law Enforcement

STUPIDITY AND INTELLIGENCE

Stupidity is practiced more than it is studied. It is probably a human cultural universal though not celebrated as such. The economic historian Carlo Cipolla sketched a framework for locating stupidity in the universe of human behavior, using a 2 × 2 graph (Pomeroy, 2016). The x-axis extends continuously from 'harmful to self' to 'helpful to self', and the y-axis from 'harmful to others' to 'helpful to others'. Those who are 'helpful to self but harmful to others' are of course bandits; those who are both self- and other-harmful are, according to this scheme, stupid. Stupidity is the B side of intelligence, and it is not unexpected that a highly credentialed generalist in the intelligence field assembled a comprehensive set of academic essays on the subject (Sternberg, 2003), examining the foibles of managers, politicians, and other foolish creatures. Stupidity also twines around the roots of humor, a rich vein of cross-cultural interplay (Yu, Jiang, Lu, & Hiranandani, 2016).

Exposition, Confrontation, and Simulation

Students can, and should, share and document experiences of stupidity. This might extend from cultural faux pas through beginners' ignorance and even to interpersonal relations. Stupid is as stupid does, as Forrest Gump said, and there are lots of videos of pratfalls and epic fails across cultures. Patricia Greenfield's *American Psychologist* article on the vagaries of intelligence and ability testing across cultures (Greenfield, 1997) neatly synthesizes, with several cogent examples, the ways in which tests can portray intelligence incompletely and inaccurately across cultures. The well-known Kpelle object-sorting study (Cole, Gay, Glick, & Sharp, 1971) and Greenfield's own studies of Piagetian conservation and collective vs. individualistic problem solving could be briefly replicated as examples for discussion and possible extension of cognitive and developmental studies across cultures. Taking tests of out-of-domain knowledge can stimulate feeling stupid in testing situations. Provide yarn and needles and see how many individuals are and are not fluent in a common task! Many tests for pilots, truckers, and other highly skilled professions, crafts, and trades are also readily available for practice on the internet. Beyond this, exploration of Cipolla's taxonomy of stupidity could be done with case studies, locating the actors in each of the four cells and, after identifying those who fall into the 'stupid' cell, examining each in more detail.

REFERENCES AND SUGGESTED READINGS

Cole, M., Gay, J., Glick, J., & Sharp, D. W. (1971). *The cultural context of learning and thinking.* New York: Basic Books.

Greenfield, P. M. (1997). You can't take it with you: Why ability assessments don't cross cultures. *American Psychologist, 52*(10), 1115–1124.

Pomeroy, R. (2016, September 14). The basic laws of human stupidity. *RealClear Science* (blog) (online). Retrieved from www.realclearscience.com/blog/2016/09/the_basic_laws_of_human_stupidity.html [Accessed August 15, 2017].

Sternberg, R. J. (Ed.) (2003). *Why smart people can be so stupid.* New Haven, CT: Yale University Press.

Yu, X., Jiang, F., Lu, S., & Hiranandani, N. (2016). To be or not to be humorous? Cross-cultural perspectives on humor. *Frontiers of Psychology, 7.* doi:10.3389/fpsyg.2016.01495

Cross-reference: Young and Old

Interpersonal
Interaction

CHARITY

Charity is prescribed by all major world religions and it is essential for economic functioning. For instance, in the area of health care, donated care by physicians is built in as an expected contribution to economic models of health care even in cultures such as the Netherlands where private insurance and public support of health expenses have reached a steady equilibrium (White & Eijkholt, 2015). Likewise, pro bono contributions are expected from other professions including law and psychology. Charity as a specific form of prosocial behavior has only recently received detailed attention in the scientific literature of psychology. The results of recent studies suggest that the determinants of charitable actions are nuanced across cultures. Peter Smith of the University of Sussex (UK), drawing on several global databases including the World Values Survey, recently analyzed data from 135 nations to test hypotheses about the effects of various structural variables (national wealth, relative income equality or inequality, trust, absence of corruption, in-group favoritism and uncertainty avoidance) on the prosocial behaviors of charitable giving, helping a stranger, and volunteering time (Smith, 2015). Regarding giving, he found that low in-group favoritism and low uncertainty avoidance most strongly predicted charitable giving. Interestingly, in view of the stress placed on charitable giving in all major world religions, he found that there was significantly more giving in less religious nations. Klein, Grossman, Uskul, Kraus, and Epley (2015) performed an experiment across seven national cultures (Austria, China, Denmark, Turkey, Russia, UK, and the United States). They presented participants with a scenario in which one of two participants in a hypothetical experiment, provided with an endowment standardized to $6 across cultures, was free to donate from 0/6 to 6/6 to the other person, described as a stranger who the giver had never met. Klein et al. asked participants to evaluate the prosociality of the giver and also his warmth and his competence. (Note: only men were represented in the scenarios.) They found an asymptotic result: after 3/6 of the endowment was shared, sharing of greater amounts did not increase the perceptions of prosociality, warmth, or competence. In fact, in some cases they found that the evaluation of the giver's competence decreased with greater hypothetical generosity, suggesting links to evaluations of rationality and intelligence accompany charitable actions.

Exposition, Confrontation, and Simulation

Both Smith and Klein et al. are excellent sources to consult to identify major cross-cultural data sources and to get an idea of how they can be used to construct variables for multivariate research. Klein et al.'s study is simple and could be replicated with or without variations in small or large classes. For instance, the factors of gender, cultural membership, and religious affiliation, among other variables, could be introduced. Examination of mutual-sharing insurance practices such as Muslim *takaful* and Amish community support for health expenses can be examined as forms of charity (Rohrer & Dundes, 2016). For instance, the benefits of working in a community-building charitable role, as a volunteer or as a salaried person taking on, in effect, a voluntary vow of relatively less affluence (though not poverty) are well described in the *Community Tool Box* produced by the Center for Community Health and Development at the University of Kansas (Center for Community Health and Development, 2017). Chapter 28 especially is a rich source for motives and strategies for innovative participation in community charity and for discussion and simulation.

REFERENCES AND SUGGESTED READINGS

Center for Community Health and Development (U. of Kansas). (2017). Community tool box (Chapter 28: Spirituality and community building). *Community Tool Box website of the KU CCHD* (online). Retrieved from http://ctb.ku.edu/en/table-of-contents/spirituality-and-community-building/being-charitable-towards-others/main [Accessed July 25, 2017].

Klein, N., Grossman, I., Uskul, A. K., Kraus, A. A., & Epley, N. (2015). It pays to be nice, but not really nice: Asymmetric reputations from prosociality across 7 countries. *Judgment and Decision Making*, 10(4), 355–364.

Rohrer, K., & Dundes, L. (2016). Sharing the load: Amish healthcare funding. *Healthcare,* *4*(4), pii E92 (online). Retrieved from www.ncbi.nlm.nih.gov/pmc/articles/ PMC5198134/ [Accessed July 25, 2017].

Smith, P. B. (2015). To lend helping hands: in-group favoritism, uncertainty avoidance and the national frequency of pro-social behaviors. *Journal of Cross Cultural Psychology,* *46*(6), 759–771.

White, B. D., & Eijkholt, M. (2015). Physician charity care in America: Almost always an illusion, ever more commercial. *Laws,* *4*, 201–215. Open access online. Retrieved from www.mdpi.com/journal/laws [Accessed July 25, 2017].

Cross-references: Conscription and Volunteerism; Religion and Law; Insurance: Risk and Future Time Orientation

COMPROMISE AND TOLERANCE

Compromise is an idea that is often, especially recently in the United States, in bad odor. From the viewpoint of the basic definition of culture adopted here, it may seem that engaging in a compromise is a downrating of or even an outright betrayal of values. Especially in the political arena, compromise may seem to threaten otherwise healthy competitiveness and thus may be vigorously resisted on that principle. From a theoretical psychological standpoint, compromise connects to ideas in the areas of negotiation, behavioral optimization, and satisficing (Brown, 2004). It is related to ideas of 'good enough' that surface from time to time in the field in connection with the ability to accept less than perfection or completeness in problem solutions. There is a natural conceptual tie between compromise and studies of tolerance. Theories of coalition building are also in play (Fine & Halkovic, 2014). Interpersonal relations are a fertile ground for theoretical examination of compromise: marriage and family counseling has a strong stream of ideas about bringing mutually conflicting parties together as do legal psychology and the psychology of conflict resolution. A recent study (Kaplan et al., 2017) confronted US, Chinese, and Iranian individuals with narratives that activated core personal values that are resistant to compromise, analyzing brain activity while doing so. More intensive processing occurred in areas of the brain connected to understanding and interpreting narrative when core values were foregrounded, differing in strength across national groups. This heightened activity may correlate with the intensity with which compromise across cultures is resisted when negotiations touch on core values, resistance that may be moderated with more attention to cultural differences (Marsella, 2015).

Exposition, Confrontation, and Simulation

Gather personal examples of compromise, interpersonal and social, attending to the circumstances in which a need for compromise arose and the ways in which it was (or was not) achieved. For more confrontation, select a controversial issue which doesn't seem to admit of compromise and discuss. Sites aimed toward secondary school students in history and government often contain materials with which historic situations of compromise can be regenerated and, as far as possible, reenacted. Extensive materials for a psychologically based course on dealing with conflict are available on the *Beyond Intractability* website (Burgess & Burgess, 2017). Consider also examining the Interpersonal Tolerance Scale (Thomae, Birtel, & Wittemann, 2016) for which materials are available for inspection online.

REFERENCES AND SUGGESTED READINGS

Brown, R. (2004). Consideration of the origin of Herbert Simon's theory of "satisficing," 1933–1947. *Management Decision, 42*(10), 1240–1256.

Burgess, G., & Burgess, H. (Eds.) (2017). Dealing constructively with intractable conflicts. *Beyond Intractability Knowledge Base* (program website) (online). Retrieved from www.beyondintractability.org/educationtraining/dealing-constructively-intractable-conflicts [Accessed October 29, 2017].

Fine, M., & Halkovic, A. (2014). A delicate and deliberate journey toward justice: Challenging privilege: Building structures of solidarity. In P. T. Coleman, M. Deutsch, & E. C. Marcus (Eds.), *The handbook of conflict resolution: Theory and practice* (3rd ed., pp. 56–75). San Francisco, CA: Jossey-Bass.

Kaplan, J. T., Gimbel, S. H., Dehghani, M., Immordino-Yang, M. H., Sagae, K., Wong, J. D., Tipper, C. M., . . . Damasio, A. (2017). Processing narratives concerning protected values: A cross-cultural investigation of neural correlates. *Cerebral Cortex, 27*(2), 1428–1438.

Marsella, A. (2015). Reflections on the cultural contexts of conflict resolution via truth and reconciliation processes. In M. Galluccio (Ed.), *Handbook of international negotiation: Interpersonal, intercultural, and diplomatic perspectives* (pp. 287–295). Cham, Switzerland: Springer International Publishing.

Thomae, M., Birtel, M. D., & Wittemann, J. (2016). *The Interpersonal Tolerance Scale (ITPS): Scale development and validation.* Paper presented at the 2016 Annual Meeting of the International Society of Political Psychology, Warsaw, Poland, 13th–16th July, 2016 (online). Retrieved from https://manuelathomae.files.wordpress.com/2016/07/the-interpersonal-tolerance-scale-ipts.pdf [Accessed October 29, 2017].

FRIENDSHIP

The title of a comprehensive recent cross-cultural psychological treatment of friendship (Harré & Moghaddam, 2013) reflects friendship's implication of a corresponding dark side of enmity. Friendships may differ in depth and intensity across culture. For instance, the Chinese conception of 'friend' is less inclusive than the Western term and is limited to "long time close friend" (Chen, 2013). Likewise, it is more likely that people will say that they have specific personal enemies in Ghana than in the United States (Stambor, 2005). However, friendship's historic and cultural universality may outweigh these region-specific nuances. Friends add to, and sometimes supplant, the social support afforded by families. Friendship, including self-friendship (Krakovsky, 2012), is a mainstay of mental health. Friendship may span species (Dunbar, 2014) and, through the medium of cultural and educational exchange, is one of the surest routes to intercultural understanding in humans (Gareis, 2017; US Department of State, n.d.).

Exposition, Confrontation, and Simulation

Examine the texture of friendships in the immediate environment by creating sociograms (Trimble, n.d.) of friend networks. Set criteria for deciding the degree to which these cross cultural boundaries and discuss those that do. Also, become familiar with psychological measurements of friendship, for example the Hawthorne Friendship Scale (Hawthorne, 2006, accessible via US Department of Defense, n.d.) and the McGill Friendship Questionnaire (Mendelson & Aboud, 2012). Use these to reveal other dimensions of friendship and, if possible, compare results across cultures. Exchange student experiences are more frequent than might be supposed. Survey to see how prevalent these are. Individuals who have been exchange students themselves or who are members of families who have been exchange hosts often have formed durable friendships, and their stories can illustrate the successes as well as the challenges of friendship across borders. For a more macrocultural approach, look into the history of bridges bearing the specific name 'Friendship Bridge' (hint: two of these connect North Korea with neighboring countries). For an artistic approach, curate and discuss the role of friendship as represented in examples of art celebrating international friendship, for instance Alfred Janniot's 1934 narrative sculpture 'Friendship Between America and France' at Rockefeller Center, New York (Rockefeller Center, n.d.), or the Statue of Liberty.

REFERENCES AND SUGGESTED READINGS

Chen, F. F. (2013). Construct equivalence. In K. Keith (Ed.), *Encyclopedia of cross cultural psychology* (pp. 235–236). New York: Wiley-Blackwell.

Dunbar, R. (2014, May 21). Friendship: Do animals have friends too? *New Scientist*(online). Retrieved from www.newscientist.com/article/mg22229700-400-friendship-do-animals-have-friends-too/ [Accessed October 8, 2017].

Gareis, E. (2017). Intercultural friendships. *Oxford Research Encyclopedias Online: Communication*. Retrieved from http://communication.oxfordre.com/view/10.1093/acrefore/9780190228613.001.0001/acrefore-9780190228613-e-161 [Accessed October 8, 2017].

Harré, R., & Moghaddam, F. M. (2013). *The psychology of friendship and enmity: Relationships in love, work, politics, and war* (2 vols.). New York: Praeger.

Hawthorne, G. (2006). Measuring social isolation in older adults: Development and initial validation of the Friendship Scale. *Social Indicators Research, 77,* 521–548.

Krakovsky, M. (2012, July 1). Self-compassion fosters mental health. *Scientific American* (online magazine). Retrieved from www.scientificamerican.com/article/self-compassion-fosters-mental-health/ [Accessed October 8, 2017].

Mendelson, M. J., & Aboud, F. (2012). McGill Friendship Questionnaire: Respondent's Affection (MFQ-RA). *Measurement Instrument Database for the Social Sciences MIDSS* (website) (online). Retrieved from www.midss.org/sites/default/files/mfq-ra.pdf [Accessed October 8, 2017].

Rockefeller Center. (n.d.). Friendship Between America and France (1934). *Rockefeller Center (NYC) website* (online). Retrieved from www.rockefellercenter.com/art-and-history/art/friendship-between-america-and-france/ [accessed October 8, 2017].

Stambor, Z. (2005, June). Perceptions of enemies differ across cultures. *Monitor on Psychology* (American Psychological Association), *36*(6), 18. Retrieved from www.apa.org/monitor/jun05/perceptions.aspx [Accessed October 8, 2017].

Trimble, J. (n.d.). How to create a more connected class. *Western Washington University, Center for Instructional Innovation and Assessment website* (online). Retrieved from http://cii.wwu.edu/cii/resources/modules/connections/default.asp [Accessed October 8, 2017].

US Department of Defense. (n.d.). Friendship Scale assessment. At *Afterdeployment. org, DCoE* (Defense Centers of Excellence for Psychological Health and Traumatic Brain Injury) *website* (US Department of Defense) (online). Retrieved from http://afterdeployment.dcoe.mil/sites/default/files/pdfs/assessment-tools/friendship-assessment.pdf [Accessed October 8, 2017].

US Department of State. (n.d.). Why participate? *Bureau of Educational and Cultural Affairs Exchange Programs, U.S. Department of State* (US Federal Government website). Retrieved from https://exchanges.state.gov/non-us/why-participate [Accessed October 8, 2017].

Cross-references: Family; Loyalty

INTERPERSONAL TRUST

O ne of the mottos of the United States blazoned on its currency (discounting the intervention of the supernatural) emphasizes the indispensability of trust in culture. Trust is a bedrock element in Erik Erikson's theory of development and is essential for carrying out human interchanges: economic, romantic, and therapeutic. As a variable in cross-cultural studies, interpersonal trust is increasingly studied across areas of psychological interest. For instance, in a case study of team building in virtual environments (Cheng et al., 2016), interpersonal trust varied depending on the degree of multicultural makeup of teams. Language and task clarity were factors that influenced trust levels. Ward, Mamerow, and Meyer(2014) found some support as well as some contrary evidence for the theoretical differentiation between 'high trust' and 'low trust' societies advanced by political scientist Francis Fukuyama (1996). Persons less likely to express trust include those with lower incomes, those who are younger, and those in poor health. Along with its being an essential element for commerce and the maintenance of social institutions, trust is also basic to more intimate interpersonal relations as well. A recent study carried out in Ethiopia (John, Tsui, Seme, & Roro, 2017) validates this claim and affirms the consensus that trust scales developed in Western cultures are cross-culturally valid.

Exposition, Confrontation, and Simulation

Seek out and become familiar with interpersonal trust scales, e.g., the Rotter Interpersonal Trust Scale (Rotter, 1967), many versions of which are available gratis online. Examine the trust variables included for the first time in the sixth and seventh waves of the *World Values Survey* (available at www.worldvaluessurvey.org/WVSOnline.jsp) and compare by country. These include 'trust in people you have met for the first time,' 'trust in neighborhood,' 'trust in people of another nationality,' 'trust in family,' 'trust in people of another religion.' A classic trust story from Ireland can be adapted for a simulation. In 1970, during a six-month strike of the Irish banks, a network of interpersonal financial trust emerged to keep the country's economy flowing more or less normally. Personal checks were exchanged, and pub owners—nodes of trust in their communities who were well acquainted with the habits of their customers and could accurately judge their trustworthiness—became intermediaries and facilitators of the process (Brancaccio, 2017; Haque, 2010; Smith, 2017). Based on this episode, conjure a scenario in which some essential element of social life is lost: a food shortage, a natural disaster, a war, a failure of government, or similar. Discuss who would be the persons most likely to be trusted to fulfill various necessary roles (communicators, expert advisors, resource providers, interpersonal supporters, etc.) and sketch out systems of trust that might potentially emerge. Could a world of Irish pubs be the future of intercultural trust?

REFERENCES AND SUGGESTED READINGS

Brancaccio, D. (2017, September 18). Using stories to teach economics. *National Public Radio Marketplace* (online broadcast transcript). Retrieved from www.marketplace. org/2017/09/18/education/economics-education [Accessed September 18, 2017].

Cheng, X., Fu, S., Sun, J., Han, Y., Shen, J., & Zarifis, A. (2016). Investigating individual trust in semi-virtual collaboration of multicultural and unicultural teams. *Computers in Human Behavior, 62,* 267–276.

Evans, A. M., & Revelle, W. (2008). Survey and behavioral measurements of interpersonal trust. *Journal of Research in Personality, 42*(6), 1585–1593.

Fukuyama, F. (1996). *Trust: the social virtues and the creation of prosperity.* New York: Simon & Schuster.

Haque, U. (2010, November 29). The Irish banking crisis: A parable. *Harvard Business Review* (online). Retrieved from https://hbr.org/2010/11/the-irish-banking-crisis-a-par [Accessed September 18, 2017].

John, N. A., Tsui, A. O., Seme, A., & Roro, M. A. (2017). Understanding the meaning of marital relationship quality among couples in peri-urban Ethiopia. *Culture, Health, & Sexuality, 19*(2), 267–278.

Rotter, J. B. (1967). A new scale for the measurement of interpersonal trust. *Journal of Personality, 35*(4), 651–665.

Smith, R. (2017, April 12). Episode 764: Pub in a box. *National Public Radio Planet Money Podcast* (online podcast/broadcast transcript). Retrieved from www.npr.org/templates/transcript/transcript.php?storyId=523653040 [Accessed September 18, 2017].

Ward, P. R., Mamerow, L., & Meyer, S. B. (2014). Interpersonal trust across six Asia-Pacific countries: Testing and extending the 'high trust society' and 'low trust society' theory. *PLoS ONE, 9*(4), e95555. doi:10.1371/journal.pone.0095555

Cross-references: Money; Sexuality; Family

LOYALTY

Loyalty is a primary virtue in the Boy Scout Law (second on the list after trustworthiness) though for some reason it's not mentioned in the Girl Scout Law. In psychology it's not featured in personality theories, though it is specifically mentioned in the '24 Character Strengths' of positive psychology (VIA Institute, 2017) in connection with justice and teamwork. Possibly this lack of attention to loyalty stems from psychology's stance as a science based on statistical decision, ready to change hypotheses based on new data. Possibly, too, it reflects an underlying US cultural attitude in which life is characterized by change, and where it's considered necessary to act according to one's self-interest as conditions alter. Choices of job, place of residence, and of relationship partners aren't meant to be permanent. There is substantial variation in marriage longevity and divorce rates worldwide (Engel, 2014): the United States is near, but not at, the top of the list in divorces. Unequivocal statements on the relative latent loyalty of gay marriages are difficult to find, though there's general agreement that same-sex couples are less likely to divorce in the United States. If PsycINFO is a good measure of research interest, the preponderant connection between loyalty and psychology is in the idea of 'brand loyalty': purchasing a product again rather than switching. This is not surprising in a culture in which success is often tied to sales. If one were looking for a clear contrast in loyalty 30 years ago, the comparison of employee loyalty to employers in Japan vs. the United States would have been a standout example. However, the idea of long-term employment, and any associated feelings of loyalty, has eroded significantly in Japan and in several other countries (Lund, 2016).

Exposition, Confrontation, and Simulation

The question of the cross-cultural status of loyalty presents many challenges for study, but also many opportunities to engage with essential questions. A start could be made by raising the question of whether loyalty is related to a specific emotion or combination of emotions, as recent research suggests (DeLeersnyder, Koval, Kuppens, & Mesquita, 2017). Discussion might also begin by inventorying and classifying the characteristics that would lead to staying loyal to family, friends, and long-term partners. A survey could be developed that could incorporate these elements and compared to the scale developed by Lugo Steidel and Contreras (2003) to measure *familismo*, a term used to describe the loyalty to nuclear and extended family in Hispanic culture, and analyzed and discussed in terms of the cultural similarities and contrasts that are revealed. Many sites and research articles in psychology deal with the question of brand loyalty worldwide and questionnaires from different countries may reveal cultural nuances of the concept. The demand for loyalty oaths continues to crop up (e.g., Owens, 2015). The question of whether loyalty can be compelled is an important one in intercultural relations in the United States, and a simulation might be based on the 1943 questionnaire presented to interned Japanese-American citizens interned in the War Relocation Authority camps in California and other states (Densho Encyclopedia, 2014). Also, searching for stories of loyalty may ultimately lead to an appreciation of the universality of this rare trait. A start could be the story of the shipwreck of the Malaysian cargo ship Selendang Ayu off the Alaska coast in December, 2004. The disabled ship's Indian Master assigned 18 of the 26 crewmen deemed non-essential to be airlifted to safety by the US Coast Guard. After the ship ran aground, the Master called for help to evacuate the remaining crew. The rescuing helicopter was swamped by a wave and crashed, and six of the seven just-rescued crew drowned. The survivor was a cadet (apprentice), from either India or the People's Republic of China, who insisted on remaining with the skeleton crew out of "loyalty to the Master" (NTSB, 2006).

REFERENCES AND SUGGESTED READINGS

DeLeersnyder, J., Koval, P., Kuppens, P., & Mesquita, B. (2017, June). Emotions and concerns: Situational evidence for their systematic co-occurrence. *Emotion, 17*(6), 895–1045.

Densho Encyclopedia contributors. (2014, May 12). Loyalty questionnaire. *Densho Encyclopedia* (online). Retrieved from http://encyclopedia.densho.org/Loyalty_questionnaire/ [Accessed July 24, 2017].

Engel, P. (2014, May 25). Divorce rates around the world. *Business Insider* (online). Retrieved from www.businessinsider.com/map-divorce-rates-around-the-world-2014-5 [Accessed July 24, 2017].

Lugo Steidel, A. G., & Contreras, J. M. (2003). A new familism scale for use with Latino populations. *Hispanic Journal of Behavioral Sciences, 25*, 312–330.

Lund, E. (2016, February 16). Study suggests Japanese workers are deeply distrustful of their employers. *Japan Today website* (online). Retrieved from https://japantoday.com/category/features/lifestyle/study-suggests-japanese-workers-are-deeply-distrustful-of-their-employers [Accessed July 24, 2017].

NTSB. (2006). Marine accident brief, Accident No. DCA-05-MM-008 (M/V Selendang Ayu). *National Transportation Safety Board.* Washington, DC (online copy). Retrieved from www.ntsb.gov/investigations/AccidentReports/Reports/MAB0601.pdf [Accessed July 24, 2017].

Owens, E. (2015, August 19). ACLU threatens lawsuit over 'McCarthy Era' loyalty oath for Nebraska teachers. *The Daily Caller* (online newspaper, Nebraska). Retrieved from http://dailycaller.com/2015/08/19/aclu-threatens-lawsuit-over-mccarthy-era-loyalty-oath-for-nebraska-teachers/ [Accessed July 24, 2017].

VIA Institute on Character. (2017). VIA classification of character strengths. *VIA Institute website* (online). Retrieved from www.viacharacter.org/www/Character-Strengths/VIA-Classification [Accessed July 24, 2017].

Cross-references: Private and Commercial Transportation; Family

THE CLUB (PRIVILEGE AND EXCLUSION)

The concepts of privilege and exclusion are central to cultural studies today. They are so essential that they probably need no introduction, since they are encountered not only in workshops on racial and gender prejudice but also in humbler settings such as farmer's markets (Rice, 2015). Rather than offering the usual sample of potentially engaging areas for interaction that appear in the other entries, here appears just one, a simple and most compelling enactment of this VICI (very important cultural issue) by my students. (Special thanks to Tyrell Hemingway, the creator of the original 'club.')

Exposition, Confrontation, and Simulation

My students created, at 2:30 in the afternoon in an otherwise ordinary classroom in our art building, a posh urban club. The room was darkened; deep violet light and slow strobes replaced the ceiling fluorescents; tables and the projector cart were turned into a DJ stand and a serving center; tables were set in enclaves around a central dance floor. Music boomed, buzzed, and thudded: outside, patrons (members of the class, numbering more than 30) lined up, hemmed in by faux velvet ropes, in front of a class door guarded by a sufficiently brooding bouncer. The club's staff emerged from inside the room and worked the line. Some individuals had special green tickets, received in advance; they were quickly pulled out and let in, free of charge, and then seated at the best tables, designated by flowers and other ornaments. Others in the line shuffled slowly forward, quizzed in depth by the bouncers and grudgingly granted admittance to less desirable locations. Some were, in advance, told to go elsewhere in the building and only much later knew that there was even a club in operation. The students mounting this presentation dressed the part of the managers, with sunglasses and sharp suits, and schmoozed the elite, plying them with perks.

When the lights went up and everyone in the class was reunited, I had to rate this dramatization of wealth inequality (the VICI subject in question) a captivating success. But the wealth hierarchy was not all that was implied. The club's dark and slightly sinister environment conveyed a sense of comfortable separateness from ordinary routine and, by extension, from ordinary law. It exuded the atmosphere of sanctioned illegality, a safe haven for covert dealing and black marketeering—easy enough for a moralistic instructor to link to the idea of corruption and its role in culture (see the Corruption entry in this book). Further connections could easily be made between the situation and the cozy clubbiness of established power networks, embodied in the inspired acting of our 'evening's' hosts. (Actually, the acting wasn't anything out of the ordinary and merely suggested subterranean connections to hidden power, but in that environment, little more was needed.) The selective process of admission and administration of comps, as well as the misdirection of others, perfectly illustrated the concepts of privilege and exclusion (Potapchuk, 2005; Minkov, 2011). I could not *require* that this pop-up club emerge again, but if in the future a student took the hint and re-created it, I'd certainly follow this activity with a viewing of The School of Life's video "Why Some Countries are Poor and Others Rich" (TSL, 2014), emphasizing especially the role corruption and insider clannishness play in social selection.

REFERENCES AND SUGGESTED READINGS

Minkov, M. (2011). *Cultural differences in a globalizing world*. Bingely: Emerald Publishing Ltd.

Potapchuk, M. (2005). What is white privilege? In M. Potapchuk, S. Leiderman, D. Bivens, & B. Major (Eds.), *Flipping the script: White privilege and community building* (Chapter 6, pp. 53–70). Silver Spring, MD: MP Associates.

TSL. (2014). Why some countries are poor and others rich. *Online Video (YouTube)*. Retrieved from www.youtube.com/watch?v=9-4V3HR696k [Accessed September 17, 2017].

Cross-reference: Corruption

RESPECT

R espect is one of the most frequently mentioned very important cultural issues, and also one of the cardinal principles in the American Psychological Association's Ethics Code. Psychological theory (Janoff-Bulman & Werther, 2008) divides respect into categorical and contingent types. Categorical respect is accorded to humans for being human and members of society; contingent respect is established within social subgroups and depends on a complex set of estimations of self and other based on rank, relative power, and degree of equality. Sara Lawrence-Lightfoot (2000), suggests that the extension of respect begins with an attitude of openness and interest and a readiness to communicate. Cross-culturally, respect is closely related with the idea of 'face' and its maintenance. The maintenance process, termed 'facework' (Ting-Toomey, 2013), involves a similarly complex set of attitudes and behaviors that maintain individuals' standing relative to each other and their group, behaviors that differ depending on whether the culture is primarily individualistic or collectivistic. The relation of respect to power and control becomes clearly visible when its opposite, disrespect, is considered. Relatively powerless groups, for instance adolescents (Barber, Xia, Olsen, McNeely, & Bose, 2012), may be especially sensitive to the absence of respect. Groups that have experienced severe social discrimination may perceive the attainment of 'respectability' to be a bad bargain involving the loss of autonomy and identity (Young, 2016).

Exposition, Confrontation, and Simulation

Some of my own best experiences in the cross-cultural class have occurred when students have reenacted situations involving disrespect. For a more theoretical approach, consider collecting and taxonomizing instances of disrespect at the hands of VE (Vulgar Euphemism) individuals as described by Howard (2016). There are several sources for facework practice: Domeneci and Littlejohn (2006) provide numerous examples for individual and group practice. Building on the material provided in Leary, Brennan, and Briggs (2005), a scale specifically focused on respect (vs. esteem) can be created, completed, and discussed.

REFERENCES AND SUGGESTED READINGS

Barber, B. K., Xia, M., Olsen, J. A., McNeely, C. A., & Bose, K. (2012). Feeling disrespected by parents: Refining the understanding and measurement of psychological control. *Journal of Adolescence, 35*(2), 273–287.

Domeneci, K., & Littlejohn, S. W. (2006). *Facework: Bridging theory and practice.* Thousand Oaks, CA: Sage.

Howard, D. J. (2016). The Vulgar Euphemism (VE) Scale: Entitled incivility in social relations. In D. J. Howard (Ed.), *The psychology of consumer and social influence: Theory and research.* Hauppage, NY: Nova Science Publishers.

Janoff-Bulman, R., & Werther, A. (2008). The social psychology of respect: Implications for delegitimization and reconciliation. In A. Nadler, T. Malloy, & J. Fisher (Eds.), *The social psychology of intergroup reconciliation* (pp. 145–170). New York: Oxford University Press.

Lawrence-Lightfoot, S. (2000). *Respect: An exploration.* Cambridge, MA: Perseus Books.

Leary, J. D., Brennan, E. M., & Briggs, H. E. (2005). The African American adolescent respect scale: A measure of a prosocial attitude. *Research on Social Work Practice, 15*(6), 462–469.

Ting-Toomey, S. (2013). Face-negotiation conflict theory. In K. Keith (Ed.), *The encyclopedia of cross- cultural psychology* (pp. 535–539). New York: Wiley-Blackwell.

Young, D. (2016, March 21). The definition, danger, and disease of respectability politics, explained. *The Root (blog)* (online). Retrieved from www.theroot.com/the-definition-danger-and-disease-of-respectability-po-1790854699 [Accessed October 22, 2017].

Cross-references: Euphemisms; Sexuality

TRIBALISM

Tribalism is among the most ancient formulations of culture study. Tribal life was equated with primitive culture in 19th century anthropology; then, tribes were viewed politically as enemies (as they were during the aggressions of the United States against its native populations in the 19th century) or, alternately and somewhat later historically, as laboratory case studies of contrast with modern conditions (for instance, Erik Erikson's studies of Hopi culture). Currently, *tribalism* and *tribes* are often used to refer to an exaggerated form of social grouping involving the formation of fragmented clusters centered around particular interests or views, hyper-exclusionary and more aggressively defended. Most definitions of tribalism emphasize the aspect of group loyalty. Today discussions of tribalism are also connected with markets and especially with the generation of temporary interest groups via social media. A central founding document for this approach is Cova and Cova (2002), and an interesting contrast between attitudes toward business formation, in which Swedes are tribal and Tanzanians more or less homogenously entrepreneurial, is drawn by Tillmar (2006). Tribalism in a more traditional sense of clannishness has been identified in other secular environments, even in higher education (Daniel & Chew, 2013). The equation of tribalism with the development of consumer communities (Skandalis, Byrom, & Banister, 2016) should not preclude seeing traditional tribalism among indigenous populations, for instance in Kenya and Ghana, or in the connection between traditional family clans and religion as in Afghanistan and other similar cultures. Nor should religious tribalism be limited to Asian and African environments: the term *tribalism* has emerged as a descriptor of the mix of religious and political value contradictions characterizing current American politics (Reich, 2014).

Exposition, Confrontation, and Simulation

Tribalism offers a naturally contentious area for interaction. While classic demonstrations of group conformity (e.g., Asch) could be done as an introduction to some of the basic psychological processes involved in group cohesion, they would probably not capture the distinguishing features of tribal behavior. For that, something like the Sherifs' 'Robbers' Cave' experiments are a historical precedent, but impractical for a time-limited interaction. A sample of tribalism might be induced simply by forming teams for any competition and observing any minor instances of trash talk during the process. Alternatively, a film of the London Marathon start described by Kovach (2017) could be procured to see if similar tribal identification with one of the starting groups occurs while watching. In an attempt to counteract religious tribalism, Ginges, Sheikh, Atran, and Argo (2016) constructed a version of the 'trolley problem' in experimental ethics, in which the opportunity to sacrifice either one's self or an in-group member is offered to save the life of an out-group member (in this case, the in-group was practicing Palestinian Muslims and the out-group Israeli Jews). They claimed that adoption of the point of view of Allah by Muslim participants lowered their willingness to sacrifice an out-group member and returned a substantial participants to a neutral state on the issue. A simulation or limited replication of their study would be reasonably simple to do and could also introduce discussion of whether the 'trolley problem' itself, widely used in studies of morals and ethics, is the most effective strategy available (Khazan, 2014).

REFERENCES AND SUGGESTED READINGS

Cova, B., & Cova, V. (2002). Tribal marketing: The tribalisation of society and its impact on the conduct of marketing. *European Journal of Marketing, 36*(5).

Daniel, D. B., & Chew, S. L. (2013). The tribalism of teaching and learning. *Teaching of Psychology, 40*(4) 363–367.

Ginges, J., H. Sheikh, S. Atran, and N. Argo. (2016). Thinking from God's perspective decreases biased valuation of the life of a nonbeliever. *Proceedings of the National Academy of Sciences, 113,* 316–319.

Khazan, O. (2014, July 24). Is one of the most popular psychology experiments worthless? *The Atlantic* (online magazine). Retrieved from www.theatlantic.com/health/archive/2014/07/what-if-one-of-the-most-popular-experiments-in-psychology-is-worthless/374931/ [Accessed August 18, 2017].

Kovach, R. (2017, July 26). How tribalism hurts companies, and what to do about it. *Harvard Business Review* (online). Retrieved from https://hbr.org/2017/07/how-tribalism-hurts-companies-and-what-to-do-about-it [Accessed August 18, 2017].

Reich, R. (2014, March 25). Robert Reich: Tribalism is tearing America apart. *Salon* (online magazine). Retrieved from www.salon.com/2014/03/25/robert_reich_tribalism_is_tearing_america_apart_partner/ [Accessed August 18, 2017].

Skandalis, A., Byrom, J., & Banister, E. (2016). Paradox, tribalism, and the transitional consumption experience: In light of post-postmodernism. *European Journal of Marketing, 50*(7–8), 1308–1325.

Tillmar, M. (2006). Swedish tribalism and Tanzanian entrepreneurship: Preconditions for trust formation. *Entrepreneurship and Regional Development, 18*(2), 91–107.

Cross-references: Disaster and War; Loyalty; Materialism and Consumer Culture

Emotion, Motivation, and Health

DISABILITIES

The concept of 'disabilities' is fraught and contested: cross-culturally there are huge gulfs in the acceptance and treatment of disability. In the United States and Canada, blindness and deafness themselves are thought to be cultures themselves (Clerc Center, n.d.; Hopfe, 1999). In Africa, stigmatization and isolation still characterize responses to deafness (Fullerton, 2013). Down Syndrome, a prime example of intellectual disability, is welcomed in some cultures. In the United States there are several organizations that encourage acceptance and even adoption of children with this condition (e.g., Global Down Syndrome Foundation, n.d.; Reece's Rainbow, n.d.) In other cultures elsewhere in the world, Down Syndrome unleashes superstition and intolerance (Bolongaro, 2016). In Europe and the United States, the lifespan of a person with Down Syndrome extends, due to the wide availability of scientifically based medicine, well past 50 years. In places where medical treatment for the congenital heart problems that accompany the syndrome in young children is available only due to donations and charity, and almost always takes place out-of-country, most children with Down Syndrome die early (Hitayezu, Ndahindwa, Murorunkwere, Uwineza, & Mu et al., 2016). Differences also exist in the willingness of cultures and countries to tolerate abortion in cases of birth defects. These wide disparities should be the starting point for any simulations or discussions in a cross-cultural format. Disabilities, since they are included in the major diagnostic systems, also stand as proxy for the full spectrum of mental disorders and an entry point for regional and cultural acceptance and treatment of these.

Exposition, Confrontation, and Simulation

No practical simulation of the full cultural experience of disability is possible short of actually living with it. Many hearing loss and vision loss simulations are available online, many times passive demonstrations of the grades of attenuation of sensation. There are many simple interactive activities that have been devised to simulate experiences of blind navigation and recognition (e.g., Willings, n.d.); there are fewer similar activities involving hearing loss, since simply plugging the ears isn't a good substitute for actual hearing loss. Possibly the closest approach to a demonstration of how hearing loss might affect social interaction and performance would be to set up some form of virtual auditory experience (Shilling & Shinn-Cunningham, 2002) in which sounds were strategically placed around a room to either distort or impede communication. Sign language is eminently teachable and would be another port of entry to understanding deaf culture. Search out, also, the very convincing account of the relation of deafness and music (Kolb, 2017) also found in the references to the Silences entry in this book. Stories of individuals who have persevered and emerged victorious over challenging sensory or intellectual conditions have always been attractive and inspiring: search these out (e.g., Gee, 2016; Karush, 2003). Likewise, blogs of persons actively challenging perceptions of disability, for instance Carrie Wade (e.g., Wade, 2016), are essential. Discussion and a simulated ratification of the United Nations Convention on the Rights of Persons with Disabilities (United Nations, n.d.) would provide a full spectrum of the ways in which disabilities integrate with all aspects of culture worldwide. In this context, a search of the range of laws protecting disability worldwide can be undertaken, and the results compared.

REFERENCES AND SUGGESTED READINGS

Bolongaro, K. (2016, August 15). Living with Down's syndrome in Kinshasa, DRC. *Aljazeera.com* (Online news source). Retrieved from www.aljazeera.com/indepth/features/2016/08/living-syndrome-kinshasa-drc-160811090938621.html [Accessed October 13, 2017].

Clerc Center. (n.d.). American deaf culture. *Laurent Clerc Education Center (Gallaudet University) website*. Retrieved from www3.gallaudet.edu/clerc-center/info-to-go/deaf-culture/american-deaf-culture.html [Accessed October 13, 2017].

Fullerton, K. (2013, August 6). Deafness in sub-Saharan Africa. *The Borgen Project* (Blog). Retrieved from https://borgenproject.org/deafness-in-sub-saharan-africa/ [Accessed October 14, 2017].

Gee, A. (2016, September 29). A world without Down's syndrome? *BBC News Magazine* (online). Retrieved from www.bbc.com/news/magazine-37500189 [Accessed October 13, 2017].

Global Down Syndrome Foundation. (n.d.). Facts and FAQ about down syndrome. *Global Down Syndrome Foundation website* (online). Retrieved from www.globaldownsyndrome.org/about-down-syndrome/facts-about-down-syndrome/ [Accessed October 13, 2017].

Hitayezu, J., Ndahindwa, V., Murorunkwere, S., Uwineza, A., & Mutesa, L. (2016). Advanced maternal age, also an important risk factor for Down Syndrome in African black population. A nine-year experience in Rwanda and burden outcome. *JSM Genetics and Genomics*, 3(1), 1012 (online). Retrieved from www.jscimedcentral.com/Genetics/genetics-3-1012.pdf [Accessed October 13, 2017].

Hopfe, A. (1999). The culture of blindness. *AEBC (Alliance for Equality of Blind Canadians) website* (online). Retrieved from www.blindcanadians.ca/publications/cbm/14/culture-blindness [Accessed October 13, 2017].

Karush, S. (2003, October 26). Disabled Russian savors his role. *The Los Angeles Times* (online newspaper). Retrieved from http://articles.latimes.com/2003/oct/26/news/adfg-disactor26 [Accessed October 13, 2017].

Kolb, R. (2017, November 3). Sensations of sound: On deafness and music. *The New York Times* (online newspaper). Retrieved from www.nytimes.com/2017/11/03/opinion/cochlear-implant-sound-music.html?_r=0 [Accessed November 4, 2017].

Reece's Rainbow. (n.d.). Who we are. *Reece's Rainbow* (organizational website). Retrieved from http://reecesrainbow.org/whoweare [Accessed October 13, 2017].

Shilling, R. D., & Shinn-Cunningham, B. G. (2002). Virtual auditory displays. In K. Stanney (Ed.), *Handbook of virtual environments: Design, implementation, and applications* (Chapter 4, pp. 65–92). Mahwah, NJ: Lawrence Erlbaum.

United Nations. (n.d.). Convention on the rights of persons with disabilities (CRPD). *Division for Social Policy and Development, United Nations* (website). Retrieved from www.un.org/development/desa/disabilities/ [Accessed October 14, 2017].

Wade, C. (2016, May 5). A letter to my able-bodied partner. *Upworthy* (online resource). Retrieved from www.upworthy.com/a-letter-to-my-able-bodied-partner?c=apstream [Accessed November 4, 2017].

Willings, C. (n.d.). Simulation activities. *Teaching Students With Visual Impairments* (website). Retrieved from www.teachingvisuallyimpaired.com/simulation-activities.html [Accessed October 13, 2017].

Cross-references: Rights, Citizenship, and Voting; Health and Sanitation; Abortion

HAPPINESS AND SADNESS

The pairing of happiness and sadness stands as proxy here for the full range of emotions expressed normally and implicated in psychopathology. In this entry, the focus will be on happiness per se and on the particular form of sadness contingent on loss and grief. Each of these has a substantial presence in the cross-cultural psychological literature (Selin & Davey, 2012; Parkes, Laungani, & Young, 2015). Early cross-cultural studies aimed at finding out whether emotional expression is universal across cultures, and up to now this has been assumed to be mostly the case. Caution should be exercised, however: a recent study comparing a relatively uncontacted group with US participants revealed that contextual cultural cues may be necessary for the interpretation of supposedly universal facial expressions (Gendron, Roberson, van der Vyver, & Barrett, 2014). Likewise the concept of happiness, always thought to be complex, is becoming more formally subdivided into distinctly different emotional states (Shiota et al., 2017). Also, cultures which emphasize balance between emotional states may not experience discrete and separable emotions. Nonetheless, there is support for the idea that emotions are, at their core, culturally universal and measureable (Bieda et al., 2017; Disabato, Goodman, Kashdan, Short, & Jarden, 2016).

Exposition, Confrontation, and Simulation

Emotion is a hub: here is a brief list of directions in which interactives can fly.

1. Examine facial expressions either pictorially or in real time with present company: compare posed emotional selfies with the classic views on Paul Ekman's website (Ekman, n.d.).

2. Find happiness/well-being/positive mental health scales: distribute, complete, and compare results. A cross-culturally validated selection is listed in Bieda et al. (2017).

3. Mine the copious data comparing rated happiness with several other dimensions of experience including GDP and other measures

of living standards across cultures on the *Our World in Data* website (Ortiz-Ospina & Roser, 2017).

4.   Discuss which features of psychiatric diagnosis might be universal and which might be culturally conditioned; use any standard text either in cross-cultural psychology, cross-cultural counseling, or cross-cultural health psychology as a guide. Note the subtle interplay between universal features of depression and psychiatrists' culturally influenced diagnoses (Jeffrey, 2015). Discuss specifically whether mania, the happiness lobe of bipolarity, is perceived differently across cultures and compare to the description in Viswanath and Chaturvedi (2012).

5.   Discuss grief and mourning in the context of its measurement: Alves, Oliveira, and Lotufo-Neto (2016) supply the elements of the frequently used TRIG (Texas Revised Inventory of Grief) scale along with cross-cultural validation.

6.   Discussion of grief and happiness may lead to considering the rituals and celebrations connected with each emotion, and to comparisons of funeral/end-of-life and birth/wedding practices: these are always rich sources of intercultural and interpersonal sharing.

7.   Finally—for this list of suggestions at least—broaden the search to include all of the other emotions, searching for cross-cultural comparisons. For a start, attempt a replication of Skolnick and Dzokoto's (2013) comparison of Ghanian and US perceptions of disgust.

REFERENCES AND SUGGESTED READINGS

Alves, T. M., Oliveira, M. C., & Lotufo-Neto, F. (2016). Diagnosis of complicated grief using the Texas Revised Inventory of Grief, Brazilian Portuguese version. *Journal of Psychology and Clinical Psychiatry* 6(1), 00316. doi:10.15406/jpcpy.2016.06.00316. Retrieved from http://medcraveonline.com/JPCPY/JPCPY-06-00316.pdf [Accessed October 23, 2017].

Bieda, A., Hirschfeld, G., Schonfeld, P., Brailovskaia, J., Zhang, X. C., & Margraf, J. (2017). Universal happiness? Cross-cultural measurement invariance of scales assessing positive mental health. *Psychological Assessment, 29*(4), 408–421.

Disabato, D. J., Goodman, F. R., Kashdan, T. B., Short, J. L., & Jarden, A. (2016). Different types of well-being? A cross-cultural examination of hedonic and eudaimonic well-being. *Psychological Assessment, 28*(5), 471–482.

Ekman, P. (n.d.). Are there universal facial expressions? Find out using this simple test. *PaulEkmanGroup* (website). Retrieved from www.paulekman.com/universal-facial-expressions/ [Accessed October 23, 2017].

Gendron, M., Roberson, D., van der Vyver, J. M., & Barrett, L. F. (2014). Perceptions of emotion from facial expressions are not culturally universal: Evidence from a remote culture. *Emotion, 14*(2), 251–262.

Jeffrey, S. (2015, May 26). Cultural differences may affect psychiatric diagnosis. *Medscape Medical News* (online news source). Retrieved from www.medscape.com/viewarticle/845329#vp_2 [Accessed October 23, 2017].

Ortiz-Ospina, E., & Roser, M. (2017). Happiness and life satisfaction. *Our World in Data* (online data source). Retrieved from https://ourworldindata.org/happiness-and-life-satisfaction/ [Accessed October 23, 2017].

Parkes, C. M., Laungani, P., & Young, B. (2015). *Death and bereavement across cultures* (2nd ed.). New York: Routledge.

Selin, H., & Davey, G. (Eds.) (2012). *Happiness across cultures: Views of happiness and quality of life in non-Western cultures.* New York: Springer.

Shiota, M. N., Campos, B., Oveis, C., Hertenstein, M. J., Simon-Thomas, E., & Keltner, D. (2017). Beyond happiness: Building a science of discrete positive emotions. *American Psychologist, 72*(7), 617–643.

Skolnick, A. J., & Dzokoto, V. A. (2013). Disgust and contamination: A cross-national comparison of Ghana and the United States. *Frontiers in Psychology, 4, 91*. doi:10.3389/fpsyg.2013.00091 (online). Retrieved from www.ncbi.nlm.nih.gov/pmc/articles/PMC3583245/ [Accessed October 23, 2017].

Viswanath, B., & Chaturvedi, S. K. (2012). Cultural aspects of major mental disorders: A critical review from an Indian perspective. *Indian Journal of Psychological Medicine, 34*(4), 306–312.

Cross-references: Health and Sanitation; Materialism and Consumer Culture; Young and Old; Pregnancy and Childbirth

HEALTH AND SANITATION

Most audiences for this text will understand health from a personal and individualistic perspective: 'my own health' encompassed by the skin and containing both the healthy mind and healthy organs envisioned in the Roman poet Juvenal's phrase *mens sana in corpore sano*. Should this focus be desired, a text in health psychology with a specific cultural flair is recommended, for example that of Regan Gurung (2013). Often, too, health, when considered in a cross-cultural context, becomes a set of contrasts between allopathic medicine (sometimes called 'Western' or 'scientific') applied in individual cases and other forms of indigenous medicine, or between sets of cultural beliefs (and sometimes superstitions) held by individuals about the causes and cures of disease. Here, the focus is instead on what Rene Dubos (1987) said were the real determinants of health: the establishment of equilibrium with pathogens through collective construction of healthy ecosystems. Turning to shit: while human 'wearing out' results in strokes and heart disease worldwide, these are the top causes of death only in highly affluent cultures. Much of the world dies because of problems of sanitation, especially in the early years of life, and billions of people worldwide have no access to sanitary toilets. Loowatt, a British company, has recently received a grant from the Bill and Melinda Gates Foundation's Reinvent the Toilet Challenge (Gates Foundation, 2011) to develop a waterless biodigesting toilet system currently being piloted in Madagascar (Zeldovich, 2017).

Exposition, Confrontation, and Simulation

Regarding individual health and health care, the discussion might start at points at which there appear to be clear cultural differences. There is a fairly sizable literature—locatable via Gurung's text as well as simple googling—on Chinese, Hispanic, and Native American medical traditions. In that context, starting a discussion with the question of what folk remedies are used by class members (and instructors) would lead naturally to a review of the range of folk wisdom (or superstition, depending on the predominance of the allopathic view). It is worth remembering that medicinal drugging emerged from the collected wisdom of indigenous healers as well as accidental encounters with naturally occurring medicinal plants. A range of cultures can be immediately encountered by reviewing any recent issue of the *International Journal of Crude Drug Research*. Nurses and other medical service providers have developed a strong commitment to addressing cultural differences in practice: chief among these over the past several decades has been Larry Purnell, whose system of cultural competences in nursing and health care extends widely beyond that sphere (Purnell, 2014). Clear differences also exist between cultures regarding the social and environmental conditions under which health care is delivered and compensated. Construction of a dramatic simulation of the respect accorded to hospitals in current warfare is recommended (e.g., Human Rights Watch, 2016). Contrast between the state of health care support in the United States and other similarly affluent countries would also be instructive and good preparation for making informed political decisions.

The subject of the hygiene side of this topic pair is selected because of its naturally discomfiting character. Not for nothing did Freud put toilet training at the heart of psychology! For one possible opener, Tyler Oakley's *Binge* contains a breezy account of the physiology of defecation in a hip and polycultural context (Oakley, 2015). For another, read selections from David Waltner-Toews's (2013) *The Origin of Feces*. Julia Scott's (2014) account of her month-long showerless existence is a great introduction to the bacterial context and a stimulant to student construction of surveys of personal hygiene. Questions of how to address the sheer magnitude of the problem of sanitation and waste disposal should lead to innovative speculations and simulations. From a cultural interventionist perspective, how do you convince a person who is used to going wherever and whenever that a toilet is a great idea? From an environmentalist perspective, what is the best way to deal with a river that is choked with fecal foam (Mallonee, 2017), next to which people take 'smog selfies'? Full discussion of questions of cultural differences in sanitation can lead to other interactive exercises in related areas, for instance trash and garbage disposal and food recycling. If these lead to discussions of population regulation, well and good.

REFERENCES AND SUGGESTED READINGS

Dubos, R. (1987). *Mirage of health: Utopias, progress, and biological change.* New Brunswick, NJ: Rutgers University Press. (Originally published 1959).

Gates Foundation. (2011). Reinvent the toilet challenge: Strategy overview. *Bill and Melinda Gates Foundation website* (online). Retrieved from www.gatesfoundation.org/What-We-Do/Global-Development/Reinvent-the-Toilet-Challenge [Accessed July 23, 2017].

Gurung, R. (2013). *Health psychology: A cultural approach* (3rd ed.). New York: Cengage.

Human Rights Watch. (2016, August 11). Syria: Government airstrikes closing down hospitals. *Human Rights Watch website* (online). Retrieved from www.hrw.org/news/2016/08/11/syria-government-airstrikes-closing-down-hospitals [Accessed July 24, 2017].

Mallonee, L. (2017, April 5). India's most polluted river actually bubbles with toxic foam. *Wired* (online magazine). Retrieved from https://www.wired.com/2017/04/zacharie-rabehi-toxic-city/ Accessed March 4, 2018.

Oakley, T. (2015). *Binge.* New York: Gallery Books.

Purnell, L. (2014). *Guide to culturally competent health care* (3rd ed.). Philadelphia, PA: F. A. Davis Co.

Scott, J. (2014, May 25). My no-soap, no-shampoo bacteria-rich hygiene experiment. *The New York Times.* Retrieved from www.nytimes.com/2014/05/25/magazine/my-no-soap-no-shampoo-bacteria-rich-hygiene-experiment.html [Accessed July 23, 2017].

Waltner-Toews, D. (2013). *The origin of feces: What excrement tells us about evolution, ecology, and a sustainable society.* Toronto, ON: ECW Press.

Zeldovich, L. (2017, June 20). Reinventing the toilet. *Mosaic Science* (online magazine). Retrieved from https://mosaicscience.com/story/poo-toilet-waste-energy-madagascar-loowatt-future [Accessed July 22, 2017].

Cross-references: Disabilities, Water and Air; Charity

HUNGER

For most of the recent past, hunger in psychology has been either a physiological or a motivational topic. Old-style behaviorism took hunger for granted in order that the animal subjects—cats, dogs, rats, and pigeons—would actively seek solutions to problems that led to relief. One of the signal achievements of mid-20th century neuroscience was the elucidation of brain mechanisms involved in controlling hunger, thirst, and other motivational states. Students of culture, however, will find only indirect paths if any between the cultural situation of hunger and the lateral hypothalamus. For a cultural view, one can start with the first level of Maslow's motivational system: little is achieved in terms of building higher cultural achievements for the self and for others if basic survival needs are not met. Beyond this truth, several paths of investigation lie open. Across cultures in the United States and worldwide, food insecurity is correlated with cultures of poverty. Grobler (2016), in a South African context, differentiates between food-secure and food-insecure low-income households in terms of the reasons for poverty, with those which are food-secure ascribing poverty to a lack of individual effort, while those who are food-insecure adopting fatalistic beliefs in environmental or social factors as causes. Similarly, chronic hunger is shown to have negative effects on both physical and mental development across subcultures in the United States (Weinreb et al., 2002). Another way in which hunger, mental state, and culture interact outside of the area of existential threat is in the process of self-control of hunger states, examples of which are dieting and religious fasting. Trepanowski and Bloomer (2010) compared Islamic Ramadan fasts, Greek Orthodox Nativity, Lenten, and Assumption fasts, and the Christian Daniel Fast. This latter ritual is based on a reading of the Biblical book of Daniel (10: 2,3) in which resistance to food as a feature of both mourning and reaction to oppression is described. They found mostly health-beneficial results of these practices, which for the most part lead to healthier food choices as well as restricted intake.

Exposition, Confrontation, and Simulation

A starting point for a discussion of hunger could be to ask whether, and under what circumstances, a day's meals or more were involuntarily missed. Surveys of food accessibility modeled on the USDA short-form food security survey (www.ers.usda.gov/media/8282/short2012. pdf) would augment a discussion along these lines. If students practice fasting, the various reasons for this can also be a starting point for further comparison among subcultures (for instance, though the practice is never recommended, certain athletic groups practice forms of enforced fasting for weight management). Dieting and other methods of controlling appetite psychologically can be introduced as topics as well. Not only are there variations in cultural dietary patterns that are considered healthier choices, but there is also a recent trend to diet less and to become more accepting of variations in normal body shape and size (Aubrey, 2017). Many good examples of the way that hunger and culture reciprocally determine themselves are contained in George Norton's recent book *Hunger and Hope* (2014).

REFERENCES AND SUGGESTED READINGS

Aubrey, A. (2017, March 8). Is dieting passe? Study finds fewer overweight people try to lose weight. *NPR Morning Edition: The Salt* (Radio program, 2017). Retrieved from www. npr.org/sections/thesalt/2017/03/08/519080766/is-dieting-passe-study-finds-fewer-overweight-people-try-to-lose-weight [Accessed July 13, 2017].

Grobler, W. C. J. (2016). Perceptions of poverty: A study of food secure and food insecure households in an urban area of South Africa. *Procedia Economics and Finance, 35,* 224–231. Retrieved from www.sciencedirect.com/science/article/pii/S2212567116000289 [Accessed July 13, 2017].

Norton, G. W. (2014). *Hunger and hope: Escaping poverty and achieving food security in developing countries.* Long Grove, IL: Waveland Press.

Trepanowski, J. F., & Bloomer, R. J. (2010). The impact of religious fasting on human health. *Nutrition Journal, 9,* 57, doi:10.1186/1475-2891-9-57. Retrieved from https://nutritionj. biomedcentral.com/articles/10.1186/1475-2891-9-57 [Accessed July 13, 2017].

Weinreb, L., Wehler, C., Perloff, J., Scott, R., Hosmer, D., Sagor, L., & Gunderson, C. (2002). Hunger: Its impact on children's health and mental health. *Pediatrics, 110*(4), e41. doi:10.1542/peds.110.4.e41. Retrieved from http://pediatrics.aappublications.org/ content/110/4/e41 [Accessed July 13, 2017].

Cross-references: Regional and Indigenous Psychology; Food and Art; Health and Sanitation; Sustainability and Population

LOVE AND HATE

Psychological attempts to quantify love began to emerge in the 1970s. A theory popularized by the Canadian sociologist John Lee (1973), partly based on classical typologies of love and partly original, identified six main types: *eros* (romantic), *ludus* (flirting), *mania* (obsession), *storge* (enduring), *agape* (selfless), and *pragma* (expedient). Robert Sternberg proposed a three-factor theory of love in the 1980s (Sternberg, 1986) that derived a similar typology of love from combinations of measured intimacy, passion, and commitment. Hatfield and Rapson (1996) specifically focused on cross-cultural dimensions of love within a two-variable framework (companionate vs. passionate love). Recent work on love has evolved a more narrative and individualized approach rather than a theoretical-empirical one. Rather than trying to establish quantitative differences between cultures' love styles, approaches like Eric Selinger's *Popular Romance Project* (Selinger, 2014) describe cultural variations in love through narrative analysis. Selinger also has an interesting take on the polycultural assemblage of the love concept.

Exposition, Confrontation, and Simulation

Love, within a United States psychological context at least, has usually been contextualized within interpersonal relations, usually sexual or marital at their core. Scales to measure Sternberg triangular factor combinations, for example, can be found in introductory psychology texts as well as on many websites: interpersonal attractiveness likewise offers several entry points in introductory and social psychology. The study of interpersonal dyads does not exhaust the meanings of love, which is as Protean a term as pleasure, to which it's semantically and emotionally related. At some level 'love' maps on to 'enjoy': a person visiting a McDonald's and 'lovin' it,' as the slogan has it, isn't looking for a long term relationship. Other linguistic traditions can be mined for words and phrases that can extend understanding of love outside of the English language cage. Don't be surprised, however, if things get lost in (back) translation: McDonalds' 'I'm lovin' it' slogan was translated for China as into an idiomatic phrase meaning "I'm lovin' it, no matter what you say" (Sant, 2015). Biblical concordances can be a starting point for extending the concept beyond romance (e.g., John 15:13; "greater love than this hath no man, that he lay down his life for his friends.") Both Louis Armstrong and John Lennon espoused universal love in song. Narratives and analyses of love in under-studied cultures, such those of Africa (e.g., Adebayo, 2017; Cole & Thomas, 2009) can be examined and discussed. The extensive anthropological and sociological cross-cultural literature on love can be engaged as well, for instance comparing what is known about the near-universality of romantic love (Sorrell, 2005) with the more subsistence-oriented factors that kick in after the honeymoon (McMullin, 2015). And, while it is not currently in fashion as a characterization of love, ambivalence is no less real, and discussion of love can lead easily to discussion of hate, for which there are better heat maps (e.g., Stephens, 2017).

REFERENCES AND SUGGESTED READINGS

Adebayo, A. (2017). *Stay with me*. New York: Knopf.

Cole, J., & Thomas, L. (Eds.) (2009). *Love in Africa*. Chicago, IL: University of Chicago Press.

Hatfield, E., & Rapson, R. L. (1996). *Love and sex: Cross-cultural perspectives*. New York: Pearson.

Lee, J. (1973). *The colors of love: An exploration of the ways of loving*. Toronto, ON: The New Press.

McMullin, Z. (2015, January 21). The married couple's 36 questions for staying in love. *Huffington Post* (online newspaper). Retrieved from www.huffingtonpost.com/zsofi-mcmullin/the-married-couples-36-questions-for-staying-in-love_b_6498012.html [Accessed August 4, 2017].

Sant, G. (2015, March 12). McDonalds' self-hating complex: Why its overseas P. R. campaign is the worst of all time. *Salon* (online magazine). Retrieved from www.salon.com/2015/03/12/mcdonalds_self_hating_complex_why_their_overseas_p_r_campaign_is_the_worst_of_all_time/ [Accessed August 4, 2017].

Selinger, E. (2014, June 12). Optimism in U.S. romance. *The Popular Romance Project: Rethinking Love and Romance* (website online). Retrieved from http://popularromanceproject.org/optimism-u-s-romance/ [Accessed August 4, 2017].

Sorrell, E. (2005). Romantic love and marriage: An analysis of the functionality of romantic love as a marital stabilizing agent. *Nebraska Anthropologist, 9*, 16–25. Open access via Digital Commons at. Retrieved from http://digitalcommons.unl.edu/cgi/viewcontent. cgi?article=1008&context=nebanthro

Stephens, M. (2017). Geography of hate: Geotagged hateful tweets in the United States. *Humboldt State University* (project website). Retrieved from http://users.humboldt.edu/ mstephens/hate/hate_map.html [Accessed August 5, 2017].

Sternberg, R. J. (1986). A triangular theory of love. *Psychological Review, 93*, 119–135.

Cross-references: Sexuality; Eye Contact

Development and Family

PREGNANCY AND CHILDBIRTH

The perinatal period is the absolute entry point for all cultures. However, while the birth process and the specific physical and psychological needs of the infant are universal, there are differences surrounding the period leading up and immediately following to birth that express cultural differences. A comprehensive reference in this area is the edited volume by Selin (2009). The decision whether or not to conceive and the use of contraception varies between cultures and is influenced by familial, social, and religious factors. Much folk tradition surrounds birth worldwide: an example is the elaborate system of beliefs about the proper foods, temperature, activity level, and spiritual invocations appropriate for a pregnant woman in China (National Library Board, 2013). The actual physical setting for birth appears to be conditional, worldwide, on relative affluence and urbanization. For example, a birth in Dakar, Senegal, to an affluent US citizen is accomplished in a private hospital with a five-day postpartum stay: conditions in public hospitals in Senegal are often vastly different and less serene (Gulia, 2015). In contrast, tradition combined with a lack of trained personnel and extreme resource depletion often lead, in Afghanistan and other remote environments, to high rates of infant and maternal mortality that are the focus of international aid interventions (USAID, 2010). Regional variations based on law embedded in custom and tradition define this area of study.

Exposition, Confrontation, and Simulation

Extending out from the foregoing, discussion of the cultural psychology of pregnancy and birth could continue this dialogue between the universal nature of the process and the extremes of the conditions under which it occurs. For example, the question of how much maternal exercise is helpful or harmful to the developing fetus can be examined in the context of extreme activity such as mountain climbing—elective (and arguably beneficial) for individuals in the United States (Rodden, 2016) and mandatory in Afghanistan. A sheer chasm between the United States and virtually all other countries in the world is reflected in the way in which pregnant women are treated in prison at and after the time of birth. Background for development of the framework for a discussion of this cultural divide can be assembled from the individual country reports contained in the US Library of Congress's document on children in prison worldwide (Library of Congress, 2014) and also Jennifer Warner's comparative study of prison treatment of pregnancy and childbirth, related to the popular television serial *Orange Is the New Black* (Warner, 2015).

REFERENCES AND SUGGESTED READINGS

Gulia, I. (2015, May 3). International birth impressions—Senegal. *The Best of Baby Blog* (online resource). Retrieved from http://thebestofbaby.com/international-birth-impressions-senegal/ [Accessed July 19, 2017].

Library of Congress. (2014, July). Laws on children residing with parents in prison. *Library of Congress (US) Law Library*. (online resource). Retrieved from www.loc.gov/law/help/children-residing-with-parents-in-prison/index.php [Accessed July 18, 2017].

National Library Board. (2013). Chinese birth rituals. *Singapore Infopedia: National Library Board of Singapore* (online resource). Retrieved from http://eresources.nlb.gov.sg/infopedia/articles/SIP_2013-05-14_113920.html [Accessed July 19, 2017].

Rodden, B. (2016, March 30). Climb ing pregnant: Medical study results. *Beth Rodden: Mother-pro climber-writer* (Personal Blog) (online resource). Retrieved from http://bethrodden.com/2016/03/climbing-pregnant-medical-study-results/ [Accessed July 19, 2017].

Selin, H. (Ed.) (2009). *Childbirth across cultures: Ideas and practices of pregnancy, childbirth, and the postpartum*. Dordrecht: Springer.

USAID. (2010, September 15). Saving newborns in rural Afghanistan. *USAID Official website* (online resource). Retrieved from www.usaid.gov/results-data/success-stories/saving-newborns-rural-afghanistan-0 [Accessed July 19, 2017].

Warner, J. (2015). Infants in orange: An international model-based approach to prison nurseries. *Hastings Women's Law Journal, 26*, 65–147 (online). Retrieved from http://repository.uchastings.edu/cgi/viewcontent.cgi?article=1159&context=hwlj [Accessed July 19, 2017].

Cross-references: Parenting; Religion and Law; Punishment and Prisons; Abortion

ABORTION

Few US textbooks in any area of psychology index abortion. This is on one hand not surprising, since in the United States it is a volatile political issue and often framed as a subject for law, but on the other, it is a glaring omission since abortion is obviously psychologically consequential and also has cross-cultural connections and implications. In the United States, abortion has led to confrontation and actual violence, with physicians and other clinic staff being assaulted and sometimes killed in workplaces and in churches. It is a prime example of an idea which is fully emotionally charged and on that basis alone is worth cognitive psychological scrutiny. Heiphetz, Strohminger, and Young (2017) continue a thread relating thoughts and decisions about moral issues, with specific reference to abortion, that has roots in the history of moral development research and especially in the conflict between legalistic and interpersonally nurturant roles exemplified by the challenge to Lawrence Kohlberg's theory of moral development raised by Carol Gilligan in the 1980s (Muuss, 1988). Cross-culturally, abortion reflects the interaction of religion, tradition, and law, and the legal status of abortion varies widely from criminalization in South America, the Middle East, and Africa, to 'constitutionalization' in Europe and the United States (Cook, Erdman, & Dickens, 2014). Depending on location, personal and health consequences vary widely. For example, Ville and Mirlesse (2015) contrast outcomes for how medical doctors interact with parents regarding prenatal diagnosis of disability. Abortion based on diagnosis of fetal pathology is legal in France while it is a crime in Brazil, and as a consequence physicians in France are less conflicted about their role in the process than those in Brazil. China's 'one child' policy, recently modified, socially compelled abortions both to regulate population numbers and to select for males over females (Fong, 2016).

Exposition, Confrontation, and Simulation

Controversy and confrontation may be at a higher pitch in this area than in others, so discussants should proceed with caution. However, proceeding with caution need not equate to avoidance. Objective approaches could include simply listing and discussing all of the cultural dimensions implicated in abortion. 'What if's abound and can be the starting point for thoughtful and critical examination. The question of prenatal diagnosis and its relation to abortion decisions can be expanded. Examination of the cognitive and emotional dimensions of the decision can be sharpened by situating it in the context of reversing an ongoing chemically induced abortion (Graham, 2017).

REFERENCES AND SUGGESTED READINGS

Cook, R. J., Erdman, J. N., & Dickens, B. M. (Eds.) (2014). *Abortion law in transnational perspective: cases and controversies.* Philadelphia, PA: University of Pennsylvania Press.

Fong, M. (2016). *One child: The story of China's most radical experiment.* New York: Houghton Mifflin Harcourt.

Graham, R. (2017, July 18). A new front in the war over reproductive rights: "Abortion pill reversal". *New York Times Magazine* (online). Retrieved from www.nytimes.com/2017/07/18/magazine/a-new-front-in-the-war-over-reproductive-rights-abortion-pill-reversal.html?_r=0 [Accessed July 18, 2017].

Heiphetz, L., Strohminger, N., & Young, L. L. (2017). The role of moral beliefs, memories, and preferences in representations of identity. *Cognitive Science, 41*(3), 744–767.

Muuss, R. E. (1988). Carol Gilligan's theory of sex differences in the development of moral reasoning during adolescence. *Adolescence, 23*(8–9), 229–243.

Ville, I., & Mirlesse, V. (2015). Prenatal diagnosis: From policy to practice. Two distinct ways of managing prognostic uncertainty and anticipating disability in Brazil and France. *Social Science and Medicine, 141,* 19–26.

Cross-references: Religion and Law; Women's Roles and Rights; Health and Sanitation; Pregnancy and Childbirth; Disability

PARENTING

Marc Bornstein, who has been writing about cross-cultural issues in child development and parenting for more than 40 years (Bornstein, 2012) quotes an oft-said line that there are only two contributions to children's development: genes and parents. Even further back in the history of psychology, Freud made plain why development should be a focus and why parents in particular were both the bringers of civilization as well as the most bitter antagonists in the developmental drama. To take up parenting in a cross-cultural class is to engage in a fascinating subject which, however, presents ambiguities that will not clear up. Thus any class on cross-cultural parenting will be founded on the principle of 'it depends.' The main theories of parenting can serve as a template. Attachment, as Peryl Agishtein and Claudia Brumbaugh have observed, in a study involving collecting data from more than 50 countries, is highly modulated by culture. For instance, they found that stronger identification with culture overall reduced attachment anxiety and avoidance (Agishtein & Brumbaugh, 2013). The classic parenting styles—authoritarian, permissive, and authoritative—are likewise affected by culture. For instance, in cultures which emphasize collectivism, a more authoritarian style may be more prevalent. However, the relation between parenting style and culture is highly nuanced: for one example, authoritarian parenting may be understood in Asian cultures as expressive of parental warmth and support, which is not how it is perceived in European and US settings (Descartes, 2012; Kim, 2005). Other variations in parenting emerge from comparative culture study, for instance the preference, in Norway, for institutionalized daycare starting at 1 year of age, a practice which emerges haphazardly in the United States based on the same economic pressures but without the foundation of substantial state supported parental leave (Choi, 2014).

Exposition, Confrontation, and Simulation

With such a great amount of individual variation and interaction between parenting styles and culture, restrained exploration with tentative conclusions should especially be sought in this area. Any course in cross-cultural parenting should view the film *Babies* (Balmes & Chabat, 2010; visit the film's website at http://focusfeatures.com/babies), which conveys both the nuances and also the universal experience of parenting across several cultures (Namibia, Mongolia, Tokyo, Japan, and San Francisco, California), filmed on site, and which can be the platform for discussion leading in several directions. For instance, the practice of accelerated childhood education in Japan and the United States is contrasted with more informal and quotidian practices in Namibia and Mongolia. Excellent insight into the environmental and social frameworks for development are likewise visible and can serve as openings not only for discussion of parenting but also of lifestyle. Classes can serve as their own laboratories as well: the thorough and well-designed training manual of the Calgary (Canada) Cross-cultural Parenting Program (www.ciwa-online.com/uploads/pdf/CCPP%20Resource%20Manual%202011.pdf) contains many simple prompts for response and discussion that draw out personal experiences and which can be interpreted from both the perspectives of monocultural, multicultural, and immigrant individuals. Finally, the focus on parenting is typically on early childhood. Classes in cross-cultural psychology can forge new research paths by concentrating on the stages of development from adolescence and beyond, on single parenting across cultures, and especially on grandparenting and other forms of extended family parental assistance.

REFERENCES AND SUGGESTED READINGS

Agishtein, P., & Brumbaugh, C. (2013). Cultural variation in adult attachment: The impact of ethnicity, collectivism, and country of origin. *Journal of Social, Evolutionary, and Cultural Psychology*, 7(4), 384–405.

Balmès, T. (dir.) Chabat, A. (producer) (2010). *Babies (Bébés)* Documentary film. Focus Features.

Bornstein, M. H. (2012). Cultural approaches to parenting. *Parenting Science and Practice*, 12(2–3), 212–221.

Choi, A. (2014). How cultures around the world think about parenting. *Ted Online* (online informational talk). Retrieved from http://ideas.ted.com/how-cultures-around-the-world-think-about-parenting/ [Accessed July 7, 2017].

Descartes, C. (2012, March). The social construction of demographic variables and parenting styles in Trinidad. *Journal of the Department of Behavioral Sciences (University of the West Indies)*, *1*(1), (online publication). Retrieved from http://libraries.sta.uwi.edu/journals/ojs/index.php/jbs/article/viewFile/21/19 [Accessed July 11, /2017].

Kim, E. (2005). Korean American parental control: Acceptance or rejection? *Ethos, 33*(3), 347–366.

Cross-references: Family; Young and Old

FAMILY

Although sexuality gets more press, family is probably the most important aspect of interpersonal relations within culture. Freudian psychology is entirely a psychology of family relations and looks backward to conceptions of primal social groups headed by powerful fathers, as well as to a body of imaginative literature that sees family conflict as eternal and inevitable. However much this anthropological conceit might be modified, the success of psychoanalysis as a means of interpreting human life rests mainly on its ability to present family dynamics dramatically as reflections of an eternal human process of enculturation. Many religions conceive of God as a father: Catholicism organizes itself around the concept of a one-child family. Until recently, and still in many cultures and many parts of the world, legal and governmental power rested with powerful families and was legally heritable rather than transferrable by popular consent. Moving from the iconography of the Madonna or the monarch to more secular current social scientific approaches to the family leads in many directions: what follows is a partial sample of the possibilities of a discussion of family within a cross-cultural framework. Leaving aside the anthropological literatures on kinship and family structure and also the equally vast sociological literature on the family as a primary socializing agent, and focusing on psychology alone, there is ample interest and impetus for discussion and further study among the at least the following areas.

Exposition, Confrontation, and Simulation

1. **Family size:** though family size has attracted attention from population theorists and economists rather than from psychologists, most individuals have an opinion about optimal family size and a survey of these opinions is a good starting point for discussion. The optimal size is usually greater than the replacement fertility rate of two children per woman: usually, lively discussion can be instigated by raising the possibility of rationing of children, such as

was officially attempted by China until recently (Hall, 2017). Family size varies world- and culture-wide due to several factors (easily accessible by cursory googling) including poverty and access to education, though the results of studies are often ambivalent in their results. Though historically poorer cultures have higher fertility rates and larger families (CIA, 2017), sometimes grinding poverty results in 'poverty Malthusianism,' that is, reducing the number of children in the family because of lack of resources or opportunities to escape. A basic decision tree incorporating factors that are influential in determining reproductive decisions can be used to simulate the way in which demographers and economists predict family size (Lawson & Mace, 2010).

2. **Paid family leave:** discussion can always be sparked by presenting data showing the United States compared to other countries in terms of how much paid parental leave is available after childbirth: the United States can be depicted as particularly heartless (e.g., Covert & Peck, 2014). However, though there isn't an official US national policy for paid leave, the situation is more nuanced, with several states and municipalities offering paid leave, as well as a number of corporations, which results in a patchwork of leave policies (Isaacs, Healy, & Peters, 2017). Further tempering of the sometimes rancorous reaction to the lack of paid leave might result from considering the results of studies that have attempted to measure psychological benefits of paid leave. A recent large scale study comparing paid leave across countries, fraught with methodological problems including a small number of studies and substantial confounds, suggests that the outcomes of family leave may not always confirm the positive sentiment that the practice arouses (Aitken et al., 2015). Most studies, too, focus on mothers rather than fathers: attention should be given to this information gap as there appear to be some psychological benefits for paternal leave as well (Coltrane, 2013).

3. **Familismo:** the generic cultural trait of 'familism' in which family predominates in individual choices and behaviors is especially

prominent in Latinx cultures, where it is called *familismo*. There are several scales for measuring it that have the virtue of simplicity: one is only five items long (the Pan-Hispanic Familism Scale, Villareal, Blozis, & Widaman, 2005). This scale includes "I am proud of my family," "My family is always there for me in times of need," "I cherish the time I spend with my family," "I know my family has my best interests in mind," and "My family members and I share similar values and beliefs." Villatoro, Morales, and Mays (2014) relate familismo to the use of informal or religious forms of psychotherapy rather than specialized psychotherapeutic or general medical services. A study of largely undocumented Latino day laborers in the United States identified familismo, along with perceptions of good general health and work satisfaction, as contributing to both life satisfaction and resistance to the bad effects of discrimination (Ojeda & Piña-Watson, 2013). Completion of the Pan-Hispanic Familism Scale and discussion of the results can open further conversations about the elements of familismo that are common to all humans in families.

4. **Family violence:** This topic has been studied cross-culturally for several years (e.g., Levinson, 1988). Recently, Leyaro, Selaya, and Trifkovic (2017) performed a field experiment investigating whether environmental and economic conditions, including apportionment of domestic responsibilities, might affect the amount of justification for violence against women in intimate or family relationships. Because of a prior observation that lower levels of altruism may be related to increased acceptance of violence, they used a version of a dictator game to gauge relative altruism between men employed in marine fishing vs. lake fishing in Tanzania, economies that differ in the relative equality of women in domestic relationships. While their results did not support a relation between altruism and violence, they did, however, show increases in perceived acceptability of violence in areas where women's roles were more unequal. Demonstration or replication of parts of this study could be a starting point both for examination of a creative way

of researching an otherwise difficult-to-view problem. It can also serve as a starting point for hypothesizing the social factors that might lead to more or less violence in families—substance abuse, for instance, or membership in subcultures such as law enforcement (Blumenstein, Fridell, & Jones, 2012).

5. **Foster, adoptive, and rescue families:** Probably the best proof of the preeminent importance placed on the family as the source of developmental support is the worldwide effort to provide care for children who have lost their families, either temporarily or permanently. Examination of Kenya's *Guidelines for the alternative family care of children in Kenya* (Republic of Kenya, 2014) linked to the tenets of the United Nations Convention on Rights of the Child, provides insight into the centrality and complexity of the system for assuring continuity of support for children. The problem of alternative family care is particularly acute there. As of 2014, Kenya—a country with a population of 40 million out of which about 40 percent are below the age of 14, counted 2.4 million orphans—mainly because of parental deaths from AIDS. The document asserts at the outset that "the family is a nurturing and caring environment and is the ideal place in which to raise a child" (p. 4), and goes on to describe in detail systems for providing care similar to those in place everywhere else in the world, yet at the same time culturally specific. For instance, primary emphasis is on kinship care and the Muslim practice of contract adoption, *kafaalah,* followed by foster care, temporary shelter, guardianship, and adoption. Special provision is made for child-headed households. Options for discussion of issues in this area could include: comparison of the Kenyan fostering system with any local system; simulating a situation in which a child from the Democratic Republic of the Congo, orphaned during ethnoreligious conflict there, finds her way to Kenya and needs placement; or tracing the path of a refugee child arriving in Italy from Africa. The Better Care Network (betttercarenetwork.org), a consortium of international organizations focused on providing alternative family care to

children who have lost their families, is a resource for information for problems such as these.

REFERENCES AND SUGGESTED READINGS

Aitken, Z., Garrett, C. C., Hewitt, B., Keogh, L., Hocking, J. S., & Kavanagh, A. M. (2015). The maternal health outcomes of paid maternity leave: A systematic review. *Social Science and Medicine, 130,* 32–41.

Blumenstein, L., Fridell, L., & Jones, S. (2012). The link between traditional police subculture and police intimate partner violence. *Policing: An International Journal of Police Strategies and Management, 35*(1), 147–164.

Central Intelligence Agency. (2017). Country comparison: total fertility rate. *CIA World Factbook* (US Government official website). Retrieved from www.cia.gov/library/publications/the-world-factbook/rankorder/2127rank.html [Accessed September 2, 2017].

Coltrane, S. (2013, December 29). The risky business of paternity leave. *The Atlantic* (online magazine). Retrieved from www.theatlantic.com/business/archive/2013/12/the-risky-business-of-paternity-leave/282688/ [Accessed September 2, 2017].

Covert, B., & Peck, A. (2014, July 30). U.S. paid family leave vs. the rest of the world, in 2 disturbing charts. *ThinkProgress* (online news source). Retrieved from https://thinkprogress.org/u-s-paid-family-leave-versus-the-rest-of-the-world-in-2-disturbing-charts-365324eeba45/ [Accessed September 2, 2017].

Hall, C. (2017, February 2). How has the end of its one-child policy affected China? *Aljazeera* (online news source). Retrieved from www.aljazeera.com/indepth/features/2017/01/child-policy-affected-china-170129130503972.html [Accessed September 2, 2017].

Isaacs, J., Healy, O., & Peters, H. E. (2017, May). Paid family leave in the United States: Time for a new national policy. *Urban Institute* (non-profit organization website). Retrieved from www.urban.org/sites/default/files/publication/90201/paid_family_leave.pdf [Accessed September 2, 2017].

Lawson, D. W., & Mace, R. (2010). Optimizing modern family size: Trade-offs between fertility and the economic costs of reproduction. *Human Nature, 21*(1), 39–61.

Levinson, D. (1988). Family violence in cross-cultural perspective. In V. B. Van Hasselt, R. L. Morrison, A. S. Bellack, & M. Hersen (Eds.), *Handbook of family violence* (pp. 435–445). New York: Springer.

Leyaro, V., Selaya, P., & Trifkovic, N. (2017, published online May 7). Culture of violence against women: Evidence from a field experiment in Tanzania. *Handelshögskolan, Goteborg University* (online publication). Retrieved from http://economics.handels.gu.se/digitalAssets/1643/1643719_89.-trifkovic-culture-of-violence-against.pdf [Accessed September 2, 2017].

Ojeda, L., & Piña-Watson, B. (2013). Day laborers' life satisfaction: The role of familismo, spirituality, work, health, and discrimination. *Cultural Diversity and Ethnic Minority Psychology, 19*(3), 270–278.

Republic of Kenya. (2014). *Guidelines for the alternative family care of children in Kenya, October, 2014*. (Official publication of the Government of Kenya in conjunction with Sweden and UNICEF) (online). Retrieved from http://bettercarenetwork.org/sites/default/files/Guidelines%20for%20the%20Alternative%20Family%20Care%20of%20Children%20in%20Kenya.pdf [Accessed September 2, 2017].

Villareal, R., Blozis, S. A., & Widaman, K. F. (2005). Factorial invariance of a pan-Hispanic familism scale. *Hispanic Journal of Behavioral Sciences, 27*, 409–425.

Villatoro, A. P., Morales, E. S., & Mays, V. M. (2014). Family culture in mental health help-seeking and utilization in a nationally representative sample of Latinos in the United States: The NLAAS. *American Journal of Orthopsychiatry, 84*(4), 353–363.

Cross-references: Young and Old; Pregnancy and Childbirth

YOUNG AND OLD

The young and the old are themselves distinct cultures, and distinctly different laws and regulations govern each of these groups within all societies. Most cross-cultural studies focus on individuals in the spectrum from late adolescence through middle adulthood. But while across the world there is no shortage of children (some countries have more than 40 percent under 14, for instance Ghana), the aged, due to medical and environmental advances and also to changes in national birth rates, are the most rapidly growing part of the human population worldwide. China's elderly population, for example, is projected to triple by 2050, becoming larger than the combined current (2017) populations of Germany, Japan, France, and Britain, or about as large as the current total population of the United States (French, 2016). The elderly are especially viewed as subjects for medical or psychotherapeutic intervention rather than a group of vibrant and autonomous individuals. Though the elderly as a group are perceived positively cross-culturally as wise and deserving of respect, this positive estimation is balanced by equivalent weights of negative impressions of unattractiveness and incompetence (Löckenhoff et al., 2009). This is true in spite of the average age of elected political representatives worldwide, which in the US Congress is nearly 60 (the British House of Lords' average age is 69, while its House of Commons is about 50)—not to mention the median age of business chief executives worldwide, which is also nearly 60 (Romei, 2015). But the prejudicial street runs both ways: age asserts restrictive legislative dominance over youth (Bessant, 2012).

Exposition, Confrontation, and Simulation

There are voluminous sources for developmental psychological issues across cultures: consult the most current culturally oriented textbooks (e.g., Arnett, 2015) for these. A little further digging will uncover articles containing materials that can be adapted to illustrate the sorts of cognitive tasks—for instance, judging relatedness in pictorial images—that are used to probe cross-cultural cognitive developmental differences (Kuwabara & Smith, 2012). For contrast with the research literature, which often focuses on children in relatively safe and affluent environments, directly examine lives of children on the edge (e.g., street children; Street Child United, 2013). Jose Solís's (2017) account of his experience seeing the Disney film Anastasia in Tegucigalpa, Honduras, as an 11-year old already conscious of his divergent gender identity, touches on immigration, discrimination, and sexuality. But it also illustrates, and can be a departure point for discussion of, the way that adult thought coalesces just at that age, and the Disney film will be easily available as well.

Regarding age, B. F. Skinner and Margaret Vaughan (1997) suggested— possibly with tongue slightly in cheek—that, to simulate old age, you should smear your glasses with butter and wear oven mitts. In fact, their highly regarded book offers an optimistic view of the aging process and numerous practical suggestions (as would be expected from one of the great practical psychologists) to cope successfully with the inevitable outcomes of aging. Positive and stereotype-mitigating discussion might turn on these: it might also be an outcome of addressing the design of products that can make older life more livable. An exercise might be designed around adaptive technology, for instance, for driving (Brody, 2017) and the relative availability of such assistive devices worldwide could be explored. The relative comfort of retirement might also be vicariously experienced via interactive websites that compare retirement conditions worldwide, for instance via the interactive map of retirement ages around the globe (Aperion, 2017) or the detailed data on social security programs worldwide provided by the US Social Security Administration (Social Security Administration (US), 2017). Finally, discussion and possible simulation/ enaction with role-playing could be designed around the intercultural patterns of socialization of elder Koreans in a Queens (New York City) McDonalds, a more complicated and continuing story than this account provides (Kimmelman, 2014).

REFERENCES AND SUGGESTED READINGS

Aperion. (2017). Retirement age around the globe (interactive map). *Aperion Care* (Corporate website) (online). Retrieved from https://aperioncare.com/blog/retirement-age-around-world/ [Accessed September 13, 2017].

Arnett, J. (2015). *Human development: A cultural approach* (2nd ed.). New York: Pearson.

Bessant, J. (2012, October 15). Seen but not heard: Age prejudice and young people. *The Canny Outlaw* (online blog, Australia: closed and archived). Retrieved from http://thecannyoutlaw.com/features/original/2012/10/seen-but-not-heard-age-prejudice-and-young-people/ [Accessed September 15, 2017].

Brody, J. (2017, August 28). Safer cars keep older drivers on the road. *The New York Times (Well Blog)* (online newspaper). Retrieved from www.nytimes.com/2017/08/28/well/safer-cars-help-keep-older-drivers-on-the-road.html?mcubz=3 [Accessed September 13, 2017].

French, H. (2016, June). China's twilight years. *The Atlantic* (online magazine). Retrieved from www.theatlantic.com/magazine/archive/2016/06/chinas-twilight-years/480768/ [Accessed September 15, 2017].

Kimmelman, M. (2014, January 28). The urban home away from home: Lessons from McDonald's clash with older Koreans. *The New York Times* (online newspaper). Retrieved from www.nytimes.com/2014/01/29/arts/design/lessons-from-mcdonalds-clash-with-older-koreans.html?mcubz=3 [Accessed September 13, 2017].

Kuwabara, M., & Smith, L. B. (2012). Cross-cultural differences in cognitive development: Attention to relations and objects. *Journal of Experimental Child Psychology, 113*(1), 20–35.

Löckenhoff, C., De Fruyt, F., Terracciano, A., McCrae, R., De Bolle, M., Costa, P. T., Aguilar-Vafaie, M. E., . . . Yik, M. (2009). Perceptions of aging across 26 cultures and their culture-level associates. *Psychology of Aging, 24*(4), 941–954.

Romei, V. (2015, September 11). Half of global CEOs are in their 50s. *Financial Times* (online newspaper). Retrieved from www.ft.com/content/226fbb53-1c36-32f0-ba15-414d8a807761[Accessed September 15, 2017].

Skinner, B. F., & Vaughan, M. E. (1997). *Enjoy old age*. New York: Norton.

Social Security Administration (US). (2017). Social security programs throughout the world. *United States Social Security Administration website* (official government website). Retrieved from www.ssa.gov/policy/docs/progdesc/ssptw/ [Accessed September 13, 2017].

Solís, J. (2017, September 13). I saw myself in "Anastasia" and I knew I had to leave Honduras. *The New York Times* (online newspaper). Retrieved from www.nytimes.com/2017/09/13/theater/anastasia-broadway-honduras.html?mcubz=3&_r=0 [Accessed September 13, 2017].

Street Child United. (2013, June 13). The story of a Rio street girl. *Street Child United* (charity website) (online). Retrieved from www.streetchildunited.org/2013/06/13/the-story-of-a-rio-street-girl/ [Accessed September 13, 2017].

Cross-references: Pregnancy and Childbirth; Ownership, Property, and Possession; Family

Government

CONSCRIPTION AND VOLUNTEERISM

Underlying conscription and volunteerism is a basic conception of shared community obligations and national service. This splits into two streams, a military and a civilian one. Compulsory military service, with or without conscription (a forced draft), is more intermittent worldwide than in the past. It is hard to predict based on national cultural characteristics whether or not compulsory service will be required. Conscription, by its nature, is perceived as intrusive and, especially in the hyper-individualistic United States, has often been resisted. In the United States, forced conscription for an unpopular war in the 1960s resulted, ultimately, in the institution of a volunteer force in 1973. But conscription and compulsory service are contingent on world conditions, and what goes away may soon return. For example Sweden, which ended a long tradition of enforced military service in 2010, will be reinstating that requirement by 2018 due to current fears about Russian aggression (Stanglin, 2017). Likewise, the requirement for mandatory non-military service is less prevalent at present worldwide. Several studies suggest that the motives for civilian volunteering in different countries are influenced by cultural values (Aydinli, Bender, & Chasiot et al., 2013; Gronlund, Holmes, Kang, & Zrinščak, 2011): presumably, these differences determine different rates of volunteering within nations as well.

Exposition, Confrontation, and Simulation

Investigate the variability in requirements for both military and civilian service worldwide using the CIA World Factbook (CIA, n.d.). Direct debates about military conscription cannot reasonably succeed at present because there is no way to comprehend involuntary conscription in current US society and no passion for the subject: probe the concept in several indirect ways, however. Simulate a draft lottery and come up with all the excuses that would exempt a person from military service. (This is pretty instinctive!) Since this is dead history at present, introduce the history of the passionate opposition to the Vietnam War and especially to the draft: Phil Ochs's song from the middle 1960s, *Draft Dodger's Rag* (Ochs, 1964) could serve as a musical theme. Address the question of whether public service or personal gain is the goal of study and life. The merits of William James's suggestion, in *The Moral Equivalent of War* (James, 1910) of a conscripted army for public service and its historic offshoots, the Peace Corps and AmeriCorps, can be evaluated: would it be possible, in the United States at current, to require public service in charitable causes such as is done in other regions of the world? Consider arguments pro and con (see e.g., Friedersdorf, 2013). Inevitably, though, the question of conscription is grounded in military service, historically and culturally, and the question of which values are worth dying for—whether in combat or in arduous national service—is the one to which those considering the subject will, and should, always return. A more upbeat approach would evaluate the opportunities for civilian volunteer service in the immediate area. In conjunction with this, use the resources provided in the Charity entry in this book. Using a list of potential volunteer activities (e.g., Center for Community Health and Development, n.d.) examine the differences between passive and active volunteering. A survey comparing the number and kind of charitable activities already done or ongoing can provide the impetus for more.

REFERENCES AND SUGGESTED READINGS

Aydinli, A., Bender, M., & Chasiotis, A. (2013). Helping and volunteering across cultures: Determinants of prosocial behavior. *Online Readings in Psychology and Culture, 5*(3). Retrieved from https://doi.org/10.9707/2307-0919.1118 [Accessed October 14, 2017].

Center for Community Health and Development. (n.d.). Community tool box (Chapter 28: Spirituality and community building). *Community Tool Box website of the KU CCHD* (University of Kansas, online). Retrieved from http://ctb.ku.edu/en/table-of-contents/spirituality-and-community-building/being-charitable-towards-others/main [Accessed July 25, 2017].

CIA. (n.d.). Military service age and obligation. *The World Factbook* (US Central Intelligence Agency online resource). Retrieved from www.cia.gov/library/publications/the-world-factbook/fields/2024.html [Accessed October 14, 2017].

Friedersdorf, C. (2013, June 26). The case against universal national service. *The Atlantic* (online magazine). Retrieved from www.theatlantic.com/politics/archive/2013/06/the-case-against-universal-national-service/277230/ [Accessed October 14, 2017].

Gronlund, H., Holmes, K., Kang, C. H., & Zrinščak, S. (2011). Cultural values and volunteering: A cross-cultural comparison of students' motivation to volunteer in 13 countries. *Journal of Academic Ethics, 9*(2), 87–106.

James, W. (1910). The moral equivalent of war. *Popular Science Monthly, 77*, 400–410. (Online at several sources, for example. Retrieved from https://en.wikisource.org/wiki/Popular_Science_Monthly/Volume_77/October_1910/The_Moral_Equivalent_of_War [Accessed October 14, 2017].

Ochs, P. (1964). *Draft Dodger's Rag.* (Musical composition.) Online version, recording from 1968. Retrieved from www.youtube.com/watch?v=tFFOUkipI4U [Accessed July 25, 2017].

Stanglin, D. (2017, March 2). Sweden reinstates military draft over concerns about Russian aggression. *USA Today* (online newspaper). Retrieved from www.usatoday.com/story/news/2017/03/02/sweden-reinstates-draft-over-concerns-russia/98641010/ [Accessed October 14, 2017].

Cross-references: Disaster and War; Charity

CORRUPTION

Corruption in an earlier, historic sense refers to the dissolution of the body after death: spoilage. It has evolved to signify a pervasive social malaise that might be an underculture or even an anticulture. Corruption subverts laws and customs and ensures beneficial returns to its lawless practitioners. From the perspective of the pervasive law-based culture inside which cultural studies in the United States are premised, corruption distorts the institutions and practices that are the basis for comparisons with other cultures. Zephyr Teachout's recent (2016) book *Corruption in America: From Benjamin Franklin's Snuffbox to Citizens United* suggests that the US constitutional government was intentionally designed to frustrate corruption, thus making outbreaks of corruption appear like virulent diseases. In other cultures, corruption is more widespread and endemic: bribery and other extra-legal work-arounds are expected and even encouraged, socially if not officially. At the Pontifical University Javieriana in Bogota, Columbia, for example, the Psychology department offers a course in The Psychology of Corruption incorporating psychological and sociological perspectives. The technical theoretical literature on corruption extends widely over the social sciences, encompassing political and economic views, and converges on corruption viewed as a cultural phenomenon. Rotondi and Stanca (2015), in the *Journal of Economic Psychology*, integrate several strands of evidence that suggest that particularism creates a framework in which individual bribery or malinfluence may occur. Kravtsova, Oshchepkov, and Welzel (2016) assert that holding 'postmaterialist' values—described by Ronald Inglehart (1977) as valuing individual self-expression over economic security and widely discussed since that time—may predispose one toward accepting corrupt behavior.

Exposition, Confrontation, and Simulation

There is probably good reason to not try to uncover evidence and information about corruption directly within either the classroom or the immediate environs, although an approach could be made in a standard academic setting by asking questions about grade inflation, television revenues for athletics, or legacy admissions. The subject of corruption leads to considerations of other pervasive ways in which societies or cultures may be metaphorically said by some to be perverted or sickened, for instance by lessening emphasis on self-reliance or on military preparedness. At the least, surveys could be conducted about the relative use of bribery and other dodgy techniques and also of the approval of those techniques. This would lead naturally to the exploration of the database used by Kravtsova et al., the 250-plus–question World Values Survey (available online for consultation and analysis, see www.worldvaluessurvey.org/WVSOnline.jsp). Question 202 in the 2010–2014 version specifically addresses acceptance of bribery as necessary in living. An excellent though grisly case study would be the Grenfell Tower fire in London in June 2017 (Erlanger, 2017). Though this may be a case of simple cost-cutting rather than outright illegality, many points of possible corruptibility exist in this situation and could be identified and discussed. Also, the contrast between different levels of legal regulation and oversight in societies puts in higher relief the underlying mechanisms that kick in when regulation and law are illegally evaded.

REFERENCES AND SUGGESTED READINGS

Erlanger, S. (2017, June 28). After Grenfell Tower fire, U. K. asks: Has deregulation gone too far? *The New York Times* (online resource). Retrieved from www.nytimes.com/2017/06/28/world/europe/uk-grenfell-tower-fire-deregulation.html?_r=0 [Accessed July 6, 2017].

Inglehart, R. (1977). *The silent revolution: Changing values and political styles among Western publics*. Princeton, NJ: Princeton University Press.

Kravtsova, M., Oshchepkov, A., & Welzel, C. (2016). Values and corruption: Do postmaterialists justify bribery? *Journal of Cross-Cultural Psychology, 48*(1).

Rotondi, V., & Stanca, L. (2015). The effect of particularism on corruption: Theory and empirical evidence. *Journal of Economic Psychology, 51*, 219–235.

Teachout, Z. (2016). *Corruption in America: From Benjamin Franklin's snuffbox to Citizens United*. Cambridge, MA: Harvard University Press.

Cross-references: Forms of Government; Rights, Citizenship, and Voting

DISASTER AND WAR

Natural disasters and war provide opportunities to confront several paradoxes of culture. Culture is pervasive and strong, and yet it is fragile, at the mercy of the violence of both the natural environment and other humans, singly or in groups (not to mention the threats of other species and diseases). A scene of natural disaster reveals humanity at its most vulnerable and defenseless points. At the same time, disasters are arenas in which the highest heroism and physical endurance are encountered. Extreme individualism—hoarding and stealing without regard for the community—is matched by extreme communalism, for instance, the outpouring of shared sympathy and resources that occurs worldwide after earthquake, flood, or storm. Over time, utter devastation gives way to rebuilding, a tribute to human resilience. Oishi and Komiya (2017) observe that the relative risk of natural disaster is positively associated with some measures of collectivism. However, this relationship is not a primary determinant of the relative individualism or collectivism present in a culture. All cultures evince adaptive collective responses to disaster. Cultures which frequently experience natural disasters get better at this situationally induced collectivism through frequent practice. Like natural disasters, war is a recurring source of devastation across the world. In some regions, war is endemic: in others, it is a theoretical possibility but mainly a historical memory, with all the distortions and inaccuracies that attend to distant memories. Whether it is a natural phenomenon like bad weather or something more intimately psychological, psychologists, especially analytic psychologists, have attested to its power and its uncanny attractiveness to the human species (Freud, 1915/1957; Hillman, 2004). Like disaster, war is a proving ground for extremes of cowardice and cruelty, and also for bravery, courage, and heroism. It is deeply woven into virtually all cultures' systems of values and collective memory. War provides a potent stimulus for changing established cultural traditions. For example, women's entry into the US workforce out of necessity during the Second World War had major and lasting social and cultural repercussions (Devonis, 2014). Tributes to the fruits of peace in the form of institutions for learning and art are matched by monuments to war. War also allows death, the ultimate natural disaster, to be publicly acknowledged and commemorated: cemeteries and monuments spread across the fields of Arlington, Virginia, and northern France as well as in North Korea and Tehran. Sometimes—for instance in Hiroshima and Nagasaki, Japan—monuments to destruction counsel peace; in other places, they suggest vigilance and preparation for future conflict.

Exposition, Confrontation, and Simulation

War and natural disasters are the focus of attention for simulators: search and find examples of each. For background on war simulation consult Michel Chossudovsky (2012) while listening to Nobel Prize winner Bob Dylan's 'Talking World War III Blues.' Of actual war games and simulations there seems to be no end: find a local expert or online group of experts. Participation in a war game may be as engaging a way to begin the conversation about the paradoxes of war as any, especially if there isn't any real war to speak of. However, don't forget that, in the United States, Canada, and other countries, there are refugees attending classes who can provide first hand accounts: utilize these for instruction. If possible, institutional investment in a disaster simulation program would be great: however, plans for simulation are available at no cost from the Pan American Health Organization, the regional affiliate of the World Health Organization, via its online publication *Guidelines for Developing Emergency Simulations and Drills* (PAHO, n.d.). Examination of the role played by international medical aid organizations, for instance Doctors Without Borders, in providing psychological counseling can aid in designing a role for counselors and other psychological specialists in the direct response to disasters. Disasters and wars result in displacement of people and the creation of refugees. There are several suggestions regarding refugee mental health services in the APA refugee mental health resources material mentioned in the Immigration and Refugees entry in this book. Likewise, discussion can include reference to the specific environmental and health consequences of physical destruction.

Discussion of war can lead directly to considering military organizations themselves as cultures: SAMHSA (the Substance Abuse and Mental Health Services Administration of the US Government) provides an informative online summary of the dimensions of military culture for basic understanding of the experience of war from a soldier's perspective (SAMHSA, 2010). Search also for specific methods in use for preparing for lifesaving operations within military organizations worldwide and compare the role of service personnel in specific disaster situations. Region-specific news accounts of the coordination between military and civilian responders can assist. The question of what to rebuild after a war is not without controversy. The rebuilding of Germany after the Second World War is well documented (e.g., Leick, Schreiber, & Stoldt, 2010) and, in that context, a discussion of priorities for rebuilding—either in an established context such as Germany or a speculative simulation based on the degree of expected destruction in the local culture—can illustrate cultural traditions and values. The question can also be raised as to whether rebuilding the physical environment alters the pattern of the society and the culture as well. Finally, questions can be raised whether, in light of its engagement with core human values, all war is 'culture war' (Malka, 2014).

REFERENCES AND SUGGESTED READINGS

Chossudovsky, M. (2012). When war games go live? "Simulating World War III". *Global Research*. Montreal, Canada: Organization website (online). Retrieved from www. globalresearch.ca/when-war-games-go-live-preparing-to-attack-iran-simulating-world-war-iii/28542 [Accessed September 20, 2017].

Devonis, D. C. (2014). *History of psychology 101*. New York: Springer Publishing Co.

Freud, S. (1915/1957). Thoughts for the times on war and death. In J. Strachey (Ed.), *The standard edition of the complete psychological works of Sigmund Freud, V. 14*. London, UK: The Hogarth Press (pp. 275–300).

Hillman, J. (2004). *A terrible love of war*. New York: Penguin Books.

Leick, R., Schreiber, M., & Stoldt, H-U. (2010, August 10). A new look at Germany's postwar reconstruction. *Spiegel Online* (online news source). Retrieved from www.spiegel. de/international/germany/out-of-the-ashes-a-new-look-at-germany-s-postwar-reconstruction-a-702856.html [Accessed September 20, 2017].

Malka, A. (2014). Political culture and democracy. In A. B. Cohen (Ed.), *Culture reexamined: Broadening our understanding of social and evolutionary influences*. Washington, DC: American Psychological Association.

Oishi, S., & Komiya, A. (2017). Natural disaster risk and collectivism. *Journal of Cross-Cultural Psychology, 48*(8), 1263–1270.

PAHO. (n.d.). *Guide for Developing Emergency Situations and Drills.* Department of Health Emergencies, Pan American Health Organization (WHO) (online). Retrieved from www.paho.org/disasters/index.php?option=com_content&view=article&id=1637%3 Aguidelines-for-developing-emergency-simulations-and-drills&Itemid=807&lang=en [Accessed September 20, 2017].

SAMHSA. (2010). *Understanding the military: The institution, the culture, and the people. Online document published by SAMHSA* (Substance Abuse and Mental Health Services Administration, US Government) (online). Retrieved from www.samhsa.gov/sites/default/files/partnersforrecovery/docs/Military_White_Paper_Final.pdf [Accessed September 20, 2017].

Cross-references: Immigrants and Refugees; Physical Toughness, Endurance, and Endurance; Health and Sanitation

FORMS OF GOVERNMENT

Abstracting from surface details of organization, forms of government distribute along two main axes: one running from oligarchy to democracy, and the other a non-polar scale indicating more or less authoritarian control. US psychology has thrived in an atmosphere of low oligarchy and relatively low authoritarianism, and theorists and researchers have mostly been concerned with explaining deviations away from this felicitous combination of factors. Authoritarian rule has been a focus of study since the middle of the 20th century, when a combination of expatriate social scientists fleeing authoritarian rule in Europe along with psychologists and others with an interest in how personality is reflected in politics, composed *The Authoritarian Personality* (Adorno, Frenkel-Brunswik, Levinson, & Sanford, 1950). Interest in authoritarianism, especially that of 'right-wing' or conservative (by US standards) governments, has continued since that time, inspired theoretically by the research program of Bob Altemeyer (1981, 2006) and exemplified by many studies of the relation of the variable right-wing authoritarianism to a wide range of behaviors and attitudes. Most cross-cultural studies in psychology involve studying interactions with culture at the individual, family, and workplace levels rather than investigating how particular forms of government can shape or create culture within and between societies. There is, however, a substantial tradition in social science of investigating the connections between politics and culture (Malka, 2014). Suffice it to say here that several key aspects of culture included in this book are inextricable from politics, for example corruption and abortion, to name just two.

Exposition, Confrontation, and Simulation

Consideration of forms of government need not focus only on right-wing authoritarianism: start by simply inventorying the ways in which government, in all of its functions (economics, defense, education, regulation of commerce, administration of justice, and enforcement of law) can impact culture: these impacts could be ranked from least to most explosive (e.g., a directive limiting family size). If right-wing authoritarianism is chosen as a focus, there is a short and reliable version of the most prominent Right Wing Authoritarianism (RWA) scale (Manganelli Rattazzi, Bobbio, & Canova, 2007) and this could be adapted for use either as a discussion tool or in a replication of a recent study (e.g., Crawford, Brandt, Inbar, & Mallinas, 2016). Most simulations of government, for instance Statecraft (Statecraft Simulations, 2017), are top-down and focus only indirectly on the individual and interpersonal psychological aspects of life in an authoritarian society. A cue toward simulating at least part of the experience could involve considering the limits to realistic simulation of oppression described in the review of the documentary recently produced for Czech television, *Holiday in the Protectorate,*" about the ways in which life was forcibly altered by the occupation of Czechoslovakia by Germany in 1939 (Lyman, 2015).

REFERENCES AND SUGGESTED READINGS

Adorno, T., Frenkel-Brunswik, E., Levinson, D., & Sanford, N. (1950). *The authoritarian personality*. New York: Harper & Brothers.

Altemeyer, B. (1981). *Right-wing authoritarianism*. Winnipeg, Canada: University of Manitoba Press.

Altemeyer, B. (2006). *The authoritarians*. Free online book. Retrieved from www.psicosocial. net/grupo-accion-comunitaria/centro-de-documentacion-gac/fundamentos-y-teoria-de-una-psicologia-liberadora/psicologia-social/626-the-authoritarians/file [Accessed July 31, 2017].

Crawford, J. T., Brandt, M. J., Inbar, Y., & Mallinas, S. R. (2016). Right-wing authoritarianism predicts prejudice equally toward 'gay men and lesbians' and 'homosexuals'. *Journal of Personality and Social Psychology, 111*(2), e31–e45.

Lyman, R. (2015, June 5). Grim reality: Czech TV makes game of Nazi era. *The New York Times* (online). Retrieved from www.nytimes.com/2015/06/06/world/europe/czech-reality-tv-show-makes-a-game-of-life-under-nazi-rule.html?_r=0 [Accessed July 31, 2017].

Malka, A. (2014). Political culture and democracy. In A. B. Cohen (Ed.), *Culture reexamined: Broadening our understanding of social and evolutionary influences*. Washington, DC: American Psychological Association.

Manganelli Rattazzi, A. M., Bobbio, A., & Canova, L. (2007). A short version of the Right-Wing Authoritarianism (RWA) Scale. *Personality and Individual Differences, 43*(5), 1223–1234.

Statecraft Simulations. (2017). Company website. Retrieved from http://statecraftsim.com/simulations/ [Accessed July 31, 2017].

Cross-references: Abortion; Punishment and Prisons; Immigration and Refugees

FREEDOM AND SLAVERY

A core value of the primary reference culture for these exercises, the United States, is freedom. The defining historical events in the United States have questions of freedom at their core: freedom from colonization at the founding and freedom from enslavement, the purpose and ostensible outcome of the US Civil War. President Franklin D. Roosevelt, while addressing the US Congress on January 6, 1941, declared that there were four essential freedoms which the United States would fight to maintain everywhere in the world: freedom of speech, freedom of worship, freedom from want, and freedom from fear (Roosevelt, 1941). Today, the US Department of State maintains an Office of International Religious Freedom headed by the Ambassador-at-Large for International Religious Freedom. This person is tasked to, among other things, "promote freedom of religion and conscience throughout the world as a fundamental human right and as a source of stability for all countries" and also to "assist religious and human rights NGOs in promoting religious freedom" (US Department of State, 2017, n.p.). The greatest contrast to freedom is slavery. The Global Slavery Index for 2013 estimated that, at that time, 29.8 million people worldwide were enslaved in some form (Datta, David, Bales, & Grono, 2013). Both freedom and slavery are implicit in psychology and yet they are addressed only obliquely. For instance, the term *freedom* does not have a stand-alone entry in the recent *APA Dictionary of Psychology* (VandenBos, 2015), while *freedom* is indexed only in conjunction with psychological reactance—resistance to authority or contrariness—in the *Encyclopedia of Cross-Cultural Psychology* (Keith, 2013).

Exposition, Confrontation, and Simulation

Although psychology has mostly compressed questions about freedom into the 'freedom vs. determinism' mold derived from the philosophy of science, there have been great advocates for freedom within the field. Readings could be drawn from classic sources, such as Carl Rogers's *Freedom to Learn* (Rogers, 1969), which encourage principles of discussion and speculation essential to learning in classrooms and also between cultures. Ranking cultures within and outside of the United States in terms of Rogers's supposed opponent B. F. Skinner's definition of freedom as the relative absence of aversive control might lead to mapping coerciveness, military rule, and other aspects of punitive government to the distribution of slavery; the ongoing Global Slavery Index along with the Global Peace Index can provide insights into the distributions of elements promoting freedom or repression worldwide. Theoretical analyses of slavery are in short supply: Hu (2003) provides an intuitive game-theoretic approach to the difference between conditions of control that lead either to slavery (absolute dominance of one player over another) or to power sharing. Possibly a video game featuring slavery could be procured, played, and discussed. Mukherjee (2016) provides some leads in this direction.

REFERENCES AND SUGGESTED READINGS

Datta, M. N., David, F., Bales, K., & Grono, N. (2013). *The global slavery index*. Annual report, Walk Free Foundation (affiliated with the Minderoo Foundation, Australia). Online open access via the Political Science Scholarship Repository, University of Richmond, VA. Retrieved from http://scholarship.richmond.edu/cgi/viewcontent. cgi?article=1031&context=polisci-faculty-publications [Accessed July 27, 2017].

Hu, X. (2003). On authority distributions in organizations: Controls. *Games and Economic Behavior, 45*(1), 153–170.

Keith, K. (Ed.) (2013). *The encyclopedia of cross-cultural psychology* (3 vols.). New York: Wiley-Blackwell.

Mukherjee, S. (2016). Video games and slavery. *Transactions of the Digital Games Research Association, 2*(3), 243–260. Available in open access PDF. Retrieved from todigra.org

Rogers, C. (1969). *Freedom to learn*. Columbus, OH: C. E. Merrill Co.

Roosevelt, F. D. (1941). The four freedoms. (Speech delivered to the US Congress, January 6, 1941). *American Rhetoric website: Top 100 Speeches* (online). Retrieved from www. americanrhetoric.com/speeches/fdrthefourfreedoms.htm [Accessed July 27, 2017].

US Department of State. (2017). Religious freedom (homepage of the Office of International Religious Freedom). *US Department of State website* (online). Retrieved from www. state.gov/j/drl/irf/ [Accessed July 27, 2017].

VandenBos, G. R. (Ed.) (2015). *APA dictionary of psychology* (2nd ed.). Washington, DC: American Psychological Association.

Cross-references: Ownership, Property, and Possession; Punishment and Prisons; Forms of Government

OWNERSHIP, PROPERTY, AND POSSESSION

Possession, it is said, is nine tenths of the law, at least in societies with a heritage in English common law. Ownership, the psychological state of feeling in possession of either goods or abilities, flows from rights and also confers rights which allow people to function unimpeded in their culture. The withering of enforced collectivism in recent political history has affirmed the strength of the private ownership concept worldwide, as has the globalization of capitalist enterprises. Owning something legally allows claims against others for theft, both of things or of services: laws protect both real and intellectual property as well as chattel goods. This is truly a cross-cutting area of study in psychology and culture. Philippe Rochat's *Origins of Possession* (2014) provides a developmental perspective on ownership. Rudmin (1996), from a combined psychological, anthropological, and historical perspective, details the cross-cultural commonalities that underlie private ownership, which include aspects of agricultural production, work specialization, family membership, patriarchy and matriarchy, and commercial principles. A free recall study of property conceptions conducted with adult Canadians (Rudmin & Berry, 1987 revealed that, while the meaning of 'property' is distributed across four semantic categories (control or possession, attachment, purchase or legal ownership, and crafting or gifting), the strongest argument for ownership was means of acquisition (purchase or gifting, for example). Cross-cultural variations in ownership are often quite striking, for instance, the comparative rates of home ownership between the United States and China.

Exposition, Confrontation, and Simulation

Several opportunities are available for simple simulation of empirical studies in the area of cross-cultural ownership and possession. If you are lucky enough to have access to young children, numerous developmental tasks may be tried out on them to illustrate the developmental aspects of research in this area. For instance, children are sensitive to the concept of 'first possession,' the idea that the first person to hold an item is its owner, and adopt a heuristic for determining ownership that embodies this (Friedman & Neary, 2008). It might be interesting to see if comparisons could be carried out between children and older persons in this regard. A study carried out by Rochat et al. (2014) on children's decisions about third-party ownership involved two identical dolls fighting over possession of a single but divisible object. Replication of this study and possible comparison with adult behaviors could affirm the study's findings of the variability in solutions to this problem across several cultures as well as illustrating experimental procedure in this area. (Apparently, Chinese children were more apt to decide like Solomon, splitting the object in two, than were children from several other cultures.) Turning toward specifically adult ideas about ownership and property and considering experimental approaches to these, simulation of the endowment effect is uncomplicated. In the endowment effect, a monetary value is assigned to an object to represent (a) what a person would pay to acquire it and (b) how a person would price it if they owned it and were selling it. Should the difference between the selling and buying prices be positive, it is a complicated indicator of both value and avarice. Gobel et al. (2014) demonstrated experimentally that persons from collective cultures in Asia achieved a substantially higher endowment effect when they visualized the priced object being used in a private setting vs. a public one. A starting point for raising the question about the emotional and interpersonal aspects of ownership could be artist David Hockney's observation, in the context of deciding to remain in a non-marital partnership, that marriage is about property and that divorce certainly proves it (Solomon, 2017). Examination of variances in divorce practices and results, comparing local experiences and settlements with the results of cross-cultural research (Greenstein & Davis, 2006; Marrs, 2009), can be instructive beyond the boundaries of cross-cultural psychology. Intellectual property is subject to piracy, an interesting psychological subject that cuts across the boundaries of property and ethics. Possible replications might involve the construction of vignettes involving opportunities for piracy and the introduction of specific moral information into the decision process, an intervention which has been shown to be effective in Arabic Muslim cultures (Brown, 2013). The study of the value of things in themselves has a moderate research history in psychology: a local replication of the study of Watson, Lysonski, Gillan, and Raymo et al. (2002) on the cross-cultural valuation of possessions can be attempted. Look into the cost of moving valued household and personal goods to, say, France: just doing the inventory and reviewing the rules for importing goods will be instructive. Good luck finding a price! Another way of looking at ownership is to break out of the individualistic framework and investigate de-ownership orientation (DOO), a form of collaborative consumption (or possibly backyard communism?) practiced by individuals who are younger, poorer, and more affected by economic downturns (Lindblom & Lindblom, 2017). Collect stories or other evidence of these informal means of adult sharing of possessions. Finally, ownership is sometimes equated with personal mastery. Scales such as the Ryff Scales of Psychological Well-Being (Seifert, 2005), which incorporate a specific environmental mastery component, can be administered and the correlation between mastery scores and number of possessions or other evidence of ownership calculated and discussed.

REFERENCES AND SUGGESTED READINGS

Brown, S. (2013). Digital piracy and the moral compass. *The Psychologist* (British Psychological Society), *26*, 528–539.

Friedman, O., & Neary, K. (2008). Determining who owns what: Do children infer ownership from first possession? *Cognition, 107*, 829–849.

Gobel, M. S., Ong, T., & Harris, A. (2014). A culture-by-context analysis of endowment effects. In P. Bello, M. Guarini, M. McShane, & B. Scassellati (Eds.), *Proceedings of the 36th annual conference of the cognitive science society* (pp. 2269–2274), Austin, TX: Cognitive Science Society.

Greenstein, T. N., & Davis, S. (2006). Cross-national divorce: Effects of women's power, prestige, and dependence. *Journal of Comparative Family Studies, 37*(3), 253–273.

Lindblom, A., & Lindblom, T. (2017). De-ownership orientation and collaborative consumption during turbulent economic times. *International Journal of Consumer Studies, 41*(4), 431–438.

Marrs, T. (2009). Money in misery. *The Economist* (online magazine). Retrieved from www.economist.com/node/13057235 [Accessed September 22, 2017].

Rochat, P. (2014). *Origins of possession: Owning and sharing in development*. Cambridge: Cambridge University Press.

Rochat, P., Robbins, E., Passos-Ferreira, C., Donato Oliva, A., Dias, M. D. G., & Guo, L. (2014). Ownership reasoning in children across cultures. *Cognition, 132*, 471–484.

Rudmin, F. W. (1996). Cross-cultural correlates of the ownership of private property: Zelman's gender data revisited. *Cross-Cultural Research, 30*(2), 171–188.

Rudmin, F. W., & Berry, J. W. (1987). Semantics of ownership: A free-recall study of property. *The Psychological Record, 37*(2), 257–268.

Seifert, T. (2005, Spring). The Ryff Scales of Psychological Well-Being. *Wabash College* (Crawfordsville, IN) *Center for Inquiry*. Retrieved from www.liberalarts.wabash.edu/ryff-scales/ [Accessed September 24, 2017].

Solomon, D. (2017, September 5). David Hockney, contrarian, shifts perspectives. *The New York Times* (online newspaper). Retrieved from www.nytimes.com/2017/09/05/arts/design/david-hockney-los-angeles-metropolitan-museum-of-art-reverse-perspective.html?mcubz=3&_r=0 [Accessed September 22, 2017].

Watson, J., Lysonski, S., Gillan, T., & Raymore, L. (2002). Cultural values and important possessions: A cross-cultural analysis. *Journal of Business Research, 55*(11), 923–931.

Cross-references: Materialism and Consumer Culture, Religion and Law

RIGHTS, CITIZENSHIP, AND VOTING

A conundrum: which comes first, citizenship or rights? On the one hand, rights are often understood, especially in countries where rights have been elemental in their creation, as primary and sometimes even 'God-given.' On the other hand, through human history rights have been granted only at the pleasure of elders or rulers, and it is just as fair to say that rights depend, even today, on citizenship. Citizenship, whether acquired through birth or naturalization, awards a package of rights all at once: awarding citizenship is a serious matter and a closely guarded process. Citizenship tests function not only as part of the ritual of naturalization but also as potential barriers and immigration controls (Etzioni, 2007). Rights and citizenship are two legs of a triangle, the last of which is free choice of political and social options by voting. Few if any countries have no form of voting at all, although it is only a recent arrival in some. For instance, elections in Saudi Arabia have been rare, and women's right to vote in them was conferred by the country's king only a few years ago (NPR Staff, 2015). The degree to which rights are enumerated and extended, the levels of citizenship, and the prevalence and practice of voting determine to a large extent the framework in which all indigenous cultures exist worldwide. Psychologists have taken an interest in voting as both a cognitive process and a social practice. Among the most prominent and accessible currently is Jon Krosnick of Stanford University (Martin, 2016).

Exposition, Confrontation, and Simulation

Taking rights, citizenship, and voting in order, a first and very typical activity is to personally enumerate rights, either as a list of known or expected rights or as a theoretical exercise. Generate lists of rights, collate them, and then compare the generated lists with the *Universal Declaration of Human Rights*, published first by the United Nations in 1948 (United Nations, n.d.). This comparison can be carried out further against local constitutions, starting with the US Bill of Rights, which is widely available. There are also several sources available to support the important collateral discussion of rights vs. privileges that usually evolves from doing this, both independent (e.g., Tokarev, 2012) and quasi-official (for instance, the various publications of the American Civil Liberties Union dealing with rights and privileges). The concept of privileges comes sharply into view when rights are curtailed: view the degree of right vs. privilege through the lens of imprisonment (ACLU, n.d.). For citizenship, review the requirements for immigration as suggested in the Immigration and Refugees entry in this book. For voting, set up a simulated election, utilize a variety of voting methods, and compare and discuss both the results and the perception of fairness of each (an overview source is Pacuit, 2017). The psychosocial arguments for voting, even in the face of its apparent futility, were made eloquently by Paul Meehl (1977) and ought to be introduced into any discussion as well.

REFERENCES AND SUGGESTED READINGS

ACLU. (n.d.). Know your rights: In prison—privileged and non-privileged mail. *ACLU website*. Retrieved from www.aclu.org/know-your-rights/prison-privileged-and-non-privileged-mail [Accessed September 26, 2017].

Etzioni, A. (2007). Citizenship tests: A comparative, communitarian perspective. *The Political Quarterly, 78*(3), 353–363.

Martin, S. (2016, October). Conversation: Five questions for Jon Krosnick. *APA Monitor* (American Psychological Association news journal), *47*(9), 27. Retrieved from www.apa.org/monitor/2016/10/conversation-krosnick.aspx [Accessed September 26, 2017].

Meehl, P. (1977). The selfish voter paradox and the thrown-away vote argument. *American Political Science Review, 71*(1), 11–30.

NPR Staff. (2015, December 19). After historic elections in Saudi Arabia, what's the future for women? *NPR* (National Public Radio online website feature). Retrieved from www.npr.org/2015/12/19/459491653/after-historic-elections-in-saudi-arabia-whats-the-future-for-women [Accessed September 26, 2017].

Pacuit, Eric. (2017, Fall). Voting methods. In E. N. Zalta (Ed.), *The Stanford encyclopedia of philosophy* (online). Retrieved from https://plato.stanford.edu/archives/fall2017/entries/voting-methods/ [Accessed October 29, 2017].

Tokarev, S. (2012, February 28). Right vs. privilege distinction. *USCivilliberties.org* (Blog). Retrieved from http://uscivilliberties.org/themes/4398-right-v-privilege-distinction.html [Accessed September 26, 2017].

United Nations. (n.d.). Universal declaration of human rights. *United Nations website*. Retrieved from www.un.org/en/universal-declaration-human-rights/ [Accessed September 26, 2017].

Weinrib, L. (2017, August 30). The ACLU's free speech stance should be about social justice, not 'timeless' principles. *The Los Angeles Times* (online newspaper). Retrieved from www.latimes.com/opinion/op-ed/la-oe-weinrib-aclu-speech-history-20170830-story. html [Accessed September 26, 2017].

Cross-references: Boundaries and Maps; Immigration and Refugees

SEPARATENESS AND SECESSION

Culture usually implies togetherness of some sort, either a collective mass or a unity of individualists as in the United States. Likewise, cross-cultural psychology tends to favor impulses toward social cohesiveness and intercultural awareness and inclusion rather than centrifugal separatist ones. Separateness fits on a continuum from individual introversion as a personality dimension to group secession. In between these poles fit exiles, hermits, or isolates by choice, intentional communities formed based on religious, lifestyle, or political bases (e.g., Green, 2017), to secession, which itself ranges from individual withdrawal from an organized system (for instance, divorce) to group secession, either small or national in scope. Isolates and hermits as well as secessionist movements provide a contrast to ordinary views of culture similar to how dystopias project a negative image of the ideals of social life. In many ways, too, they reflect the ways that cultures oppress and how individuals and groups can, by their actions, increase separation, engender cultural unity, or resist perceived oppression. Indeed, while these words are being written the US president has just called, in the wake of a lone shooter's violent acts, for a renewal of unity around shared cultural values (Landler & Sullivan, 2017).

Exposition, Confrontation, and Simulation

Following the pattern set out in the introduction to this entry, the psychology of the introvert can be considered: suggested paths are reading drawn from the recent popular book *Quiet* (Cain, 2013) and also examination of the personality variable introversion via many available assessment instruments. This may also be a starting point for consideration of personality within and between cultures, taking cues from the procedures for cross-cultural comparison via personality measures described in the open-source publication of Afshan, Askari, and Manickam (2015). Biographies of productive (Emily Dickinson) and destructive (Ted Kaczynski) loners can be read and discussed in relation to the ways that these individuals reflected as well as remained separated from the culture of their times. Start the process of becoming a hermit monk: there are many sites that give instructions and advice for this (e.g., Anonymous, 2012). Look into other religious communities as well (e.g., Amish Christians) and compare their rules and expectations for joining with those expected for citizenship or immigration. Likewise, sketch out a plan for an intentional community and then compare with the brochures, websites, and manuals available from the many intentional communities worldwide with web presences (e.g., Milagro Cohousing near Tucson, Arizona, United States; http://milagrocohousing.org). For a historical psychological take on intentional communities, return to Skinner's (1948) *Walden Two* and the literature that describes its status, and that of related successor communities, as varieties of this species (Breshears & Devonis, 2015). At the macrosocial, national level, secession usually involves a tragic fate, while successful secession is venerated as the achievement of independence. Independence histories and myths are loci for interaction in this area. Regarding unsuccessful secession, start the discussion here with consideration of the destruction of already separate and autonomous communities or peoples by colonizers or invaders, for instance the genocide of the Ovaherero by Germany in Africa in 1904 (Steinmetz, 2005) or the persistent revengeful memory of the Conquistadores in New Mexico (Romero, 2017). The controversy over the recent Catalonian vote to secede from Spain has overtones of US Civil War history, and for those who want to take the widest view of the issue this is one of the most currently active areas. For those who desire a more limited and simplified secession episode, consider one that occurred in Oregon in 2016. A group of individuals intending to resist what they perceived as federal government oppression of their rights as independent rural ranchers maintained an occupation in force of the Malheur National Wildlife Refuge in eastern Oregon (Oregonian Staff, 2017). Their siege was broken by local, state, and federal law enforcement after 41 days: a subsequent trial found the leaders of the occupation not guilty of conspiracy (Bernton, 2016). The ambiguous ending to this episode adds complexity to a story that I have used at the beginning of cross-cultural courses to illustrate the problems of understanding the United States in terms of a single aspect of the individualist–collectivist polarity. The occupiers bore hallmarks not only of independent libertarians but also of a family clan. The verdict suggests some level of official tolerance for the action, and illustrates well the tension between the collectivism of the law and the individual liberty that it is designed to protect.

REFERENCES AND SUGGESTED READINGS

Afshan, A., Askari, I., & Manickam, L. S. S. (2015, April–June). Shyness, self-construal, extraversion-introversion, neuroticism, & psychoticism: A cross-cultural comparison across college students. *Sage Open* (online open-source journal), 1–8. Retrieved from http://journals.sagepub.com/doi/pdf/10.1177/2158244015587559 [Accessed October 2, 2017].

Anonymous. (2012). How I became a medieval-style anchorite. *Catholic Herald* (online newspaper). Retrieved from www.catholicherald.co.uk/news/2012/02/29/how-i-became-a-medieval-style-anchorite/ [Accessed October 2, 2017].

Bernton, H. (2016, October 27). Jury acquits leaders of Malheur wildlife-refuge standoff. *The Seattle Times* (online newspaper). Retrieved from www.seattletimes.com/seattle-news/crime/verdict-near-in-malheur-wildlife-refuge-standoff-trial/ [Accessed October 2, 2017].

Breshears, J., & Devonis, D. (2015). The Wright stuff? Architectural influences in Walden Two. *Operants* (online journal of the B. F. Skinner Foundation), Fourth Quarter, 59–65. Retrieved from www.bfskinner.org/wp-content/uploads/2015/12/OPERANTS_Q4.pdf [Accessed October 2, 2017].

Cain, S. (2013). *Quiet: The power of introverts in a world that can't stop talking.* New York: Broadway Books.

Green, E. (2017, January 15). Seeking an escape from Trump's America. *The Atlantic* (online magazine). Retrieved from www.theatlantic.com/politics/archive/2017/01/anarchism-intentional-communities-trump/513086/ [Accessed October 2, 2017].

Landler, M., & Sullivan, E. (2017, October 2). Trump, after Las Vegas shooting: "Our unity cannot be shattered by evil." *The New York Times* (online newspaper). Retrieved from www.nytimes.com/2017/10/02/us/politics/trump-las-vegas-mass-shooting.html?action=click&contentCollection=US&module=RelatedCoverage&region=Marginalia&pgtype=article [Accessed October 2, 2017].

Oregonian Staff. (2017, February 15). Oregon standoff timeline: 41 days of the Malheur refuge occupation and the aftermath. *The Oregonian/OregonLive* (online newspaper). Retrieved from www.oregonlive.com/portland/index.ssf/2017/02/oregon_standoff_timeline_41_da.html [Accessed October 2, 2017].

Romero, S. (2017, September 30). Statue's stolen foot reflects divisions over symbols of conquest. *The New York Times* (online newspaper). Retrieved from www.nytimes.com/2017/09/30/us/statue-foot-new-mexico.html?mcubz=3&_r=0 [Accessed October 2, 2017].

Skinner, B. F. (1948). *Walden Two*. New York: Palgrave Macmillan.

Steinmetz, G. (2005). The first genocide of the 20th century and its postcolonial aftermath: Germany and the Namibian Ovaherero. *The Journal of the International Institute* (University of Michigan) (online institutional journal). Retrieved from https://quod.lib.umich.edu/j/jii/4750978.0012.201/-first-genocide-of-the-20th-century-and-its-postcolonial?rgn=main;view=fulltext [Accessed October 2, 2017].

Cross-references: Freedom and Slavery; Immigration and Refugees; Religion and Law; Rights, Citizenship, and Voting; Dystopias and Utopias

Law

FIREARMS

Firearms have a long history. For now, the focus will be on the current US prototype concept of 'firearms': a portable personal weapon firing a projectile. Included in this would be pistols, shotguns, and rifles, automatic or not: excluded would be artillery and rocketry. The *APA Dictionary of Psychology* (APA, 2014) doesn't have an entry for firearms but does have one for the weapon effect (the observation that aggression increases on the sight of a weapon) and one for the weapon-focus effect (the tendency of eyewitnesses to attend more to weapons than to other elements of the environment). Weapons-effect studies generalize the idea of 'weapon' across several different types of object, though firearms and knives are those that are most often cited. It may be that the weapon and weapon-focus effects emerge universally but research in this area has focused more on gender and race rather than cultural variables. Expanding this forensic psychological focus toward a more hybridized cultural one, an interesting take on the idea of 'culture as a weapon' to be deployed alongside actual firearms emerges from an analysis of the way that the US Army homogenized and distorted the diversity in Iraqi culture in its training manuals (Davis, 2010). In the United States, gun ownership and especially the degree to which the right to possess, use, and display a gun can be granted are the basis of what Lemieux (2014) terms "gun culture." Within gun culture, subcultures of gun enthusiasts support fewer limitations while gun-control advocates support tighter restrictions. This polarity contributes to political conflict and differentials in the enactment and enforcement of gun law based on the prevalent local or regional attitude toward guns. (As might be expected, gun enthusiasm is associated with increases in firearm-caused deaths and gun control with decreases.) US gun culture projects a romantic frontier image with a long historical lineage (Russell, 1980) and this along with its relatively less restrictive firearms policies makes the United States a destination for gun tourism, for example from highly gun-restrictive China (Gardner, 2017). Internationally, guns are regulated more stringently elsewhere than in the United States, which stimulates booming illegal gun markets. For example, in India, although a person is only one-twelfth as likely to be killed by a firearm there than in the United States, more than 90 percent of those deaths are due to illegal guns (FirstPost, 2016). At present—as through all of modern history—arms manufactured in the United States, Europe, Russia, and Asia are dumped in Africa and fuel civil strife and terrorism.

Exposition, Confrontation, and Simulation

US gun culture can be debated within and outside the United States: a comprehensive background source is Utter (2015). Simulating the process of applying for a permit to purchase a gun will graphically illustrate the baseline characteristics of responsible citizenship in the United States and in any other culture for which the process can be initiated online: view Person (2013) for examples of how stringent gun laws are outside of the United States. Elsbach and Bhattacharya's (2001) contention that people will develop their own identity within culture by adopting attitudes and behaviors contrary to the stated goals of particular organizations— their example was people resisting the values of the (US) National Rifle Association—can be explored and replicated as well.

REFERENCES AND SUGGESTED READINGS

APA. (2014). *APA dictionary of psychology* (2nd ed.). Washington, DC: American Psychological Association.

Davis, R. (2010). Culture as a weapon. *Middle East Research and Information Project*, No. 255, Vol. 40 (online). Retrieved from www.merip.org/mer/mer255 [Accessed August 19, 2017].

Elsbach, K. D., & Bhattacharya, C. B. (2001). Defining who you are by what you're not: Organizational disidentification and the National Rifle Association. *Organization Science, 12*(4), 393–413.

FirstPost. (2016, June 14). Americans 12 times vulnerable to gun violence than Indians: UP, Bihar lead in illegal arms: report. *FirstPost* (online news source). Retrieved from www.firstpost.com/world/americans-12-times-vulnerable-to-gun-violence-than-indians-up-bihar-lead-in-illegal-arms-report-2834730.html [Accessed November 1, 2017].

Gardner, H. (2017, April 29). In gun-taboo China, tourism to U.S. firing ranges grows. *USA Today* (online newspaper). Retrieved from www.usatoday.com/story/news/world/2017/04/09/beijing-china-guns-united-states-tourism/99121058/ [Accessed August 19, 2017].

Lemieux, F. (2014). Gun violence and mass shootings in the United States: A multi-level quantitative analysis. *International Journal of Criminal Justice Sciences, 9*, 74–93.

Person, C. (2013, December 10). Legally owning a gun in Japan is really, really hard. *Kotaku* (online magazine). Retrieved from https://kotaku.com/legally-owning-a-gun-in-japan-is-really-really-hard-1479865283 [Accessed August 19, 2017].

Russell, C. P. (1980). *Guns on the early frontiers: A history of firearms from Colonial times through the years of the Western fur trade.* Lincoln, NE: University of Nebraska Press.

Utter, G. (2015). *Guns in contemporary society: The past, present, and future of firearms and firearm policy* (3 vols). New York: Praeger/ABC-Clio.

Cross-references: Tourism; Borders and Boundaries; War; Surveillance and Eyewitnessing

LAW ENFORCEMENT

To the extent that culture is a creation of law, it owes its survival to some form of enforcement. We hardly think of the punishments and sanctions for rule breaking carried out by families and schools as law enforcement, though these are the first line of this cultural defense. In current societies, worldwide, beyond this locally intimate level, law enforcement is a function of policing by force of arms, carried out either by an officially sanctioned governmental institution (for example, a state police force) or, during an emergency, an arm of a national military force. Enforcement can also be carried out by armed enforcers operating outside the law for the benefit of opposition forces within a state (e.g., a militia connected to a radical opposition group) or, sometimes, for its own benefit (e.g., a group of pirates). Consideration of the rules of engagement for organizations at an international level (e.g. a United Nations Peacekeeping Unit in Africa) or for lawless enforcers (e.g., a criminal mob) may be interesting and appropriate, but for most individuals studying cross-cultural psychology the face of law enforcement meeting culture in the United States is embodied in the patrol officer in a municipal police force. Police, like the military, are a culture unto themselves and discussion of policing can be an entry point to a discussion of military culture as well. In the United States, Ellen Kirschmann's 2006 book *I Love a Cop* is a requisite introduction to the insular and defensive world of enforcers. Recently, consideration has expanded to the specific concerns and stresses on members of other national or social cultures in policing. Police in interaction with other cultures function either as occupying forces or as negotiators: episodes differ in their relative crudity and cruelty of approach. Looking at the situation from the perspective of those who are on the receiving end of law enforcement techniques, policing is a flash point revealing the cultural tensions that smolder in US society. Through the current decade, visible cases—made more so by the introduction of car and body cameras—have rendered a picture of a volcanically active edge between several cultures in the United States and the gunfire of enforcers. Background reading on the conditions of arbitrary punishment and inflexible enforcement leading to this could start with Victor Rios's *Punished: Policing the Lives of Black and Latino Boys* (2011).

Exposition, Confrontation, and Simulation

It's not typical that many students of culture in the United States will have had experiences with law enforcement in other countries, but that does not mean that there will be no place to start with basic discussion and information gathering. At the outset, sharing of experiences about encounters with law enforcement can set a context. Simulation of the perception of danger from an officer's point of view can be helpful in gaining perspective. In my classes we have had success with simply role-playing a traffic stop; this can work well even if it is seriously done by members of similar cultures, but in the context of cross-cultural learning it works even better if the person being stopped has the features and language of 'otherness.'

REFERENCES AND SUGGESTED READINGS

Kirschmann, E. (2006). *I love a cop: What police families need to know* (2nd revised ed.). New York: Guilford Press.

Rios, V. (2011). *Punished: Policing the lives of Black and Latino boys*. New York: New York University Press.

Cross-references: Forms of Government; Petty Crime; Punishment and Prisons; Immigration and Refugees; Safety and Danger; Disaster and War; Parenting

PETTY CRIME

Cross-cultural approaches to crime are reflected in both comparative criminology and media studies (e.g., Evans & White, 2013). The focus in most studies of criminology is typically on highly visible and violent crime. Murder and its prohibition are probably culturally universal (Rachels, 1999). But what of pickpocketing, shoplifting, and other more common but less glamorous crimes? In the case of pickpocketing in the United States, the increased use of debit and credit cards, heightened surveillance, more severe penalties, dismantlement of the previously existing system of apprenticeship in the pickpocketing trade, and also the increased availability of firearms and the consequent increase in armed robberies led to pickpocketing dropping from sight between 1970 and 2010 (NPR Staff, 2011). However, worldwide, pickpocketing is viewed—at least by online travel advisors—as ubiquitous (Potter, 2016). The question of whether a crime is 'petty' depends on the society in which it happens: for instance, petty theft might draw a fine (Denmark) or, in Indonesia, a severe beating before a prison sentence (Wockner, & Erviani, 2016). In some parts of the world, petty thievery is less a crime than a part of the informal economy. For instance, in Swaziland, shoplifters camp in the central markets and are a source of desirable consumer goods, paying a nominal fine if and when they are caught. Prosecution is rare (Zwane, 2014).

Exposition, Confrontation, and Simulation

Discussion could start by trying to establish at least a local norm for petty crime. What behaviors constitute petty crime, and when does 'unauthorized use of a vehicle' become 'Grand Theft Auto'? After this, the variation of consequences for petty crimes should be researched and compared, within and across nations. At the very least this could be an exercise in beginning comparative legal scholarship and would dovetail with discussion of law and penalties in other exercises in this book. Also, it would reveal divergences of opinion about whether any crimes at all are petty or insignificant. In some cultures severe punishment for minor offenses is common, while in others, some forms of petty crime are essentially tolerated. This could be a good springboard for examination of informal, off-the-books economies as well as the texture of criminality worldwide. Some attention could be given to the correlation of petty crime with economic deprivation. Examination of the ways that neighborhoods change from crime-ridden to relatively crime-free could be undertaken, using the process of gentrification as an example to tie together many strands of economic and social factors determining the petty crime rate (Rotondaro & Ewing, 2013). To promote empathy, role-playing the situation of an impoverished 16-year old with a 1-year-old child in Indonesia engaging in petty stealing, as in the example mentioned earlier (Wockner & Erviani, 2016), could involve the calculation of risk and benefit for snatching a cellphone. There are many YouTube videos providing demonstrations of defenses against pickpockets and snatchers: simulation of such situations could be a possibility with proper safeguards and spotters.

REFERENCES AND SUGGESTED READINGS

Evans, L., & White, M. (Eds.) (2013). Crime across cultures. *Moving Worlds: A Journal of Transcultural Writings, 13*(1) (online). Retrieved from www.movingworlds.net/ [Accessed July 31, 2017].

NPR Staff. (2011, March 6). Pickpocketing: An art that's stealing away. *NPR (National Public Radio), All Things Considered* (transcript of radio broadcast) (online). Retrieved from www.npr.org/2011/03/06/134298101/pickpocketing-an-art-thats-stealing-away [Accessed July 31, 2017].

Potter, E. (2016, May 11). Five myths about pickpockets. *USA Today* (online newspaper). Retrieved from www.usatoday.com/story/travel/advice/2016/05/11/pickpockets/ 84179812/ [Accessed July 31, 2017].

Rachels, J. (1999). *The challenge of cultural relativism* (online). Retrieved from http:// faculty.uca.edu/rnovy/Rachels--Cultural%20Relativism.htm [Accessed July 31, 2017]. (Adapted from Rachels, J. (1986). *The elements of moral philosophy* (Chapter 2). New York: McGraw-Hill).

Rotondaro, V., & Ewing, M. (2013, January 15). The ins and outs. *Narratively* (online literary magazine). Retrieved from http://narrative.ly/the-ins-and-the-outs/ [Accessed August 1, 2017].

Stamatel, J. (2011). Cross-national crime. *Oxford Bibliographies Online* (digital resource). Retrieved from www.oxfordbibliographies.com/view/document/obo-9780195396607/obo-9780195396607-0082.xml (subscription required) [Accessed July 31, 2017].

Wockner, C., & Erviani, K. (2016, November 30). Bali teen accused of stealing mobile from Australian woman 'beaten' by security. *News.com.au* (online newspaper). Retrieved from www.news.com.au/world/asia/bali-teen-accused-of-stealing-mobile-from-australian-woman-beaten-by-security/news-story/ecc135bf846f93477c7027aa247b675b [Accessed August 1, 2017].

Zwane, A. (2014, October 25). Shoplifters beating all odds. *Swazi Observer* (online newspaper). Retrieved from www.observer.org.sz/news/pick-of-the-day/67138-shoplifters-beating-all-odds.html [Accessed August 1, 2017].

Cross-references: Punishment and Prisons; Religion and Law

PUNISHMENT AND PRISONS

Prisons evolved along with law and have existed since at least the time of ancient Athens (Allen, 2003). In the United States, which currently has one of the highest incarceration rates in the world, psychology—though its most famous 20th century experiments involved simulations of punishment delivery and imprisonment—has not evolved a consistent or subtle theory of punishment. And regarding prisons, psychologists interested in reform have fought a continual uphill battle (Devonis & Triggs, 2017). Perhaps psychology's single most glaring ethical problem of the past two decades has been the involvement of psychologists in the design and implementation of overt torture in the US military prison maintained as a military-colonial enclave in Cuba (Risen, 2015). Extreme variations exist between regions and cultures in the style and frequency of prison punishment. A recent study compared three European or European-derived cultures (the United States, Canada, and Germany) with widely different incarceration rates (currently—2017—US, 666/100,000; Canada 114/100,000; and Germany, 77/100,000). The results suggest that even though there are some individual-level cultural differences in punitiveness in these societies, they are not the main driver of differential incarceration rates. However, these statistics probably reflect more the social endorsement of the status quo established by lawmakers' choices of punishment strategies (Kugler, Funk, Braun, Gollwitzer, & Kay, 2013).

Exposition, Confrontation, and Simulation

No credible simulation of prisons that captures the full cruelty of the experience can be done either in a classroom or in a laboratory. Consideration of prison issues must rely on the testimony of past and current prisoners, family members, prison staff members and administrators, and other interested individuals. Begin by examining the data available for prisons worldwide at the *World Prison Brief* website (www.prisonstudies.org). This resource not only ranks basic prison statistics (total number of prisoners, rate per 100,000 population, percentage under 18, female, etc.), but it also hosts a series of international prison reports including downloadable *Guidance Notes on Prison Reform*, with chapters on demilitarization of prisons, overcrowding, and pre-trial detention, a nagging worldwide problem. After this, search for comparisons between cultural attitudes toward prisoners, especially toward prisoners returning to society. One such comparison could be between 'Miriam,' the pseudonym of an illiterate woman incarcerated in Sierra Leone because of her ignorance of the meaning of her plea, who was glad to have learned to write during her time in prison, and Michelle Jones, incarcerated in the United States for 20 years for killing her child and released. Jones's rehabilitation was complete, and her academic work in prison qualified her for admission to Harvard University, which rejected her, demonstrating the US cultural belief in crime as a permanent moral stain (Hager, 2017).

REFERENCES AND SUGGESTED READINGS

Allen, D. S. (2003, March 23). Punishment in Ancient Athens. In A. Lanni (Ed.), *Athenian law in its democratic context* (Center for Hellenic Studies Online Discussion Series). Republished in C. W. Blackwell, ed., *Dēmos: Classical Athenian Democracy* (A. Mahoney & R. Scaife, Eds. The Stoa: A consortium for electronic publication in the humanities) (online). Retrieved from www.stoa.org/projects/demos/article_punishment?page=5 [Accessed September 15, 2017].

BBC. (2017, September 14). 100 Women: I didn't mean to plead guilty. *BBC News Magazine* (online magazine). Retrieved from www.bbc.com/news/magazine-40881469 [Accessed September 15, 2017].

Devonis, D. C., & Triggs, J. (2017). Prison break: Karl Menninger's *The Crime of Punishment* and its reception in US psychology. *History of Psychology, 20*(1), 92–121.

Hager, E. (2017, September 13). From prison to Ph. D: The redemption and rejection of Michelle Jones. *The New York Times* (online newspaper). Retrieved from www.nytimes.com/2017/09/13/us/harvard-nyu-prison-michelle-jones.html?mcubz=3 [Accessed September 15, 2017].

Kugler, M. B., Funk, F., Braun, J., Gollwitzer, M., & Kay, A. C. (2013). Differences in punitiveness across three cultures: A test of American exceptionalism in justice attitudes. *The Journal of Criminal Law and Criminology, 103*(4), 1071–1114.

Risen, J. (2015, April 30). American Psychological Association bolstered torture program, report says. *The New York Times* (online newspaper). Retrieved from www.nytimes.com/2015/05/01/us/report-says-american-psychological-association-collaborated-on-torture-justification.html?mcubz=3 [Accessed September 15, 2017].

Cross-reference: Religion and Law

RELIGION AND LAW

Neither religion nor law can be treated in any degree of detail in a cross-cultural psychology course. Like marriage, money, or privilege, religion and law are part of the expected framework in which any such course will take place. Presumably both law and religion stem from a primordial source of the evolution of human social behavior: both Freud (in his rarely read *Group Psychology and the Analysis of the Ego* as well as in his frankly anthropological *Totem and Taboo*) and more recent commentators (e.g., Facchini, 1991) offer insights on this. From a cultural psychological point of view, it is where law intersects with religion that offers the best starting point for discussion. It is a highly contested area, a primary source for culture war, and would be ideal for a course that treats culture as evolving from conflict, but less so for other less warlike approaches.

Exposition, Confrontation, and Simulation

First, achieve some basic familiarity with law's incorporation of religion. Shariah is a good starting point since many essential legal issues are influenced by religious principles in Muslim cultures, including marriage and divorce, inheritance, finance, and insurance. There are several reasonably accurate and simple summaries available of the ways in which Muslim legal practice depends on religious tenets (e.g., Rashid, 2012). There are similar intersections between traditional Jewish religious law and current secular law, and sources detailing aspects of these (e.g., Greenberg-Kobrin, 2014) can be mined for discussable examples, for instance, the *get*. In the same spirit as the suggestions for approaching rights and citizenship, students should be encouraged to draft codes of laws de novo, and then to compare these with the structure of secular and religious codes. Beyond this, case studies can be developed for examination. The following two recent US cases have a good deal of documentation, so a convincing interactive exercise can be developed from the evidence, either simulation of some stage of the legal proceedings or posing of the ethical problems involved. These are the Nickel

Mines school shooting that occurred in 2006 (Kocieniewski & Gately, 2006) and the controversy over a display of a Ten Commandments stele in front of an Alabama courthouse in 2001. The Nickel Mines case, one of many well publicized terroristic events involving shootings at schools over the past 20 years, is notable because its targets forgave the shooter (Shapiro, 2007). The judge in the Ten Commandments case, Roy Moore of Alabama, was ordered to remove the large monument displaying the Decalogue, refused, and was ultimately removed from office over the issue (CNN, 2003). Since that time he has established a national profile and following, and is a public voice for the polar position that "God's law comes first" (Scherer, 2017).

REFERENCES AND SUGGESTED READINGS

CNN. (2003, November 14). Ten Commandments judge removed from office. *CNN* (Cable News Network) (online news source). Retrieved from www.cnn.com/2003/LAW/11/13/moore.tencommandments/ [Accessed September 24, 2017].

Facchini, F. (1991). The roots of ethics: An anthropological approach. *Human Evolution*, 6(5–6), 461–469.

Greenberg-Kobrin, M. (2014). Religious tribunals and secular courts: Navigating power and powerlessness. *Pepperdine Law Review*, 41, 997–1012.

Kocieniewski, D., & Gately, G. (2006, October 3) Man shoots 11, killing 5 girls, in Amish school. *The New York Times* (online newspaper). Retrieved from www.nytimes.com/2006/10/03/us/03amish.html?mcubz=3 [Accessed September 24, 2017].

Rashid, Q. (2012, November 4). Shariah law: The five things every non-Muslim (and Muslim) should know. *Huffington Post (The Blog)* (online news source). Retrieved from www.huffingtonpost.com/qasim-rashid/shariah-law-the-five-things-every-non-muslim_b_1068569.html [Accessed September 23, 2017].

Scherer, M. (2017, September 22). Roy Moore disrupts U.S. Senate race in Alabama—and prepares for new level of defiance in Washington. *The Washington Post* (online newspaper). Retrieved from www.washingtonpost.com/politics/roy-moore-disrupts-alabama-senate-race--and-prepares-for-new-level-of-defiance-in-washington/2017/09/21/2a88a4a2-9e38-11e7-9083-fbfddf6804c2_story.html?utm_term=.b5d26cdaace4 [Accessed September 24, 2017].

Shapiro, J. (2007, October 2). Amish forgive school shooter, struggle with grief. *NPR* (National Public Radio) *All Things Considered* (online broadcast transcript). Retrieved from www.npr.org/templates/story/story.php?storyId=14900930 [Accessed September 24, 2007].

Cross-references: Punishment and Prisons; Rights, Citizenship, and Voting; Separateness and Secession

Economics and Work

CORPORATE AND WORK CULTURE

The idea of corporate culture emerges from organizational sociology, which itself is an outgrowth of the main historical roots of that field in the work of Emile Durkheim and Max Weber (Lincoln & Guillot, 2006). The idea that corporations shape character has circulated in social science since the 1950s, when the concept of the 'organization man' was current (Whyte, 1956). It has persisted through the recent update of Arlie Russell Hochschild's *The Managed Heart* (2012), which portrays the ways that corporations can compel conformity to not only corporate policies but also to regulations which ultimately define, and may deform, human interaction. Organizational culture extends across cultures (Gelfand, 2007) and distinct national differences in corporate styles emerge in interaction with regional and national cultural characteristics. Geert Hofstede (2011) observes that the culture of specific occupations is a new frontier for cross-cultural studies. At the level of work itself rather than its larger social organization, the individual again emerges. Individuals bear the marks of their professions, as Sherlock Holmes often astutely observed. They are shaped not only by their home culture but also by the universal demands of their jobs (driving and plumbing are the same wherever they are practiced, subject only to specific environmental constraints) and by their interactions with apprentice masters, co-workers, and customers.

Exposition, Confrontation, and Simulation

"Corporations are people," said Mitt Romney, a candidate for president of the United States during a visit to the Iowa State Fair in 2011. He probably meant only that corporations are a convenient way of collectively referring to groups of people. However, he was vilified in the press and by the opposing party for what seemed to be an endorsement of extending legal rights that properly belong to free human individuals to abstract legal fictions ramifying soulless corporate behemoths (Rucker, 2011).

Romney's statement could introduce the concept of 'corporate personhood' as a discussion topic, which could be amplified by a replication of the findings of Mentovich, Huq, and Cerf (2014) that individuals are unlikely to grant this status to corporations, especially large, profit-making ones. Older generations may still remember when a job in the United States promised support for a long time, often a lifetime. However, today, even in some cultures where the idea of long-term employment was bolstered by collective pressure to stay in place, job security has been replaced by transience and uncertainty. One place where this uncertainty becomes visible is during corporate mergers and acquisitions, whose pace has increased over the past few decades. M&As, as these are called, are observed to be active sites of culture clashes that can render mergers unworkable (Stafford & Miles, 2013). Most students of culture, at least in college, will not have much experience with employment or corporate culture, and most graduates will tend to stay in their home culture rather than becoming involved with a multinational enterprise, although this is becoming more likely as globalization progresses. As it stands, M&As are probably the best place to observe the power of organizational culture, but for persons without experience and outside of the corporate environment, it might be difficult to imagine why a job transition might be traumatic. Probably the best advice would be to structure discussion around situations in which the rules have changed. A corporate case in point could be the unsuccessful merger of automakers Daimler and Chrysler in the first decade of this century, a widely documented episode (Watkins, 2007). Other ways to conceptualize the psychological effects of a bad merger are to compare it to a bad divorce or a bad remarriage in terms of the rancor involved, viewed from the perspective of any of the parties involved. Many of the same events—arbitrary changes of roles and rules; introduction of new and possibly foreign values; and changes in organizational aim— can be easily analogized to the elements that cause mergers to founder (Jacobsen, 2012).

To get at what Hofstede (2011) is suggesting when he suggests looking into the culture of individual professions, choose one that is accessible and concrete: plumbing, for example. Water doesn't run uphill in Nigeria, nor does it behave under pressure there any differently than it does in Britain. And plumbing, from the standpoint of public health at least, is a universal need, although plumbing with pipes and running water is itself not universal, not even in the United States (Ingraham, 2014). Investigate how plumbing can cross cultures by following the stories of Anselm Okoukoni, who parlayed training he received as an illegal immigrant in Britain into professionally bringing competent plumbing to Nigeria, where it is in short supply (Nwaubani, 2015). Also follow the story of Safa'a, a Syrian refugee starting a new life as a plumber in Jordan (Rescue.org, 2016).

REFERENCES AND SUGGESTED READINGS

Gelfand, M. J. (2007). Cross-cultural organizational behavior. *Annual Review of Psychology,* *58*, 479–514.

Hochschild, A. R. (2012). *The managed heart: The commercialization of human feeling.* (Update with a new preface). Berkeley, CA: University of California Press (Originally published 1983).

Hofstede, G. (2011). Dimensionalizing cultures: The Hofstede Model in context. Online Readings in *Psychology and Culture, 2*(1). Retrieved from https://doi. org/10.9707/2307-0919.1014; http://scholarworks.gvsu.edu/cgi/viewcontent. cgi?article=1014&context=orpc [Accessed September 24, 2017].

Ingraham, C. (2014, April 23). 1.6 million Americans don't have indoor plumbing. Here's where they live. *The Washington Post* (online newspaper). Retrieved from www. washingtonpost.com/news/wonk/wp/2014/04/23/1-6-million-americans-dont-have-indoor-plumbing-heres-where-they-live/?utm_term=.f4be37168458 [Accessed September 24, 2017].

Jacobsen, D. (2012, September 26). 6 big mergers that were killed by culture (and how to stop it from killing yours). *Globoforce* (online blog). Retrieved from www.globoforce. com/gfblog/2012/6-big-mergers-that-were-killed-by-culture/ [Accessed September 24, 2017].

Lincoln, J. A., & Guillot, D. (2006). A Durkheimian view of organizational culture. In M. Korczynski, R. Hodson, & P. Edwar (Eds.), *Social theory at work* (pp. 88–120). Oxford: Oxford University Press.

Mentovich, A., Huq, A., & Cerf, M. (2014). The psychology of corporate rights. *University of Chicago Public Law & Legal Theory Working Paper No. 497* (Online). Retrieved from http://chicagounbound.uchicago.edu/cgi/viewcontent. cgi?article=1956&context=public_law_and_legal_theory [Accessed September 24, 2017].

Nwaubani, A. T. (2015, December 21). Illegal migrant makes good as plumber in Nigeria. *BBC News* (online news magazine, British Broadcasting Corporation). Retrieved from www.bbc.com/news/world-africa-35131170 [Accessed September 24, 2017].

Rescue.org. (2016, September 28). The plumber: An unexpected path. *Rescue.org* (nonprofit organization website). Retrieved from www.rescue.org/article/plumber-unexpected-path [Accessed September 25, 2017].

Rucker, P. (2011, August 11). Mitt Romney says 'corporations are people'. *The Washington Post* (online newspaper). Retrieved from www.washingtonpost.com/politics/mitt-romney-says-corporations-are-people/2011/08/11/gIQABwZ38I_story.html?utm_term=.fbf899758c6e [Accessed September 24, 2017].

Stafford, D., & Miles, L. (2013, December 11). Integrating cultures after a merger. *Bain Brief* (Bain & Company Corporate website). Retrieved from www.bain.com/publications/articles/integrating-cultures-after-a-merger.aspx [Accessed September 24, 2017].

Watkins, M. D. (2007, May 18). Why DaimlerChrysler never got into gear. *Harvard Business Review* (online). Retrieved from https://hbr.org/2007/05/why-the-daimlerchrysler-merger [Accessed September 24, 2017].

Whyte, W. H. (1956). *The organization man.* New York: Simon & Schuster.

Cross-references: Hiring and Firing; Health and Sanitation; Rights, Citizenship, and Voting

HIRING AND FIRING

Especially in the United States, little else defines the self at its most basic motivational levels as does work. Yet it is unusual to encounter many of the actual practices of work in cross-cultural course settings, especially at the level of non-management employees needing to fit into a culture's economic system to survive. This unintentional blindness to the cultural pervasiveness of work and its importance to basic life systems (e.g., the linkage of health insurance to employment in the United States) makes this a provocative area for attention. From a perspective of US industrial/organizational psychology, most treatments of work focus on hiring and evaluation, less on termination and job loss, and are pitched to more or less permanent employment situations in corporate settings. The realities of the growing temporariness and unpredictability of work, gender inequality in work, and the replacement by automation of the traditional conceptions of jobs—not only in manufacturing but in almost every other aspect of employment (for instance, the projected near-total automation of banking and the replacement of the department store by e-commerce)—signalize seismic cultural shifts.

Over the past quarter century, many corporations worldwide have taken seriously the need to expand operations into other countries and have taken a lead in making at least their own internal corporate cultures plain. An excellent example of this is the 'culture deck' generated by Netflix (Netflix Corporation, 2009). The explicit statement of Netflix's value system—which emphasizes directness, speed, efficiency, self-direction, and public criticism and evaluation—allows it to be easily contrasted with the values implicit in other cultures. For instance, Netflix encountered resistance to its conception of rapidly terminating 'B-level' performance—albeit with generous severance pay—in Japan, where employment, especially in a corporate setting, is often for life. Other cultures, for example Islamic culture, place at least as strong an emphasis on morality and social solidarity as on trade (Ali & Al-Owaihan, 2008), and may place more emphasis on maintaining personal relationships rather than adopting the attitude that 'being let go from an Olympic team makes one no less great,' a prevalent attitude in Netflix's corporate culture toward termination (Fairchild, 2016, n.p.).

Exposition, Confrontation, and Simulation

Employment law is complex no matter what the culture. One approach to understanding this highly regulated area of human behavior is to review employment law (and laws protecting employees from unfair dismissal) across cultures—many examples worldwide are available online by googling 'termination law' along with the country of interest. Likewise, all other aspects of the employment process—from the search through the interview, and from apprenticeship to promotion to dismissal—are treated extensively online, providing fruitful sources for comparative analysis of at least the explicit legal aspects of culture. Another approach would be to take the perspective of an immigrant to a new culture needing to find work, for instance a US citizen intending to become employed in Portugal (necessary first step: applications and resumes need to be prepared in Portuguese!). Confrontation and simulation can be blended here and can, for purposes of starting discussion, focus on the immediate cultural environment rather than comparing across cultures. For example, try simulation or role-playing of termination scenarios across several types of organization: for example, an informal very small business setting, such as a lawn and landscaping business with five employees, compared with a fast-food restaurant with explicit and strict policies (publicly available on the net), compared with a Netflix or other advanced corporate setting. Attention can be given not only to the interaction of explicit rules with unstated underlying family or personal dynamics between the persons involved, but also to the emotions that may be expressed when personal values conflict with corporate ones.

REFERENCES AND SUGGESTED READINGS

Ali, A. J., & Al-Owaihan, A. (2008). Islamic work ethic: A critical review. *Cross-cultural Management, 15*(1), 5–19.

Fairchild, C. (2016). Netflix redefined American company culture: Will it do the same abroad? *CNBC MakeIt* (online resource), June 20, 2016. Retrieved from www.cnbc.com/2016/06/20/netflix-redefined-american-company-culture-will-it-do-the-same-abroad.html [Accessed June 29, 2017].

Netflix Corporation (2009). Culture deck (online power point presentation). Retrieved from www.slideshare.net/reed2001/culture-1798664 [Accessed March 4, 2018].

Cross-reference: Corporate and Work Culture

INSURANCE: RISK AND FUTURE TIME ORIENTATION

Insurance, though it is not typically considered in cross-cultural context, offers a launching point for discussion of several factors that may be related to insurance-related decisions, including obtaining and maintaining insurance coverage. The debate about the structure of health insurance coverage in the United States, for the most strident recent example, has generated vast amounts of public attention and irritated fundamental cultural sores. The rancor can be tuned down by focusing instead on more prosaic forms of insurance that may be more frequently encountered by students of culture. Automobile liability insurance has been compulsory in most countries for generations: few if any countries in the world do not have an official policy mandating at least third-party coverage. Interesting cross-national and inter-regional variations exist. Likewise, extreme variations exist in the numbers of individuals who avoid obtaining coverage, again regionally as well as cross-nationally. For example, in the United States, the percentage of uninsured drivers ranges from a low of 4 percent (in Maine and Massachusetts) through an average of 15 percent (in California, Texas, Washington D. C., and Wisconsin) up to more than 25 percent (in New Mexico and Mississippi). Sometimes the percentage is not even officially known. In Ontario, Canada, which has very strict requirements to carry insurance and high fines for noncompliance, uninsurance is growing. Officials recently could not say what the percentage of uninsured motorists is, since they are "off the radar" (Miller, 2016). In contrast, Pakistan, where third-party insurance is also mandatory, reportedly has a rate of as high as 75 percent of drivers without insurance (KarloCompare, n.d.).

Exposition, Confrontation, and Simulation

Taking these widely varying rates of uninsurance across cultures as a starting point for discussion, some factors that have cross-cultural relevance can be probed for a basic level of familiarization with explanatory variables as well as for speculative in-class correlation with individual insurance-related behavior. Relative perception of risk has been shown to vary across cultures. For instance, Li (2017) cites data showing that risks are rated differently by Japanese and US student participants, with Japanese rating more risks as uncontrollable, dreaded, and catastrophic. Examination of measurement scales for risk—for instance, the widely available DOSPERT scale (Weber, Blais, & Betz, 2002) and several links at the scale's home site (www8.gsb. columbia.edu/decisionsciences/research/tools/dospert)—are excellent resources for learning about scale composition as well as the dimensions of risk overall. Another plausible theoretical variable related to insurance is future time perspective. For this, the Hofstede dimensions can be a takeoff point. However, there doesn't seem to be a high degree of correlation between a nation's future time orientation and the rate at which its population observes insurance laws. Pakistan, for instance, doesn't vary widely on this factor from the United States, even though insurance compliance is substantially different. In the case of Pakistan, again, many cars are obtained as used cars (Ansari, 2015), outside of the scrutiny of dealerships and official registration procedures. Also, it is likely that some forms of informal accommodation to this official regulation are present. Pakistan's relative poverty compared to the United States may also be a factor influencing noncompliance with insurance, while in the United States, affluence may be less a factor than specific attitudes toward future time. One time-perspective factor that is probably involved is related to the ages of individuals who need to purchase insurance. Local regulations can be examined to see at what age individuals can begin to drive, and at what age and under what circumstances they obtain vehicles. In this context, completion and discussion of the Philip Zimbardo's time perspective scale, contained in *The Time Paradox* (Zimbardo & Boyd, 2008) and available online (www.thetimeparadox.com/zimbardo-time-perspective-inventory/) can form the basis for another set of correlations between adolescent/young adult attitudes toward time and economic security. From this point discussion may be extended to other aspects of risk and future-orientation concerns, for example obtaining contraceptives (Baum et al., 2016). If the conclusion reached in discussion is that being uninsured is the result of a constellation of factors rather than a combination of a couple of salient ones, this would probably be sufficiently correct. Compare this with a recent study of why people avoid medical care, conducted across several US demographic groups (Taber, Leyva, & Peroskie, 2015). It describes a mix of factors, among which cost and no access to insurance combine to describe only 30 percent of the reasons behind treatment avoidance. This would at least result, after the discussion, in more familiarity with some important variables in cross-cultural research.

REFERENCES AND SUGGESTED READINGS

Ansari, N. (2015, September 7). Need a ride? Here's the ultimate guide to buying used cars in Karachi. *Dawn* (online news source). Retrieved from www.dawn.com/news/1204648/[Accessed November 1, 2017].

Baum, S., Burns, B., Davis, L., Yeung, M., Scott, C., Grindlay, K., & Grossman, D. (2016). Perspectives among a diverse sample of women on the possibility of obtaining oral contraceptives over the counter. *Women's Health Issues, 26*(2), 147–152.

KarloCompare. (n.d.). Five things you should know about auto insurance in Pakistan. *KarloCompare* (consumer website). Retrieved from www.karlocompare.com.pk/blog/five-things-you-may-not-know-about-motor-insurance-in-pakistan/ [Accessed November 1, 2017].

Li, E. P. H. (2017). Cognitive styles and personality in risk perception. In G. Emilien, R. Weitkunat, & F. Ludicke (Eds.), *Consumer perception of product risks and benefits* (pp. 267–282). Basle, CH: Springer International Publishing AG.

Miller, T. (2016, December 29). Driving without insurance risky in many ways. *Toronto Star* (newspaper) R.9 (online). Retrieved from http://pqasb.pqarchiver.com/thestar/doc/1853622475.
html?FMT=ABS&FMTS=ABS:FT&type=current&date=Dec+29%2C+2016&author=Miller%2C+Tim&pub=Toronto+Star&edition=&startpage=R.9&desc=Driving+without+insurance+risky+in+many+ways [Accessed July 15, 2017].

Taber, J., Leyva, B., & Peroskie, A. (2015). Why do people avoid medical care? A qualitative study using national data. *Journal of General Internal Medicine, 30*(3), 290–297.

Weber, E. U., Blais, A-R., & Betz, N. (2002). A domain-specific risk-attitude scale: Measuring risk perceptions and risk behaviors. *Journal of Behavioral Decision Making, 15*, 263–290. Available with several other cognate scales at. Retrieved from www8.gsb.columbia.edu/decisionsciences/research/tools/dospert

Zimbardo, P., & Boyd, J. (2008). *The time paradox: The new psychology of time that will change your life.* New York: Atria Books.

Cross-references: Health and Sanitation; Safety and Danger; Pregnancy and Childbirth

MATERIALISM AND CONSUMER CULTURE

Materialism can take a couple of paths into philosophical deep water. It can lead to contrasts with idealism or spiritualism and to conflict with hard determinists (one wonders whether there are many of these still around, 50 years after behaviorism's heyday), or it can lead to consideration of the ethical and moral proposition that the best life is the one that is most well-equipped with physical comforts and goods. For the purposes of this brief introduction the latter will be followed. The extreme form of goods-based materialism is the cargo cult, which has a more complicated history than the usual account of the veneration of the litter of war by credulous Pacific Islanders as gifts sent directly from heaven and obtainable again by invocation (Dunning, 2010; Raffaele, 2006). Less extreme forms of materialism connected to ordinary consumer economics have been measured and those measurements are prominent in the consumer behavior and marketing literature. Cross-cultural comparisons have proved to be difficult to make on psychometric grounds, although the effort continues to establish differences (Masoom, Sarker, & Liu, 2017; Watchravesringkan, 2012).

Consumer culture as a specific term can be found in use in several contexts. It can be understood as a force which differentiates groups within a society. For instance, art historian Pamela Karini locates the tension between traditional religion and modern secularization in Iran specifically in the ways that ordinary Iranian citizens made choices about household design and household equipment (Karimi, 2013). Larger scale analyses of ongoing modernization in the same region (e.g., Bill, 1972) also tied class differences to consumption differences. Consumerism can also be understood as one of the core elements of a whole society: many scholars have described (or dismissed) the United States as a consumer culture, dedicated to a cycle of production and consumption that has multiple psychological outcomes. Searching on 'mental health' crossed with 'consumer culture' in PsycINFO leads to hundreds of hits leading to critiques varying in emphases from the commodification of health care services and those who consume them (Sturgeon, 2014), to the promotion in popular music lyrics of overconsumption of intoxicants (Holody, Anderson, Craig, & Flynn, 2016), to the interpretation of seduction by product advertising as a form of classic Freudian hysteria (Castro, 2016).

Exposition, Confrontation, and Simulation

Most psychological studies of consumer materialism refer to the scale developed in the early 1990s by Marsha Richins and Scott Dawson, the Material Values Scale (MVS; see Richins & Dawson, 1992; Richins, 2004). The contents of the MVS can be deduced from these published materials, and discussion of individual questions from the MVS and/or examination of the results of its group administration can provide a baseline for materialistic value orientation in the immediate environment. The connection of materialism and consumerism with psychological well-being has been meta-analyzed (Dittmar, Bond, Hurst, & Kasser, 2014) and the scales used in that analysis can be tracked down, examined, and discussed as well: among them are, along with the MVS, the Money Ethic Scale, the Money over Mind Questionnaire, the Spending Tendency Scale, and the Compulsive Buying Scale. Consider visiting the *Society for Neuroeconomics* website (https://neuroeconomics.org) and using the Find function to search for 'culture', 'cross-cultural', and related terms in the conference abstracts. This will unveil a new frontier for cross-cultural studies. Further discussion of the consumer concept can be engendered by following up on Sturgeon 2014 article and asking, in the context of psychology becoming more and more closely aligned with the health care system worldwide, whether health care is best considered a commodity, and persons seeking contact with therapists, consumers. Turning to more mundane and material matters, examination of the provenance of the clothing worn by members of the immediate group will certainly locate the world centers of apparel production. Consider also the question of luxury consumption vs. subsistence. Seek where the largest markets for luxury German auto brands are (hint: China) and how luxury consumption might square with typical characterizations of that society as collectivistic. Ask (and research) why Louis Vuitton has comparatively few outlets in Africa. For a lighter touch, visit the IKEA website (www.ikea.com), which contains catalogs specialized for each of its many countries of operation (and production as well). Access them and compare the iconography, product descriptions, and relative availability of products. Also examine the distribution, worldwide, of Costco outlets.

REFERENCES AND SUGGESTED READINGS

Bill, J. (1972). *The politics of Iran: Groups, classes, and modernization.* Columbus, OH: Charles E. Merrill Publishing Co.

Castro, J. C. L. (2016). The discourse of hysteria as the logic of mass consumption. *Psychoanalysis, Culture, and Society, 21*(4), 403–421.

Dittmar, H., Bond, R., Hurst, M., & Kasser, T. (2014). The relationship between materialism and well-being: A meta-analysis. *Journal of Personality and Social Psychology, 107*(5), 879–924.

Dunning, B. (2010, March 30). Cargo cults. *Skeptoid Podcast.* Skeptoid Media (online source). Retrieved from http://skeptoid.com/episodes/4199 [Accessed September 11, 2017].

Holody, K. J., Anderson, C., Craig, C., & Flynn, M. (2016). 'Drunk in love': The portrayal of risk behavior in music lyrics. *Journal of Health Communication, 21*(10), 1098–1106.

Karimi, P. (2013). *Domesticity and consumer culture in Iran: Interior revolutions of the modern era.* New York: Routledge.

Masoom, M. R., Sarker, M. M., & Liu, G. (2017). Rising materialism in the developing economy: Assessing materialistic value orientation in contemporary Bangladesh. *Cogent Business and Management, 4*(1) (Published online 7/5/2017). Retrieved from www.tandfonline.com/doi/full/10.1080/23311975.2017.1345049 [Accessed September 11, 2017].

Raffaele, P. (2006, February). In John they trust. *Smithsonian Magazine* (online). Retrieved from www.smithsonianmag.com/history/in-john-they-trust-109294882/ [Accessed September 11, 2017].

Richins, M. L. (2004). The material values scale: Measurement properties and development of a short form. *Journal of Consumer Research, 31*(1), 209–219.

Richins, M. L., & Dawson, S. (1992). A consumer values orientation for materialism and its measurement: Scale development and validation. *Journal of Consumer Research, 19*(3), 303–316.

Sturgeon, D. (2014). The business of the NHS: The rise and rise of consumer culture and commodification in the provision of healthcare services. *Critical Social Policy, 34*(3), 405–416.

Watchravesringkan, K. (2012). Cross-cultural equivalence of Materialistic Values Scale (MVS): An exploratory study between the United States and Thailand. *Journal of Targeting, Measurement, and Analysis for Marketing, 20*(3–4), 235–253.

Cross-references: Housing, Personal Space, and Segregation; Religion and Law, Globality, Multiculturality, and Biculturality

MONEY

No culture is without some means of exchange, and the presence or absence of money is a prime conditioner of cultural differences. Typical readers and users of this set of exercises will usually be familiar with systems of money and credit similar to those in the United States. Also, many will not have experienced money except as a constant background fuel supply for cultural life, since they have not had too much experience in not having it. However, in many cultures, scarcity both of resources and money is the rule, and in those situations mutual aid, barter, and other forms of adaptation to the challenge of obtaining basic goods emerge. Also, religious prohibitions against lending at interest that exist in strictly Muslim cultures, for example, change fundamental perceptions of the availability of money and the means for its repayment (Alexander, 2011). Relative levels of wealth within and between cultures can determine the view that insiders have of outsiders' personalities (Chan et al., 2011). Informal economies outside of the ordinary channels of exchange develop under poverty conditions, in the United States as well as elsewhere (Bonnet & Venkatesh, 2016; Glinton, 2017). Economic sociology reveals many other ways in which the perception of money and wealth is conditioned by culture, including gender factors (e.g., Zelizer, 2005, 2011).

Exposition, Confrontation, and Simulation

Depending on the experience of the group, some basic familiarization with money economies compared with barter economies might be advised at the start. There are elementary simulations of barter contrasted with money (e.g., Carolina K-12, 2012). For a more ambitious project, imagine a culture in which forms of microfinance, interest-free credit, illegal trade, and barter are the main ways in which goods are obtained by persons outside of the elite. Local accounts from cultures with extreme wealth differentials (for example Ghana, Dadzie, 2015) can assist in setting a context. Simulate a susu collective money pool (Kunzemann, 2010): use play money or chips, and set up a market with desirable goods to buy at local prices depending on the culture or region. Throw in a few medical supplies and automotive repairs or transportation as desirable goods, and set up both barter and black market systems on the side. Assign players to be possessors of goods and others to be seekers, a few with no ready cash and a few others with some cash or other resources. Operate this set of simulated markets for a short while and take specific note not only of the relative amounts gained by individuals, but also of any sign of coalition or alliance building, development and utilization of bargaining techniques, and skill in detecting which form of exchange is desired by each possessor. If poverty is the focus, then starting with a questionnaire about poverty experiences could start the conversation about wealth differentials in the immediate environment: section VII of the somewhat dated but still applicable NPR-Kaiser Family Foundation-Kennedy School of Government Poverty Study (NPR, 2001) is a short and efficient path toward revealing histories and attitudes.

REFERENCES AND SUGGESTED READINGS

Alexander, D. (2011, May 16). Understanding how money works in different cultures. *The Chronicle of Philanthropy* (online magazine). Retrieved from www.philanthropy.com/article/Understanding-How-Money-Works/196039 [Accessed August 28, 2017].

Bonnet, F., & Venkatesh, S. (2016). Poverty and informal economies. In D. Brady & L. M. Burton (Eds.), *Oxford handbook of the social science of poverty* (pp. 637–659). Oxford: Oxford University Press.

Carolina K-12. (2012). Barter and money. *Carolina Public Humanities* (online educational resource). Retrieved from http://civics.sites.unc.edu/files/2012/05/Money10.pdf [Accessed August 28, 2017].

Chan, W., McCrae, R. R., Rogers, D. L., Weimer, A. A., Greenberg, D. M., & Terracciano, A. (2011). Rater wealth predicts perceptions of outgroup competence. *Journal of Research in Personality, 45*(6), 597–603.

Dadzie, E. (2015, January 19). Working for poor wages: Ghana's example stinks. *MyJoy Online* (online newspaper). Retrieved from www.myjoyonline.com/opinion/2015/January-19th/working-for-poor-wages-ghanas-example-stinks.php [Accessed August 28, 2017].

Glinton, S. (2017, October 27). Some black Americans turn to informal economy in the face of discrimination. *NPR (National Public Radio) All Things Considered* (Broadcast transcript). Retrieved from www.npr.org/2017/10/27/560239264/some-black-americans-turn-to-informal-economy-in-the-face-of-discrimination?utm_

source=facebook.com&utm_medium=social&utm_campaign=npr&utm_
term=nprnews&utm_content=2054 [Accessed November 1, 2017].

Kunzemann, T. (2010, February 10). Microfinance: Do you susu? *Allianz Knowledge* (Allianz Bank website) (online). Retrieved from www.allianz.com/en/about_us/open-knowledge/topics/finance/articles/100220-microfinance-do-you-susu.html/ [accessed August 28, 2017].

NPR (National Public Radio). (2001). *The NPR-Kaiser family foundation-Kennedy school of government poverty study* (online). Retrieved from www.npr.org/programs/specials/poll/poverty/poll.html [Accessed August 29, 2017].

Zelizer, V. (2005). *The purchase of intimacy*. Princeton, NJ: Princeton University Press.

Zelizer, V. (2011). *Economic lives: How culture shapes the economy*. Princeton, NJ: Princeton University Press.

Cross-references: Insurance: Risk and Future Time Orientation; Hunger; The Club (Privilege and Exclusion)

Environment

FUEL

Fuel is a ubiquitous necessity intermixed with air, water, and food as a potent force both in structuring and maintaining cultures as well as hastening their change. Any fuel will serve as a starting point: here are some examples of how coal connects with culture. Coal mining in the United States, a physically demanding and dangerous trade, is associated with a set of cultural values that result in a fatalistic and traditionalist mindset (Law, 2012) that is resistant to the introduction of new fuel technologies and new ways of thinking about energy in a larger framework than that of the immediate region. In an entirely different region, as a perceptive essay by Derks (2015) demonstrates, coal in Vietnam has served as a way out of economic privation, by preserving forests which were in danger of destruction because of overuse of wood for fuel. But, at the same time, coal is devalued as a survival of an older, dirtier past that is being replaced, symbolically and actually, by the use of gas as a fuel for cooking. Architects and planners are determining that coal, which needs to be burned outside because of the threat of carbon monoxide poisoning, will not be prominent as a fuel in the future since new apartments are being built that incorporate indoor kitchens integrated with the living space, each equipped with gas and electric appliances. In this case, within a couple of generations, an older way of life centered around fire-tending and slow cooking has been replaced with a lifestyle incorporating elements of European and American speed, efficiency, and relative cleanliness in both household and environmental terms.

Exposition, Confrontation, and Simulation

Most US and West European readers won't have much experience with fuel famine. A start could be made by simulating a power outage, a common occurrence in Iraq (cut the lights and, if possible, the A/C—but beforehand, let people know that a power outage might be imminent and that the use of open flames is not permitted during the outage). Observe closely and note the reactions, emotional, cognitive, and behavioral. Fuel use is a habit, so a thought experiment could be done imagining what might happen if oil, for instance, or natural gas were restricted in supply. What strategies would come into play that would be different under those changed conditions? An actual demonstration of learning new fuel use habits can be done (outdoors!) with a Coleman stove equipped with the baking oven attachment. My own experience with baking soda bread when using this device for the first time resulted in a loaf that was exactly 1/2 raw and 1/2 charred. Keep a stock of edible versions of whatever is attempted on hand to alleviate any disappointment with the experimental product. Alternatively, discussion could center around what happens when a new energy source is introduced into a culture. Sketch a vignette in which electricity is delivered for the first time to a Muslim village in East Africa: list as many consequences of this event as possible, and also place the consequences in order of their occurrence, immediate to delayed. After this, compare the list with the consequences described by Tanja Winther (2013), especially noting whether anyone mentioned the specific consequences described on pages 167 and 168. The entire edited volume from which Winther's essay is drawn (Strauss, Rupp, & Love, 2013) provides a rich variety of examples of how cultural traditions are being modified by worldwide energy needs and extractive practices, which can be drawn on and modified for discussion as well.

REFERENCES AND SUGGESTED READINGS

Derks, A. (2015). Fueling change: A biography of the beehive coal briquette in post Đổi Mới Vietnam. *Journal of Material Culture, 20*(3), 331–349.

Law, B. M. (2012). Coal miners' dilemma: In West Virginia, the demise of rehab programs for coal miners means a reduced likelihood of psychological treatment. *APA Monitor on Psychology, 43*(4), 40. Retrieved from www.apa.org/monitor/2012/04/coal-miners.aspx [Accessed August 18, 2017].

Strauss, S., Rupp, S., & T. Love, T. (Eds.), *Cultures of energy: Power, practices, technologies.* Walnut Creek, CA: Left Coast Press.

Winther, T. (2013). Space, time, and sociomaterial relationships: Moral aspects of the arrival of electricity in rural Zanzibar. In S. Strauss, S. Rupp, & T. Love (Eds.), *Cultures of energy: Power, practices, technologies.* Walnut Creek, CA: Left Coast Press.

Cross-references: Regional and Indigenous Psychology; Physical Toughness, Endurance, and Resilience; Gambling: Fate, Play, Chance, and Luck; Water and Air; Disaster and War

HOUSING, PERSONAL SPACE, AND SEGREGATION

Housing is part of the universal set of human environmental needs. Historically, cultures have developed unique ways of solving the shelter problem utilizing locally available materials and creating distinct cultural architectural styles. However, as population expands and technology globalizes, traditional ways of dealing with the universal problem of shelter are giving way to modularization. Even so, the utilization of standardized architectural spaces, for example the modernist apartment block (Lara & Kim, 2010) or the stylized public space that remains after apartments are erected (Qian, 2014), are conditional on culture. In the same way, space, whether for housing (Marquardt, 2016) or just for ordinary living, has an emotional dimension, and deprivation of it, or violation of it, provokes a visceral response. The combination of housing and space can lead in several productive directions, as follows.

Exposition, Confrontation, and Simulation

For demonstrating personal space, an ancient sociological concept, consult any of the numerous sources detailing cross-cultural comparisons of standing distance and touching rules (e.g., IIMN, n.d.). For a striking visual rendition of personal space, attach flexible strips of tubing or heavy cardboard to caps in an umbrella-like arrangement such that the circumference of the outer edge approximates the personal space radius for various cultures. Regarding housing itself, search comparatively across regions for typical housing, condition, and prices. Compare, for example, the factors leading to housing crises in Botswana (Ngowi, 2015) with those operating on the Pine Ridge Reservation in South Dakota (Strickland, 2016). Regarding housing combined with space, consult any of the numerous sources offering comparative data on average square area and costs for living worldwide (e.g., Christie's, 2016; Mallon, 2015). It is effective, if in a space that is large enough, to take a 25-foot or 10-meter tape measure and lay out a typical living room in a high vs. low space environment, marking the limits with painter's tape. If there are sufficient people to simulate a party, put them in the largest space and gradually compress them. It could be more amusing if furniture could be brought in as well: utilize the IKEA catalog for creative ideas on how to equip a living room space of 100 square feet or 9 square meters (this would be comparatively large in some regions). Switching from the micro to the macrosocial level, investigate the relative willingness of individuals to live outside the boundaries of their cultures by consulting recent maps detailing the relative cultural or ethnic segregation of US cities (e.g., Bloch, Cox, & Giratikanon, 2015; Vanhemert, 2013). Print (or arrange to project) the individual maps and set up a matching task for identifying the cities or regions most to least segregated by proximity.

REFERENCES AND SUGGESTED READINGS

Bloch, M., Cox, A., & Giratikanon, T. (2015, July 8). Mapping segregation (online interactive map). *The New York Times* (online newspaper). Retrieved from www.nytimes.com/interactive/2015/07/08/us/census-race-map.html?mcubz=3&_r=0 [Accessed September 30, 2017].

Christie's. (2016, November 15). The price of luxury: A global comparison of square foot prices. *Christie's International Real Estate website (luxurydefined)* (online). Retrieved from http://luxurydefined.christiesrealestate.com/blog/market-insights/the-price-of-luxury-a-global-comparison-of-square-foot-prices [Accessed September 30, 2017].

IIMN. (n.d.). Body language and personal space. *International Institute of Minnesota website (Culture at Work: Finding Common Understanding)* (online organizational website). Retrieved from http://iimn.org/publication/finding-common-ground/culture-at-work/body-language-personal-space/ [Accessed September 30, 2017].

Lara, F., & Kim, Y. (2010). Built global, lived local: A study of how two diametrically opposed cultures reacted to similar modern housing solutions. *Journal of Architectural and Planning Research, 27*(2), 91–106.

Mallon, B. (2015, August 26). How big is the average house size around the world? *ElleDecor* (online magazine). Retrieved from www.elledecor.com/life-culture/fun-at-home/news/a7654/house-sizes-around-the-world/ [Accessed September 30, 2017].

Marquardt, N. (2016). Learning to feel at home. Governing homelessness and the politics of affect. *Emotion, Space, and Society, 19*, 29–36.

Ngowi, K. (2015, April 27). There's no place like home: Botswana's housing problem. *UrbanAfrica.net* (online news source). Retrieved from www.urbanafrica.net/news/theres-no-place-like-home/ [Accessed September 30, 2017].

Qian, J. (2014). Performing the public man: Cultures and identities in China's grassroots leisure class. *City and Community, 13*(1), 26–48.

Strickland, P. (2016, November 2). Life on the pine ridge native American reservation. *AlJazeera* (online news source). Retrieved from www.aljazeera.com/indepth/features/2016/10/life-pine-ridge-native-american-reservation-161031113119935.html [Accessed September 30, 2017].

Vanhemert, K. (2013, August 26). The best map ever made of America's racial segregation. *Wired* (online news source). Retrieved from www.wired.com/2013/08/how-segregated-is-your-city-this-eye-opening-map-shows-you/ [Accessed September 30, 2017].

Cross-references: Privacy; Water and Air; Private and Commercial Transportation

PRIVATE AND COMMERCIAL TRANSPORTATION

Transportation, a complex subject, divides roughly into halves: private or individual transportation, from walking and Segways to cars and (comparatively few) private airplanes, and commercial transportation, involving either human passengers or other sorts of freight. A complication of this last category is that some part of commercial transportation is a highly subsidized public convenience or good, while other parts of it are for-profit. The line between public and private blurs further when, for instance, a national airline (e.g., Air France) enters into partnerships with commercial carriers inside and outside of its home country.

The prototypical form of individual transportation is the personal automobile. Much has been said about US 'car culture' for many years (Flink, 1976): few regions in the world are immune from this. Economic, space, resource, and other factors have determined that some cultures will favor smaller versions of the car or even smaller individual conveyances, for instance the motorbike and the bicycle. In some places the motorbike was the first vehicle to thoroughly motorize the culture (e.g., Vietnam) and is still prevalent. Cultural preferences for motor vehicles are reinforced, not only in Los Angeles but also in Malaysia, by the lack of sidewalks: only 7 percent of the roads in Malaysia have walkable paths alongside them (Cochrane, 2017). In many rapidly modernizing countries, traffic forced onto inadequate roads can become picturesquely chaotic.

Cars demand resources: space for parking as well as driving, and—almost exclusively—fossil fuels. Transportation uses about 29 percent of the total energy available in the United States, with about 3/4 of that proportion gasoline and diesel fuel (USEIA, 2017). Cars are also expensive. Initial vehicle cost usually must be amortized worldwide (the maximum loan for a car in Russia via Sberbank at the time of this writing is the equivalent of $84,000 USD for five years) and further outlays are necessary for maintenance and insurance. Thus, many people in the world are priced out of auto culture: even in the United States as recently as 2009, one household in 12 does not own a car (PBIC, 2017). Recently in the United States a group called Biciculture has brought together environmental activists and advocates for marginalized urban communities to campaign for the development of social and physical infrastructure to make bicycling a more viable alternative than cars (Lugo, Golub, Hoffman, & Sandoval, 2016). However, local movements toward two-wheeled independence are counteracted in other places by the continual growth of car culture in places where bicycling was previously dominant. For instance, China, which quickly developed a strong bicycle culture after 1949, has experienced steep downturns in commuter cycling. Even though wide landscaped bicycle paths still exist, trips made on them have declined between one-half to three-quarters over the past two decades (Lusk, Xu, & Lijun, 2014). Northern European cultures are leaders not only in cycle commuting but also in accessible and frequent public passenger transportation. Trams, for instance, are beloved enough to have museums and even rodeos featuring tram bowling, where tram drivers compete to knock down inflatable pins with large inflatable balls (Giaimo, 2017). Yet across the Euro-28 the car is dominant. In 2014, 83 percent of all passenger transport on average was by private car (Eurostat, 2017a, 2017b).

Turning to commercial transportation, air transportation has become the overwhelming means of getting people between widely different cultures. Air transport is a prime area for promotion of safety culture, which sometimes conflicts with cultural traditions of longer standing. Cultural differences, for instance power distance and communication style in Korean culture, may have played roles in several aircraft accidents (Wee, 2013). Roads have been as important as rivers in bringing cultures together: the Roman roads and the Silk Road (Harrison, 2016) are historic examples. Trucks mix with cars in traffic worldwide: the legendary phrase "Horn OK Please" is an Indian cultural tagline, painted in folk style and color on the tailgates of trucks. Small trucks are the transport of choice for both farmers and terrorists (Engel, 2015). Long haul trucking—a culture that is itself undergoing substantial change in the United States (Viscelli, 2016)—intersects with immigration, both as a source of immigrant jobs (Gonzalez, 2016) and also exploitation, and, sadly, as a part of the pipeline of extra-legal immigration, visible when an occasional trailerload of hopeful travelers suffocates in a parking lot (Montgomery, Fernandez, & Joseph, 2017). Sea transportation is another multicultural area, already alluded to in this book in the Loyalty entry.

Exposition, Confrontation, and Simulation

As can be seen from the cross-references, transportation can be integrated into lots of different cross-cultural subjects. Experiences with long distance air travel can be discussed, and the question can be raised as to whether airports—boundary nodes—themselves share a common culture (Eriksen & Døving, 1992). Many statistical sources are available to conduct comparisons between the modes of transport of countries and regions. YouTube videos of trains from the cab as well as the passenger compartments and platforms are widely available. Free flight simulators (Digital Trends Staff, 2017) might be employed in a simulation of some aspects of power distance's effect on cockpit communication (actually, any kind of kibitzing could probably be adapted to demonstrating teamwork-friendly vs. teamwork-resistant environments). Try setting up an appointment for car service in Mumbai or Jakarta: there are lots of sites to do this. Follow the Malaysian tuk-tuk debate (user Elex, 2015). Simulate the situation facing a Nigerian city bus driver (Olapoju, 2016). It's not only cellphones that can distract a driver, but also swarming crowds, narrow streets, crazy traffic, and having to collect fares, monitor stops, and scan for passengers that present a safety challenge worldwide. Suggested: set up a driving simulator and have individuals play the role of the driver while the rest of the group creates various mayhem: use scrap cardboard for bus doors and bring lots of party horns.

REFERENCES AND SUGGESTED READINGS

Cochrane, J. (2017, August 20). Jakarta, the city where nobody wants to walk. *The New York Times* (online newspaper). Retrieved from www.nytimes.com/2017/08/20/world/asia/jakarta-walking-study-sidewalks.html?mcubz=3&_r=0 [Accessed September 1, 2017].

Digital Trends Staff. (2017, March 31). Take to the virtual skies with these free flight simulators. *Digital Trends* (online magazine). Retrieved from www.digitaltrends.com/gaming/best-free-flight-simulators/ [Accessed August 25, 2017].

Engel, P. (2015, October 7). These Toyota trucks are popular with terrorists worldwide: Here's why. *Business Insider* (online magazine). Retrieved from www.businessinsider.com/why-isis-uses-toyota-trucks-2015-10 [Accessed August 25, 2017].

Eriksen, T. H., & Døving, R. (1992). In limbo: Notes on the culture of airports. *Eriksen's Site* (online blog). Retrieved from http://hyllanderiksen.net/Airports.html [Accessed August 25, 2017].

Eurostat. (2017a). Passenger cars in the EU. *Eurostat: Statistics Explained* (online statistical information site for the European Union). Retrieved from http://ec.europa.eu/eurostat/statistics-explained/index.php/Passenger_cars_in_the_EU [Accessed September 1, 2017].

Eurostat. (2017b). Transportation statistics. *Eurostat: Statistics* explained (website) (online). Retrieved from http://ec.europa.eu/eurostat/statistics-explained/index.php/Passenger_transport_statistics [Accessed August 25, 2017].

Flink, J. (1976). *The car culture*. Cambridge, MA: MIT Press.

Giaimo, C. (2017, June 8). Europe hold an annual tram-driver Olympics. *Atlas Obscura* (online magazine). Retrieved from www.atlasobscura.com/articles/tram-olympics-europe-bowling [Accessed September 1, 2017].

Gonzalez, S. (2016, April 21). America's trucking industry faces a shortage: Meet the immigrants helping fill the gap. *PRI Global Nation* (radio broadcast transcript). Retrieved from www.pri.org/stories/2016-04-21/america-s-trucking-industry-faces-shortage-meet-immigrants-helping-fill-gap [Accessed August 25, 2017].

Harrison, K. (2016). *Mongols on the silk road: Trade, transportation, and cross-cultural exchange in the Mongol empire*. New York: Rosen Young Adult.

Lugo, A., Golub, A., Hoffman, M., & Sandoval, G. (Eds.) (2016). *Bicycle justice and urban transformation: Biking for all?* New York: Routledge.

Lusk, A. C., Xu, W., & Lijun, Z. (2014). Gender and used/preferred differences of bicycle routes, parking, intersection signals, and bicycle type: Professional middle class preferences in Hangzhou, China. *Journal of Transport and Health, 1*(2), 124–133.

Montgomery, D., Fernandez, M., & Joseph, Y. (2017, July 23). Journey fatal for 9 migrants found in truck in a San Antonio parking lot. *The New York Times* (Online newspaper). Retrieved from www.nytimes.com/2017/07/23/us/san-antonio-truck-walmart-trafficking.html?mcubz=3&_r=0 [Accessed August 25, 2017].

Olapoju, O. M. (2016). Culture of distracted driving among intra-city commercial bus drivers in Ile-Ife, South-Western Nigeria. *Transportation Research Part F: Traffic Psychology and Behaviour, 42*(3), 425–432.

PBIC. (2017). Who's walking and bicycling. *Pedestrian and Bicycle Information (PBIC)* (US Department of Transportation/Federal Highway Administration website). Retrieved from www.pedbikeinfo.org/data/factsheet_general.cfm [Accessed September 1, 2017].

(user Elex). (2015, January 13). Tuk Tuk to be in Malaysia? Cheap but congest the road. *Lowyat.net* (online community). Retrieved from https://forum.lowyat.net/topic/3468279/all [Accessed September 1, 2017].

USEIA (2017). Use of energy in the United States, explained (website of the United States Energy Information Administration). Retrieved from https://www.eia.gov/energyexplained/?page=us_energy_transportation [Accessed March 4, 2018].

Viscelli, S. (2016, May 10). Truck stop: How one of America's steadiest jobs turned into one of its most grueling. *The Atlantic* (online magazine). Retrieved from www.theatlantic.com/business/archive/2016/05/truck-stop/481926/ [Accessed August 25, 2017].

Wee, H. (2013, July 9). Korean culture may offer clues in Asiana crash. *CNBC* (online news source). Retrieved from www.cnbc.com/id/100869966 [Accessed September 1, 2017].

Cross-references: Boundaries and Maps; Forms of Government; Immigration and Refugees; Sustainability and Population; Safety and Danger; Insurance: Risk and Future Time Orientation; Loyalty

SUSTAINABILITY AND POPULATION

As defined on the *Circular Ecology* website (Circular Ecology, 2017), *sustainability* is actually a composite of three different elements: economic sustainability, meaning the maintenance of an ongoing positive balance sheet between all aspects of production and consumption; environmental sustainability, meaning the conservation (and so far as possible the increase) of natural resources; and social sustainability, or the ability of groups to manage their resources to produce a stable level of well-being. Often, discussions of sustainability focus on one or another of these elements, and most often (at least in the United States at present) on the environmental ones, for which the evidence of imbalance are steadily mounting in the form of gradual temperature increases, sea level rises, and other effects of changing climate. At the core of the question of sustainability—apart from the question of what is to be sustained (Current levels of economic growth? Current levels of military expenditures? Current levels of automotive production? Current lifestyles and levels of consumption?), is a clash between two different worldviews or, one might also say, between two cultures. On one side (to put it perhaps too simply) are groups that see resources as limited and endangered, and which recommend policies limiting expectations and the extent of economic growth. The other side sees fewer to no limits to growth and reads the evidence for resource depletion as a temporary aberration if not entirely fabricated. These sides do not map neatly onto particular subgroups or regions, and they shift over time. Worldwide attitudinal support for environmental conservation and other sustainability-related beliefs has been documented for several years (Schultz, 2002) and major international accords under the aegis of the United Nations resolving to limit greenhouse gases were recently (in 2016) put in force. However, local politics as well as differing attitudes within diverse demographic groups in different regions (e.g., Bronfman, Cisternas, López-Vázquez, de la Maza, & Oyanedel, 2015) weaken the unanimity of resolve.

Fifty years ago, on publication of Garrett Hardin's *The Tragedy of the Commons* (Hardin, 1968), overpopulation was widely seen as an imminent threat. But since that time world population has more than doubled and increases are projected confidently rather than feared. The world is on track at this writing to reach 8.5 billion by 2030 (United Nations, 2015). Population growth mirrors the tensions within sustainability debate. As noted earlier in this text in connection with the Family entry, fertility rates vary widely across the globe. Lower fertility rates, some below the replacement level, characterize more affluent and educated regions. The more people become educated and affluent, the fewer children they have, and the more resources they direct to each child. The highest fertility rates are in the poorest areas, and even though infant mortality is also highest in those areas, they are still the most energetic drivers of world population growth. Population growth correlates with sustainability concerns: increasing population density connects to deforestation and soil erosion even in otherwise affluent countries; in poorer ones it leads to food shortages that become acute during periodic droughts. Famine and poverty lead to migration and its consequences. The desire to limit population is strong in most poor countries. However, this aim is impeded by the lack of access to contraception as well as by cultural traditions that insist on women's primary role as childbearers and caregivers. It might seem at first that limiting population everywhere in the world is as necessary as limiting fuel use practices that lead to global warming. However, it's sometimes the case that increases in population may also lead to improved living conditions. China's recent reversal of its long-standing one-child policy is said to have occurred in order to have a larger younger working population to support its increasingly aged population, one consequence of too few births coupled with longer life spans. At the same time, an increase in population in a now highly urbanized and relatively affluent society will lead to a demand for more consumer goods and cars, and thus contribute further to threats to environmental sustainability.

Exposition, Confrontation, and Simulation

While sustainability and population growth are usually featured in environmental psychology, addressing these subjects in a cross-cultural psychology context will make it plain that cross-cultural issues are not confined to boardroom behavior or interpersonal dyads. Sustainability and population are transcultural issues that will eventually impact every culture on earth. A starting point for establishing basic terminological and conceptual infrastructure for discussion of both population and sustainability could be the open-source text *Population and Culture* available from the University of Minnesota Libraries (University of Minnesota, 2017). Among other things, this text clearly presents the subject of ethnic cleansing, which is one of the ways in which cultures manage populations and for which the most current example at this writing is the expulsion of the Rohingya religious minority from Myanmar (Ponniah, 2017). Appropriate demonstration or discussion materials are always available on websites related to genocides, past and present. One way to conceive the relation between sustainability and population is to see each as demanding action to control growth based on different sets of attitudes and habits. At the outset, ask students to imagine that they have to make a decision about (a) buying a car and (b) having a child. In which ways (if any) will sustainability and population concerns be considered in making your decision? Compare results. Search the research literature for comparative data on perceptions of climate change threats in different world regions: a recent article on climate change and its effects in Pakistan also contains a chart of the 10 countries most affected by climate change worldwide (Sukhera, 2017). Specific attention could be directed to China as a test case for both sustainability and population issues. Culture is often equated with values, and sustainability and other environmental aspects of psychology have a heavy investment in value description and clarification. Examination of overall value systems in an environmental context can be done by taking advantage of the scales provided in Dietz, Fitzgerald, and Shworn (2005). Speculate also on whether human populations have to be as large as they now are in order for humans to be as advanced (i.e., technologically interconnected, knowledge-rich, etc.) as they are now. How large must the world be, in terms of the people in it, to be a complete world? Examine, in this context, the articles available on the website of the Ten Million Club (The Ten Million Club Foundation, 2017).

REFERENCES AND SUGGESTED READINGS

Bronfman, N. E., Cisternas, P. C., López-Vázquez, E., de la Maza, C., & Oyanedel, J. C. (2015). Understanding attitudes and pro-environmental behaviors in a Chilean community. *Sustainability, 7*(10), 14133–14152. doi:10.3390/su71014133

Circular Ecology. (2017). What is sustainability and what is sustainable development? *Sustainable Ecology website* (online resource). Retrieved from www.circularecology.com/sustainability-and-sustainable-development.html#.WbRZ_eQUjIU [Accessed September 9, 2017].

Dietz, T., Fitzgerald, A., & Shworn, R. (2005). Environmental values. *Annual Review of Environment and Resources, 30*(1), 335–372.

Hardin, G. (1968). The tragedy of the commons. *Science, 162*(3859), 1243–1248.

Ponniah, K. (2017, January 10). Who will help Myanmar's Rohingya? *BBC News* (online news source and broadcast transcript). Retrieved from www.bbc.com/news/world-asia-38168917 [Accessed September 11, 2017].

Schultz, P. W. (2002). Environmental attitudes and behaviors across cultures. *Online Readings in Psychology and Culture, 8*(1) (Online resource, International Association for Cross-Cultural Psychology. https:doi.org/10.9707/2307-0919.1070). Retrieved from http://scholarworks.gvsu.edu/cgi/viewcontent.cgi?article=1070&context=orpc [Accessed September 9, 2017].

Sukhera, N. (2017, March 27). The perils of inaction on climate change in Pakistan. *Dawn* (online newspaper). Retrieved from www.dawn.com/news/1322335 [Accessed September 9, 2017].

The Ten Million Club. (2017). *The Ten Million Club Foundation website* (online). Retrieved from www.overpopulationawareness.org/en/articles/ [Accessed September 9, 2017].

United Nations. (2015, July 29). World population projected to reach 9.7 billion by 2050. *United Nations Department of Economic and Social Affairs website* (online). Retrieved from www.un.org/en/development/desa/news/population/2015-report.html [Accessed September 9, 2017].

University of Minnesota. (2017). *World regional geography: People, places, and globalization (Chapter 1.3, population and culture).* Minneapolis, MN: University of Minnesota Libraries Publishing (online). Retrieved from http://open.lib.umn.edu/worldgeography/chapter/1-3-population-and-culture/ [Accessed September 8, 2017]. This is a derivative of World Regional Geography: People, Places, and GlobAlization by a publisher who has requested that they and the original author not receive attribution, which was originally released and is used under CC BY-NC-SA. This work, unless otherwise expressly stated, is licensed under a Creative Commons Attribution-NonCommercial-ShareAlike 4.0 International License.

Cross-references: Family; Pregnancy and Childbirth; Private and Commercial Transportation; Fuel; Water and Air

TECHNOLOGY AND CONNECTEDNESS

Technology is one of the intellectual roots of cultural studies, evidenced by the connection of the term *technology* specifically to culture (in the title—*Technology and Culture*—of the journal of SHOT, the Society for the History of Technology) and to civilization (Mumford, 1934/2010). Up until comparatively recently, the term *technology* was virtually equivalent to 'mechanization' (e.g., Giedion, 1948/2013). Gradually, over the past two decades especially, technology has risen to equivalence with the mathematized sciences in the field of education, evidenced by the current acronym STEM, standing for Science, Technology, Engineering, and Mathematics. It has also become equated in the popular mind with digitization and its outcomes and consequences, from robotics to the dominance of the computer and the internet in human affairs. Any technology—medical, food, or manufacturing—could be considered from a comparative cultural and historical perspective (for instance, the persistence of bullock and donkey carts in India and Africa alongside modern transportation in the context of transportation in culture; Iyer, 2017). For the following examples of potential interactives, the focus will be on what is probably the most ubiquitous element of digital technology in use worldwide today: the cellphone.

Exposition, Confrontation, and Simulation

Cellphone use parallels the historic growth of trade along transportation routes. In Africa today, where in Burkina Faso, for example, almost half the population has access to cellphones (though not to computers or the internet), that growth is centered on main highways. Search, display, and compare relative availability of power grid and cellphone coverage (coverage may be assessed for virtually the whole world via the *OpenSignal* [2017] website, which collates crowdsourced data on towers and signal strength from users of its app). Investigate both the electricity gap, a major constraint on expansion of digital applications (Gronewold, 2009), and also determine the level of potential *digital nativity* in various populations. Theoretical background can be found in the annual International Telecommunications Union (ITU) reports available online (www.itu.int/en/ITU-D/Statistics/Pages/publications/mis2017.aspx); for digital natives see especially Chapter 4 of the 2013 Annual Report. An underlying psychological scale has been developed by Timothy Teo at the University of Macao (Teo, 2013), validated in other places, and can be a source, if accessed and completed, for discussion of the digital nativity concept. Cyberbullying is one of the less pleasant cross-culturally relevant consequences of electronic technology use: for background for the discussion of this aspect of the subject, consult Barlett et al. (2014). Finally, it would be engaging and fun to replicate, as far as possible, the studies of Ma, Yang, and Wilson (2017), who have found differences between Chinese and British selfie takers, with differences in both composition and redaction (image editing) related to underlying cultural characteristics.

REFERENCES AND SUGGESTED READINGS

Barlett, C. P., Gentile, D. A., Anderson, C. A., Suzuki, K., Sakamoto, Yamaoka, A., & Katsura, R. (2014). Cross-cultural differences in cyberbullying behavior. *Journal of Cross-Cultural Psychology*, 45(2), 300–313.

Giedion, S. (2013). *Mechanization takes command*. Reprint edition: Minneapolis, MN: University of Minnesota Press. (Originally published in New York by Oxford University Press, 1948).

Gronewold, N. (2009, November 24). One-quarter of world's population lacks electricity. *Scientific American* (web magazine). Retrieved from www.scientificamerican.com/article/electricity-gap-developing-countries-energy-wood-charcoal/ [Accessed September 24, 2017].

Iyer, S. (2017, June 16). From bullock cart to bullet train: Transportation in India has indeed come a long way! *India.com* (online news source). Retrieved from www.india.com/news/india/from-bullock-cart-to-bullet-train-transportation-in-india-has-indeed-come-a-long-way-1403645/ [Accessed September 24, 2017].

Ma, J. W., Yang, Y., & Wilson, J. A. J. (2017). A window to the ideal self: A study of UK Twitter and Chinese SinaWeibo selfie-takers and the implications for marketers. *Journal of Business Research*, 74, 139–142.

Mumford, L. (2010). *Technics and civilization*. Reprint edition: Chicago, IL: University of Chicago Press (originally published in London UK by Routledge Kegan Paul in 1934).

OpenSignal Corporation. (2017). *OpenSignal website* (online). Retrieved from https://opensignal.com/ [Accessed September 15, 2017].

Teo, T. (2013). An initial development and validation of a Digital Natives Assessment Scale (DNAS). *Computers & Education, 67,* 51–57.

Cross-references: Private and Commercial Transportation; Fuel

VANDALISM

Vandalism—briefly, the intentional defacement or destruction of property—began to be studied seriously by psychologists in the 1950s in connection with juvenile delinquency. Later, in the late 1960s and early 1970s, Philip Zimbardo, among others, examined the power of environmental situations to influence (anti)social behavior by setting up conditions for vandalism to occur (Zimbardo, 1973). Vandalism since that time has usually been considered a species of petty crime. In criminology vandalism was a stimulant to the creation of an influential theory of policing, "broken windows theory" (Kelling & Wilson, 1982), which viewed acts like property destruction as the tinder for neighborhood deterioration and increases in major crime levels. In psychology, vandalism continues to be viewed as a marker of adolescent maladjustment, but it is a more complex concept socially and cross-culturally. The threat of vandalism may be a pretext for repressing adolescent girls' development of identity and autonomy in street culture (Bottrell, 2008). Stickers with wry comments (e.g., "Press Until Shiok"), pasted on pedestrian traffic signals in Singapore by Samantha Lo resulted in her arrest for vandalism under strict Singaporean law. This notoriety fueled her development into a recognized urban artist (Ubersnap, 2015). The term *cultural vandalism* is used to describe anti-cultural acts. These are similar to antisocial behavior, but aimed at cultural products. One example of this is *Elginism*, a term coined to name the practice of expropriation of significant cultural products, based on the removal of the marble sculptures from the Parthenon in Greece to Great Britain by Lord Elgin between 1801 and 1812. A blog with this name (Various, 2002–2017) has had 245 pages of commentary since 2002. Other recent examples are the destruction of ancient sites in Syria during the recent civil war there, and the passage of laws denying access to information necessary to counteract the effects of climate change (Crease, 2015).

Exposition, Confrontation, and Simulation

Since this issue is redolent of at least minor criminality, confession will be good for the soul at the outset—but strictly anonymously! Survey to see whether acts of vandalism have been committed, and analyze for intent vs. negligence, creative destruction vs. the other sort, etc. No culture is immune from vandalism and a further expedition can be made to gather as many instances as are necessary to demonstrate the breadth and diversity of vandalism worldwide. As case studies, consider graffiti: is the widespread decoration of building surfaces in Berlin (Arms, 2011) expressive art or a crime? Is the recent vandalism of the Tejas Express in India (Bhattacharya, 2017) really 'vandalism' or just thoughtlessness? Or, following the research of Philipps, Scholzel, and Richter et al. (2016), draw a mustache or other decoration on a portrait of a local politician: disrespect, or deserved?

REFERENCES AND SUGGESTED READINGS

Arms, S. (2011, July 13). The heritage of Berlin street art and graffiti scene. *Smashing Magazine* (online magazine). Retrieved from www.smashingmagazine.com/2011/07/the-heritage-of-berlin-street-art-and-graffiti-scene/ [Accessed August 9, 2017].

Bhattacharya, R. (2017, May 22). The vandalism of the Tejas Express proves that we Indians just don't deserve good things. *Scoop Whoop* (online news magazine). Retrieved from www.scoopwhoop.com/why-we-dont-deserve-good-things/ [Accessed August 9, 2017].

Bottrell, D. (2008). TGG: Girls, street culture, and identity. In A. Harris (Ed.), *Next wave cultures: Feminism, subcultures, activism* (pp. 37–62). New York and London: Routledge.

Crease, R. P. (2015, September 3). Cultural vandalism in America. *Project Syndicate* (online magazine). Retrieved from www.project-syndicate.org/commentary/lamar-smith-us-congress-war-on-science-by-robert-p--crease-2015-09?barrier=accessreg [Accessed August 9, 2017].

Kelling, G. L., & Wilson, J. Q. (1982). Broken windows: The police and neighborhood safety. *Atlantic Monthly, 249*(3), 29–38.

Philipps, A., Scholzel, H., & Richter, R. (2016). Defaced election posters: between culture jamming and moral outrage. *Communication, Politics, and Culture, 49*(1), 86–109.

Ubersnap. (2015, November 27). Sam Lo: Life after "Sticker Lady". *Vulcan Post* (online magazine). Retrieved from https://vulcanpost.com/463621/sam-lo-sticker-lady-interview/219201/infographic-keep-in-mind-life/463621/sam-lo-sticker-lady-interview/ [Accessed August 9, 2017].

Various. (2002–2017). *Elginism* (online blog). Retrieved from www.elginism.com/ [Accessed August 9, 2017].

Zimbardo, P. G. (1973). A field experiment in auto shaping. In C. Ward (Ed.), *Vandalism* (pp. 85–90). London: The Architectural Press.

Cross-references: Forms of Government; Cartoons; Petty Crime; High and Low Culture; Private and Commercial Transportation; Materialism and Consumer Culture

WATER AND AIR

Water and air are symbolically central in culture (two of the four elements) as well as in psychology. Freud intuited, though he did not himself experience it, an 'oceanic' feeling connected to religion; Jung understood water as symbolic of the unconscious and air as related to the soul, as did the ancient Greeks. Descending from these heights to more practical cultural psychology, the way that water is used may convey messages about the user and be a factor in cultural solidarity. For example, homeowners in the Southwestern United States may feel pressure to use water-intensive landscaping to be positively evaluated by peers, rather than using more environmentally sound water-conserving plantings (Neel, Sadalla, Berlin, Ledlow, & Neufeld, 2014). As the climate changes, drought along with rising temperatures becomes a more frequent environmental event. A recent study by Pachter et al. (2016) surveyed three Latinx populations in Guatemala, Mexico, and the United States (Texas) about their folk beliefs regarding sunken fontanel, a depression of the skull in infants that is due to dehydration. While the individuals surveyed related sunken fontanel to illness, they rarely assigned the correct cause or treatment for it (rehydration): a demonstration of the interaction of environmental change and folk medicine. Their beliefs did not extend to thinking in terms of environmental cause and effect. Another example of the interaction of culture, environment, and psychology is due to dehydration related to climatic change in El Salvador. The ingrained ethos of hard work leads farm workers accustomed to long hours and stoic persistence to either not notice or override any signals from ambient temperatures now dangerously elevated due to climate change. This then leads to epidemic kidney failure (Palmer, 2017). Air, as well, is under assault from climate change interacting with the emissions of modern culture worldwide (e.g., Anand, 2017).

Exposition, Confrontation, and Simulation

A starting point for discussing the role of water in culture could be a comparison of individual and group water use in the immediate environment. There are several sites available that detail the amount of water consumed in everyday activities (e.g., Clift, Cuthbert, & Green, 2009). Put these totals against lists of water consumption in other regions worldwide (e.g., The Water Information Program, 2017). Demonstrations and simulations involving chemically compromised air would be too dangerous to attempt: the study of Berry et al. (2017)comparing the relative rate of delay discounting for air vs. money could be simply done, and also add water to the mix. Another interesting and simple replication would be to follow up the experiments of Mony et al. (2013). They note that European and Asian people prefer room temperature water or hot beverages (tea) with meals, and that the temperature of water accompanying various foods (including chocolate!) affects several sensory and affective dimensions of the consumption experience. Since iced water, preferred by North Americans, reduces the perception of sweetness, this may be one variable explaining the desire for more highly sweetened foods in the United States.

REFERENCES AND SUGGESTED READINGS

Anand, G. (2017, February 14). India's air pollution rivals China's as world's deadliest. *The New York Times* (online). Retrieved from www.nytimes.com/2017/02/14/world/asia/indias-air-pollution-rivals-china-as-worlds-deadliest.html?_r=0 [Accessed July 25, 2017].

Berry, M. S., Friedel, J. E., DeHart, W. B., Mahamane, S., Jordan, K. E., & Odum, A. L. (2017). The value of clean air: Comparing discounting of delayed air quality and money across magnitudes. *The Psychological Record, 67*(2), 137–148.

Clift, J., Cuthbert, A., & Green, C. (2009, August 4). How much water do you use? Here's some quick numbers. *AlterNet* (online media). Retrieved from www.alternet.org/story/141751/how_much_water_do_you_use_here%27s_some_quick_numbers [Accessed July 25, 2017].

Mony, P., Tokar, T., Pang, P., Fiegel, A., Meullenet, J-F., & Seo, H-S. (2013). Temperature of served water can modulate sensory perception and acceptance of food. *Food Quality and Preference, 28*(2), 449–455.

Neel, R., Sadalla, E., Berlin, A., Ledlow, S., & Neufeld, S. (2014). The social symbolism of water-conserving landscaping. *Journal of Environmental Psychology, 40*, 49–56.

Pachter, L. M., Weller, S. C., Baer, R. D., Garcia de Alba Garcia, J. E., Glazer, M., Trotter, R., Klein, R. E., & Gonzalez, E. (2016). Culture and dehydration: A comparative study of *Caída de la Mollera* (Fallen Fontanel) in three Latino populations. *Journal of Immigrant and Minority Health, 18*(5), 1066–1075.

Palmer, J. (2017, April 18). Climate change is turning dehydration into a deadly disease. *BBC Earth* (Radio program transcript, online). Retrieved from www.bbc.com/earth/story/20170418-climate-change-is-turning-dehydration-into-a-deadly-disease [Accessed July 26, 2017].

The Water Information Program. (2017). Water facts. *The Water Information Program: Providing Water Information to the Communities of Southwest Colorado.* (Informational website, online). Retrieved from www.waterinfo.org/resources/water-facts [Accessed July 25, 2017].

Cross-references: Sustainability and Population; Health and Sanitation

Animals and Other Species

ANIMALS

Historically, animals have been deified, and they continue to be symbolic in many ways, as sports totems, as allegorical characters, and as deliverers of alternative points of view on the human experience, e.g., the narrator in *War Horse* (Malone & Jackman, 2016). Practically speaking, animals integrate at all levels with human society and with many of the topics in this book. They are utilized as beasts of burden as food and combated as pests, loved as pets, hunted for sport, exhibited in zoos, empathized with in pain and suffering (Specia, 2017), and utilized in many other ways. Animals do not have a specific presence at the core of cross-cultural psychology, but anthropologists in the specific area of anthrozoology have filled this gap, revealed by recent work on the human–animal connection (Hurn, 2012; Murray, 2016). Likewise, comparative psychologists have pursued the question of whether animals themselves, individually or collectively, form cultures (Laland & Galef, 2009), and have probed the degree to which they are to be included in human moral systems (Gluck, 2016).

Exposition, Confrontation, and Simulation

The chapter titles in Hurn (2012) identify the following areas among others as important sites of animal-human cultural interaction: "The West and the Rest," "Domestication," "Food," "Pets," "Communication," "Intersubjectivity," "Humans and Other Primates," "Science and Medicine," "Conservation," "Hunting and Blood Sports," and "Animal Rights and Wrongs." These could form the basis of an inventory and discussion of the multiple cultural roles of animals in the immediate environment and could be treated individually in interactive presentations. Individual stories of human–animal connectedness can be solicited and shared. On the principle that a culture is a system that confers particular rights on its members, examination and discussion of various initiatives for animal rights could be introduced. Neumann (2012) provides the text of both the 1978 UNESCO Universal Declaration of Animal Rights and its later revisions, along with a comprehensive historical account of the development of formal proclamations of animal rights. A draft of a 'bill of animal rights' could be undertaken in a class and then compared to these texts. Actual involvement with animals, while it could be extraordinarily revealing of layers of culture, needs to be crafted with some care. For example, in a recent environmental psychology course in our University my co-instructors and I, along with the class, raised 'rescue chickens,' castoff genetically modified broilers that reach a somewhat grotesque maturity in nine weeks. We participated, along with a local aviculture expert, in the rearing, feeding, housing, and ultimately in the slaughtering. We took every precaution along the way to ensure that everyone was fully informed of all aspects of the process, and while signed informed consent to all aspects of the activity was obtained (and opting-out was respected). Nonetheless, official policy now demands that any future activity like this be passed through an Institutional Animal Care and Use Committee (IACUC) that was formed—necessarily and wisely, in my opinion—in response to these activities. Perhaps some semblance of the interaction of human and animal can be gained by the employment of virtual pets. Perhaps recent research (Aguiar & Taylor, 2015) which suggests that children detect different affordances from stuffed animals (friendship) vs. virtual pet animals (entertainment) could be replicated, with a cross-cultural component if circumstances permit.

REFERENCES AND SUGGESTED READINGS

Aguiar, N. R., & Taylor, M. (2015, April). Children's concepts of the social affordances of a virtual dog and a stuffed dog. *Cognitive Development, 34,* 16–27.

Gluck, J. P. (2016). *Voracious science and vulnerable animals: A primate scientist's ethical journey.* Chicago, IL: University of Chicago Press.

Hurn, S. (2012). *Humans and other animals: Cross-cultural perspectives on human-animal interactions.* London: Pluto Press.

Laland, K. N., & Galef, B. G. (Eds.) (2009). *The question of animal culture.* Cambridge, MA: Harvard University Press.

Malone, T., & Jackman, C. (2016). *Adapting war horse: Cognition, the spectator, and a sense of play.* London: Palgrave Macmillan.

Murray, L. (2016). Animals and anthropology. *AnthroPod: The SCA Podcast* (*Cultural Anthropology* website) (online). Retrieved from https://culanth.org/fieldsights/1119-animals-and-anthropology [Accessed August 2, 2017].

Neumann, J-M. (2012). The Universal Declaration of Animal Rights or the creation of a new equilibrium between species. *Animal Law Review of the Lewis & Clark University, 19*(1), 359–396. Retrieved from https://law.lclark.edu/live/files/22931-191-neumannpdf

Specia, M. (2017, July 27). Animals, abandoned and starving, are evacuated from zoo in Syria. *The New York Times* (online). Retrieved from www.nytimes.com/2017/07/27/world/middleeast/syria-zoo-animals-rescued-aleppo.html?_r=0 [Accessed August 2, 2017].

Cross-references: Robot Culture; Pest Control; Pets; Sports and Spectators; Brooms (Animism, Anthropomorphism, and Dehumanization)

PEST CONTROL

From far back in history, humans have been at war with nature in the form of other species called pests. These include crop eaters, disease vectors, and people biters. The history of physical and chemical combat of agrarian and domestic pests stretches back far before the ancient Greeks, to the beginnings of cultivation and medicine. Sumerians used sulphur compounds for insect control, while in China ca. 2000 BC arsenic and mercury are said to have been used on lice (Unsworth, 2010). The recent history of pest control leads through the development of DDT and other synthetic insecticides, the bad consequences of which led to the development of less toxic varieties as well as heightening consciousness of the effects of humans on the environment. It also leads, via the preparation Zyklon-B, originally an insecticidal fumigant employed against typhus-carrying lice, through the history of Shoah in Central and Eastern Europe. The similar ways that humans combat the worldwide distribution of rodents, insects, and microorganisms reflects the struggle of human culture against other cultures—and not only non-human ones—that must have been the impetus for the pessimistic views of both James and Freud on the likelihood of the eradication of war. In terms of current psychological theory, "cultural pest control" (USDA, 2009), which technically means establishing alliances with other organisms (bacteria, insects, and predators) to eradicate organisms we don't like, opens a window on the cultural forces carving out our human niche.

Exposition, Confrontation, and Simulation

John Henrich, among others, sees evolution originating in cultural adaptations transmitted by imitation and learning (Henrich, 2011). Discussion could focus on Henrich's theory in which cultural practices begin as adaptations to environmental conditions, pass through a stage of cultural evolution, and lead to an interaction between genes and culture that produces both a more culturally capable human as well as one that becomes more diffusely integrated with its environment over time. Bottom line: every action we take with regard to the environment will result in automatic coadaptation (think pesticide resistance, or the gradual decrease in antibiotic effectiveness). Bedbugs and mosquitoes themselves are far more stimulating for discussion than theory, so one could start with surveys of local pest control and branch outward to see the marvelous similarity between cultures worldwide in terms of the regionally specific pests they combat. Termite exterminators are employed on every continent, and according to their websites they all drive panel trucks! For a simulation, consider raising the issue of the cultural meaning of 'pests.' An example from Australia involving a plan to reduce a water buffalo herd believed to be a vector of tuberculosis and brucellosis met strong resistance from indigenous populations who saw the buffalo in a very different light (Robinson & Whitehead, 2003). In the US context, game management might be easier to simulate and promote the same interaction of different cultural views. And, while otherwise little is said directly about agriculture in this book, the combating of agricultural pests can be a place where a foothold for discussion of the larger cultural issues surrounding agriculture, society, and sustainability can be established.

REFERENCES AND SUGGESTED READINGS

Henrich, J. (2011, November). A cultural species: How culture drove human evolution. *APA Psychological Science Agenda* (online resource). Retrieved from www.apa.org/science/about/psa/2011/11/human-evolution.aspx [Accessed July 14, 2017].

Robinson, C. J., & Whitehead, P. (2003). Cross-cultural management of pest animal damage: a case study of feral buffalo control in Australia's Kakadu National Park. *Environmental Management, 32*(4), 445–458. Retrieved from www.ncbi.nlm.nih.gov/pubmed/14986894 [Accessed July 14, 2017].

Unsworth, J. (2010). History of pesticide use. *IUPAC (International Union of Pure and Applied Chemistry) website: Agrochemicals* (online). Retrieved from http://agrochemicals.iupac.org/index.php?option=com_sobi2&sobi2Task=sobi2Details&catid=3&sobi2Id=31 [Accessed July 14, 2017].

USDA. (2009). What is cultural pest control? *Extension* (online publication of the USDA/NIFA Cooperative Extension) (online resource). Retrieved from http://articles.extension.org/pages/43672/what-is-cultural-pest-control [Accessed July 14, 2017].

Cross-references: Regional and Indigenous Culture, Disaster and War; Sustainability and Population

PETS

This entry and its recommendations focus specifically on animals as pets in contrast to animals considered in other ways, treated earlier in this section. Domestication of animals evolved to animals kept solely for their value as companions. This change of function is explained, psychologically, in terms of animals being recognized for their emotional connection, valued as sources of unconditional positive regard or solace, and even accepted as family members (McConnell, Lloyd, & Buchanan, 2016). Some have even held that animals may be important adjuncts in psychotherapy, but according to stringent research this may be overstating the case (see e.g., Lilienfeld & Arkowitz, 2008). Only very recently has an effort been made to summarize the cross-cultural presence of pets. Gray and Young (2011), using a probability sample drawn from the Human Relations Area Files (HRAF, Yale University), accessed a great deal of detailed information about the presence, treatment (including living conditions and feeding), and ultimate disposition of pets and presented it in tabular form. Dogs, cats, and birds are, not surprisingly, the most commonly kept pets worldwide, ever more frequently since they take up less room in a world under pressure of population increase and land loss (horses, for instance, need much more room). Pets are also a marker of economic advance. Formerly the privilege of the rich in mostly European settings, pets, especially dogs, now accompany the rapid reconfiguration of Chinese society into a heavily urbanized one. Gray and Young also note many anthropologically interesting pet sidelights such as human breastfeeding of dogs and the relation of dogs and cats to the spirit world.

Exposition, Confrontation, and Simulation

Oddly, Gray and Young (2011) do not tabulate fish as pets, although their presence is widespread in US culture (any Walmart has a bank of fish tanks in its pet section). Discussion might focus not only on this omission but on the vagaries of using a large database containing an indiscriminate mix of very old and very modern data as an information source. Another line of discussion might focus on the enculturation of certain types of pets (e.g., very small ornamental dogs in specific urban neighborhoods; particularly aggressive breeds favored by similarly aggressive people; or the personality characteristics of individuals who might keep armadillos or wallabies as pets). The question of the emotional connection between pets and humans might be introduced in context with the question of eating cats and dogs, considered both by Gray and Young and also by Podberscek (2009). A mordant simulation might involve re-creating the situation faced by Victor Klemperer, a scholar-professor who survived the period 1933 through 1945 as an assimilated (he thought) Jew in Dresden, Germany, keeping a diary of his successive stages of dehumanization. In May, 1942, he tragically decided that he would euthanize his and his wife's pet cat, since it would no longer be allowed to have any official food rations (Klemperer, 1942/1995). This could be a springboard for discussion not only of the human–pet bond but also of the particular inhumanity of the Nazi *Kultur* of that time (Mosse, 2003). Klemperer's ordeal, as described in his diaries, has also been adapted as a full-length play (Bartenieff & Malpede, n.d.).

REFERENCES AND SUGGESTED READINGS

Bartenieff, G., & Malpede, K. (n.d.). *I will bear witness: The diaries of Victor Klemperer.* Stage play, adapted from the nonfiction work of the same title. Brooklyn, NY: Theatre Three Collaborative. Retrieved from http://theaterthreecollaborative.org/theater-three-collaborative/

Gray, P. B., & Young, S. M. (2011). Human-pet dynamics in cross-cultural perspective. *Anthrozoös, 24*(1), 17–30.

Klemperer, V. (2001). *I will bear witness 1942–1945: A diary of the Nazi years.* New York: Modern Library.

Lilienfeld, S., & Arkowitz, H. (2008, June 1). Is animal assisted therapy really the cat's meow? *Scientific American Mind* (online). Retrieved from www.scientificamerican.com/article/is-animal-assisted-therapy/ [Accessed July 11, 2017].

McConnell, A. R., Lloyd, E. P., & Buchanan, T. M. (2016). Animals as friends: Social psychological implications of human-pet relationships. In M. Hojjat & A. Moyer (Eds.), *Psychology of friendship* (pp. 157–174). New York: Oxford University Press.

Mosse, G. L. (2003). *Nazi culture: Intellectual, cultural, and social life in the Third Reich.* Madison, WI: University of Wisconsin Press. (Originally published 1966).

Podberscek, A. L. (2009). Good to pet and eat: The keeping and consuming of dogs and cats in South Korea. *Journal of Social Issues, 65*(3), 615–632.

Cross-reference: Animals

ROBOT CULTURE

Though named *robots* only comparatively recently, mechanical stand-ins for humans have existed for millennia. Currently, robots are used extensively in surgery and are proving superior to humans in this domain (Strickland, 2016), similar to the way in which computer chess programs have outstripped human brain power (Baraniuk, 2015). More that 10 years ago Sherry Turkle (2006) explicitly named the developing relation between humans and humanoid machines "cultural,'" and since that time robotic companionship has extended from robotic pets and conversing heads to robotic elder-caregivers to robotic sex (Sharkey, van Wynsberghe, Robbins, & Hancock, 2017). Robots plus humans are evolving a worldwide superculture as previously labor-intensive complex tasks are progressively automated (Bradsher, 2017). Even psychotherapy (Costescu, Vanderborght, & David, 2014) may involve robotic components.

Exposition, Confrontation, and Simulation

Two approaches follow, the first conceptual. Historian of science Sophia Roosth (2015) suggests that designing synthetic biological systems ultimately reveals new biological knowledge: the synthetic precedes the actual. Consider a robot that is programmable to simulate any conversation with any human. Should this robot be programmed to reflect a particular cultural origin and membership? If so, which culture—and what elements would need to be included? If not, why should (or could) this not be done? The second is practical. An object that might be more available in teaching settings in the next few years would be a 3-D printer. The printer could be set up to produce a product that is or could be currently produced in a manufacturing facility involved in injection molding. The steps of injection molding, which itself is dependent on several machines similar in complexity to the printer, can be detailed and the number of individual machine tenders reduced ad lib depending on the number of steps selected. It's recommended to choose a site from a company in China or India (e.g., AcoMold, 2017). It would also help to synergize with individuals in computer science and robotics. A clunkier but just as effective demo could involve setting up a dramatized assembly line for folding charity T-shirts as described in this book's introduction. Removal of individuals from the line based on randomized assignment of steps to a machine could physically dramatize the number of individuals who would be inactive. Inactivity, as Daniel Lieberman says, is a natural condition, a result of a built-in drive toward entropic stasis or, in evolutionary terms, a necessary tendency to rest after hunting and gathering (Itkowitz, 2016). Discussion could move to what might replace work, or what might occupy leisure for individuals with varying capabilities and talents. Maybe, as Bradsher (2017) opines, there will be a proliferation of robot factories that will employ all skilled workers who are displaced by machines. What will a culture without much physical work at all look like? The question of what cannot be automated is a natural offshoot as well: start with commercial fishing (SmartCatch, 2017).

REFERENCES AND SUGGESTED READINGS

AcoMold. (2017). Injection mold making. *AcoMold website* (company website). Retrieved from www.acomold.com/mold-making.html [Accessed July 25, 2017].

Baraniuk, C. (2015, December 4). The cyborg chess players that can't be beaten. *BBC Future* (online magazine). Retrieved from www.bbc.com/future/story/20151201-the-cyborg-chess-players-that-cant-be-beaten [Accessed August 9, 2017].

Bradsher, K. (2017, May 5). A robot revolution, this time in China. *The New York Times Magazine* (online). Retrieved from www.nytimes.com/2017/05/12/business/a-robot-revolution-this-time-in-china.html?_r=0 [Accessed August 9, 2017].

Costescu, C., Vanderborght, B., & David, D. O. (2014). The effects of robot-enhanced psychotherapy: A meta-analysis. *Review of General Psychology, 18*(2), 127–136.

Itkowitz, C. (2016, September 15). This Harvard professor explains why we were born to resist working out. *The Washington Post: Inspired Life* (newspaper, online). Retrieved from www.washingtonpost.com/news/inspired-life/wp/2016/09/15/this-harvard-professor-knows-why-you-skipped-the-gym-this-morning-it-is-natural-and-normal-to-be-physically-lazy/?utm_term=.98a896f0c571 [Accessed July 25, 2017].

Roosth, S. (2015). *Synthetic: How life got made*. Chicago, IL: University of Chicago Press.

Sharkey, N., van Wynsberghe, A., Robbins, S., & Hancock, E. (2017). Our sexual future with robots. *Foundation for Responsible Robotics Consultation Report* (online). Retrieved from http://responsiblerobotics.org/wp-content/uploads/2017/07/FRR-Consultation-Report-Our-Sexual-Future-with-robots_Final.pdf [Accessed August 9, 2017].

SmartCatch. (2017). DigiCatch: Digital catch monitoring system. *SmartCatch website* (commercial site, online). Retrieved from http://smart-catch.com/#catch_cam [Accessed July 25, 2017].

Strickland, E. (2016, May 4). Autonomous robot surgeon bests humans in world first. *IEEE Spectrum* (online magazine). Retrieved from http://spectrum.ieee.org/the-human-os/ robotics/medical-robots/autonomous-robot-surgeon-bests-human-surgeons-in-world- first [Accessed August 9, 2017].

Turkle, S. (2006). A nascent robotics culture: New complicities for companionship. *AAAI Technical Report Series* (online). Retrieved from http://web.mit.edu/~sturkle/www/ nascentroboticsculture.pdf [Accessed July 25, 2017].

Recreation and Sports

GAMBLING: FATE, PLAY, CHANCE, AND LUCK

Although the forms it might take would be different from the familiar casino games, gambling is likely a universal human activity. Games of chance (*alea*) are one part of a universal classification of games offered many years ago by Roger Caillois that still proves practically useful in classifying games both in their substance and purpose (Caillois, 2001; Robison, 2007). Bramham and Wagg (2014), from a leisure studies perspective, cite other anthropological work that suggests that preliterate cultures may engage in games of chance to the extent that beliefs in fate predominate in them (Sutton-Smith & Roberts, 1971; Sutton-Smith, 2001). Though Western-style casino gambling, now considered an 'industry,' has spread its stereotyped and largely automated activities along with its garish tastelessness globally, some measure of primitive superstition remains along with more socially acceptable aspects (i.e., making money) of engaging in what might be otherwise seen as purposeless play (Kim, Ahlgren, Byun, & Malek, 2016). Further evidence for gambling's universality is its resistance to regulation and prohibition. Islam and B. F. Skinner (Knapp, 1997) argue against gambling, both on moral grounds, to little use. Remarkably, horse racing (sans betting) is central to Saudi Arabian culture, while Turkey, though it recently closed the window to horse racing and casino gambling as quickly as it opened it, still maintains, as do other cultures that officially ban gambling, a state lottery.

Exposition, Confrontation, and Simulation

As the complicated title of this entry suggests, discussion could take many directions depending on the interests and tastes of the audience. Examination of play, for instance, could entirely take the place of a focus on gambling if social constraints limit its direct consideration.

Cross-cultural studies of children's play have been widely available for a long time and children's games and toys contain much adaptable material for demonstrations (Edwards, 2000). Possibly an activity could be introduced where locally available toys could be modified to be more culturally universal—or for that matter, how toys available in other cultures could be modified to be more indigenous, rather than representing the average corporate idea of toys: consult Amazon.in, for example, for raw material. For example, the 'Burka Barbie' story could be a focus of discussion. A claim emerged during the past decade that the Mattel Toy Corporation had introduced a 'Burka Barbie' as part of the 50th anniversary of the popular doll. Though this never happened and was debunked, there was at least a germ of truth in the assertion as an Italian artist/designer had clad a Barbie in traditional Islamic dress as part of an exhibit of several hundred differently decorated dolls being offered in a charity auction by the Save The Children foundation (Sandel, 2009). Even though scientific psychological research is based on probabilistic principles and admits to being wrong 5 percent of the time or less, theoretical accounts of fate, luck, and fortune per se, although they have been adduced as topics in the field (Adler & Gielen, 2001), are mostly absent from current US and related psychology. One way to enter this area directly would be to consider Albert Bandura's view on the role of chance in life direction (Bandura, 1982). Other paths might be derived from the literature on cross-cultural cognitive differences. These can include differences in probability estimation and their relation to logical vs. holistic modes of thought (Lechuga & Wiebe, 2011), or differences in susceptibility to common statistical errors related to gambling (Ji, McGeorge, Li, Lee, & Zhang, 2015). Simulation or replication of experiments in this domain could be attempted. In this connection it may be interesting to think how cultures that are "anumeric" (Everett, 2017) participate in games of chance, or understand probability. With regard to familiar US games of chance, the specific insights of Arthur Reber on gambling should not be ignored. Reber, by turns cognitive psychologist and expert poker player and horse handicapper, has written extensively on the ways in which gambling and cognition interact (Reber, 2012).

Turning to gambling itself, surveys could be conducted to see how far, for instance, Peter Gray's observation of the over-representation of young males among gambling populations (Gray, 2004) or the observation of cross-cultural gender differences in risk perception (Lam, 2015) matches the local population. Games can be played without betting to get a feel for the cognitive and social aspects that, alongside with avarice, propel players. Poker is easy to set up and learn, while Mah-Jongg is a little more complicated; both and more are available online. Edgier approaches to interaction around this topic could involve examination and comparison of online gambling options, the preferred escape for those gamblers who are residents of cultures officially banning betting, for instance China. Mention of these here does not constitute an endorsement! However, some searching in this area could lay the foundation for a better appreciation of clandestine markets worldwide as well as for the profusion of culturally related games (Pearson, 2016).

REFERENCES AND SUGGESTED READINGS

Adler, L. L., & Gielen, U. P. (Eds.) (2001). *Cross-cultural topics in psychology*. New York: Greenwood.

Bandura, A. (1982). The psychology of chance encounters and life paths. *American Psychologist, 37,* 747–755.

Bramham, P., & Wagg, S. (2014). *An introduction to leisure studies*. London: Sage.

Caillois, R. (2001). *Man, play, and games*. Champaign, IL: University of Illinois Press. (Originally published in French, 1958).

Edwards, C. P. (2000). Children's play in cross-cultural perspective: A new look at the Six Cultures Study. *Cross-Cultural Research, 34*(4), 318–338.

Everett, C. (2017, April 25). 'Anumeric' people: What happens when a language has no words for numbers? *The Conversation* (online magazine). Retrieved from http://theconversation.com/anumeric-people-what-happens-when-a-language-has-no-words-for-numbers-75828 [Accessed September 1, 2017].

Gray, P. (2004). Evolutionary and cross-cultural perspectives on gambling. *Journal of Gambling Studies, 20*(4), 347–371.

Ji, L-J., McGeorge, K., Li, Y., Lee, A., & Zhang, Z. (2015). Culture and gambling fallacies. *Springerplus* (online) 4, 510. doi:10.1186/s40064-015-1290-2. Retrieved from www.ncbi.nlm.nih.gov/pmc/articles/PMC4573969/ [Accessed September 1, 2017].

Kim, J., Ahlgren, M. B., Byun, J-W., & Malek, K. (2016). Gambling motivations and superstitious beliefs: A cross cultural study with casino customers. *International Gambling Studies, 16*(2), 296–315.

Knapp, T. (1997). Behaviorism and public policy: B. F. Skinner's views on gambling. *Behavior and Social Issues, 7*(2), 129–139.

Lam, D. (2015). Gender differences in risk aversion among Chinese university students. *Journal of Gambling Studies, 31*(4), 1405–1415.

Lechuga, J., & Wiebe, J. S. (2011). Culture and probability judgment accuracy: The influence of holistic reasoning. *Journal of Cross Cultural Psychology, 42*(6), 1054–1065.

Pearson, S. (2016, September 5). Brazil hopes gambling will reverse its fortunes. *Financial Times* (online newspaper). Retrieved from www.ft.com/content/646bac98-6d72-11e6-a0c9-1365ce54b926 [Accessed September 1, 2017].

Reber, A. (2012). *Poker, life, and other confusing things.* Pittsburgh, PA: ConJelCo.

Robison, A. (2007, Fall). *Course materials for CMS.600/CMS.998, Videogame theory and analysis.* MIT OpenCourseWare, Massachusetts Institute of Technology (online). Retrieved from https://ocw.mit.edu/courses/comparative-media-studies-writing/cms-600-videogame-theory-and-analysis-fall-2007/projects/w1.pdf [Accessed September 1, 2017].

Sandel, A. (2009, December 10). Muslim world: Barbie's 50th anniversary Islamic makeover. *The Los Angeles Times: Babylon and Beyond Blog* (online newspaper) Retrieved from http://latimesblogs.latimes.com/babylonbeyond/2009/12/arab-world-burka-barbie-iconic-doll-gets-an-islamic-makeover-for-50th-anniversary.html [Accessed March 31, 2018].

Sutton-Smith, B. (2001). *The ambiguity of play.* Cambridge, MA: Harvard University Press.

Sutton-Smith, B., & Roberts, J. M. (1971). The cross-cultural and psychological study of games. *International Review of Sport Sociology, 6,* 79–87.

Cross-references: Insurance: Risk and Future Time Orientation; Religion and Law

PHYSICAL TOUGHNESS, ENDURANCE, AND RESILIENCE

Cultures, it is true, survive in their records, their institutions, and their practices, whether these are explicitly recorded (as in texts or artistic creations) or implicit in daily activities. Not always noticed, though essential to cultures, is the hardiness of their members and their resistance to the many dangers and threats that cultures face. When conditions become tough, humans have to become tougher. History records many events of survival that seem miraculous. For one instance, during the 1941–1943 siege of Leningrad (now again St. Petersburg, Russia), every conceivable thing that could be eaten, and many things that were thought impossible to eat, were consumed in the interests of bare existence (Salisbury, 2003). One way that cultures have acknowledged this need to develop the strength to survive is in their development of contests of physical stamina and endurance. These are often embodied across cultures in sporting events of long duration in inhospitable conditions, for instance long distance races (Pierce, Stillner, & Popkin, 1982) or in shorter bursts, as in the yearly dips of members of 'polar bear' clubs (Weisberger, 2016). Other ways in which this need is expressed involve the ritualization of challenge and toughness in adolescent initiations (Warner, 2013) as well as other professional initiations like military boot camps and medical school training. (Bullying may be a darker side of this impulse toward toughening.) An outward reflection of the value placed on physical heroics is the veneration of soldiers, police, and firefighters (for an example outside of Western and Northern European culture and its derivatives, where such admiration is common, see Batdorff, n.d.). Connected to this is the cultural prominence of sports involving intense physical contact or prolonged exertion, ranging from US football to Japanese *keirin* (Glasscock, 2015). Exercise training for endurance is common and not without drawbacks, including possible decreases in male libido (Hackney, Lane, Register-Mihalik, & O'Leary, 2017). Individual endurance is also tested throughout the lifespan by disease: the strongest, both physically and socially, survive longest (Surbone & Halpern, 2016). The focus here so far has been on strictly physical aspects of endurance, but mental endurance is equally important. Patience and resilience are necessary internal dispositions for endurance. Patience is said to be a difficult cross-cultural achievement (Hudson, 2016), and in time-driven Western cultures it is often in short supply. Resilience, the ability to take shocks and rebound, is an important protective factor against stress and mental illness across cultures (Ungar, 2005).

Exposition, Confrontation, and Simulation

There is a substantial literature on survival training and physical endurance boosting in physical education, sports medicine, and other related fields that can be consulted for examples of exercise that can be undertaken (or at least admired) individually or collectively in the instructional setting. Websites of the various armed services worldwide offer at least minimal information about the basic physical requirements necessary for induction and retention. Seek out veterans for actual details. Inventory the favorite contact sports and subdivide by participant, observer, or both. A brief simulation of a marathon—if only lining up for one—or of exposure to the cold can be a fulcrum for exploration. Initiation experiences can be collected and shared: these need not be violent or painful ones (although it could be argued that even beautiful ceremonies such as the *quinceañera* are preparation for strenuous adult roles such as marriage, childbearing, and work). Medical survivorship stories are virtually universal and another point of entry into discussion of endurance. Patience scales (e.g., Schnitker, 2012) may be located, obtained, completed, and discussed with reference to the local and the extended environment. For those less patient, Vischer et al. (2013) offer an ultra-short version. The concept of patience can be related to the question of medical survivorship as well as medical care rationing by linking it to wait times for cancer care (for example) and seeking out comparative data across cultures (Elit, 2015). Several resilience scales are available, and some cross-cultural validation data is available on these. A very short (two-question!) resilience scale that can be easily employed for illustration and discussion is embedded in the text of Vaishnavi, Connor, and Davidson (2007).

REFERENCES AND SUGGESTED READINGS

Batdorff, E. (n.d.). The bomberos of Guatemala City. *Shatter the Looking Glass* (online travel magazine). Retrieved from www.shatterthelookingglass.com/the-bomberos-of-guatemala-city/ [Accessed September 29, 2017].

Elit, L. (2015). Wait times from diagnosis to treatment in cancer. *Journal of Gynecologic Oncology, 26*(4), 246–248.

Glasscock, T. (2015, December 4). Inside the wild world of *keirin,* Japan's brake-free bicycle racing. *Wired* (online magazine). Retrieved from www.wired.com/2015/12/jasper-clarke-inside-the-fast-paced-world-of-japanese-keirin/ [Accessed September 29, 2017].

Hackney, A. C., Lane, A. R., Register-Mihalik, J., & O'Leary, C. B. (2017). Endurance exercise training and male sexual libido. *Medical Science of Sports and Exercise, 49*(7), 1383–1388.

Hudson, V. F. (2016, April 27). Patience across cultures: The power of observation and planning. *High Road Global Services Blog* (online). Retrieved from www.highroaders.com/blog/patience-across-cultures-the-power-of-observation-and-planning/ [Accessed September 29, 2017].

Pierce, C. M., Stillner, V., & Popkin, M. (1982). On the meaning of sports: Cross cultural observations of super stress. *Culture, Medicine, & Psychiatry, 6*(1), 11–28.

Salisbury, H. (2003). *The 900 days: The siege of Leningrad* (2nd ed.). Boston, MA: Da Capo Press.

Schnitker, S. A. (2012). An examination of patience and well-being. *The Journal of Positive Psychology, 7*(4), 263–280.

Surbone, A., & Halpern, M. T. (2016). Unequal cancer survivorship care: Addressing cultural and sociodemographic disparities in the clinic. *Supportive Care in Cancer, 24*(12), 4831–4833.

Ungar, M. (2005). Introduction: resilience across cultures and contexts. In M. Ungar (Ed.), *Handbook for working with children and youth: pathways to resilience across cultures and contexts* (pp. xv–xxxix). Thousand Oaks, CA: Sage.

Vaishnavi, S., Connor, K., & Davidson, J. R. T. (2007). An abbreviated version of the Connor-Davidson Resilience Scale (CD-RISC), the CD-RISC2: Psychometric properties and applications in psychopharmacological trials. *Psychiatry Research, 152*(2–3), 293–297.

Vischer, T., Dohmen, T., Falk, A., Huffman, D., Schupp, J., Sunde, U., & Wagner, G. G. (2013). Validating an ultra-short survey measure of patience. *Economics Letters, 120*(2), 142–145.

Warner, G. (2013, November 1). How one Kenyan tribe produces the world's best runners. *NPR (National Public Radio) Parallels* (radio broadcast transcript) (online). Retrieved from www.npr.org/sections/parallels/2013/11/01/241895965/how-one-kenyan-tribe-produces-the-worlds-best-runners [Accessed September 29, 2017].

Weisberger, M. (2016, January 1). Everybody freeze! The science of the Polar Bear Club. *Scientific American LiveScience* (online magazine). Retrieved from www.scientificamerican.com/article/everybody-freeze-the-science-of-the-polar-bear-club/ [Accessed September 29, 2017].

Cross-references: Disaster and War; Young and Old

SPORTS AND SPECTATORS

Spectator sports were known in ancient China (Crowther, 2007): now they are a modern industry. Sports and games are conceptually related in that they both are rule-governed and competitive, and both may be played individually or in teams. Perhaps the only difference is that sports involve more of the body and may also be more physically demanding and dangerous (see the Physical Toughness, Endurance, and Resilience entry in this book). Sports participation and performance have attracted psychological interest for more than a century (Green & Benjamin, 2009) and have their own division in the American Psychological Association (Division 47). Recently, sports has garnered attention from evolutionary psychological theorists who see in sports the outlines of processes of mate selection (Apostolou, 2015). Sports has been a pivotal force in bringing cultures and groups together. Jackie Robinson's signing a major league baseball contract in 1947 delivered a stinging blow to racial segregation in the United States, while Muhammad Ali, the US heavyweight boxing champion, became the public face of challenges to Anglo domination of all aspects of American culture. Internationally, the modern Olympic games have served as symbolic arenas for acting out cultural conflict. The triumph of Jesse Owens in the Berlin Olympics of 1936, the defiance of Black athletes at the Mexico City games in 1968, and the tragedy of terrorism at the Munich games in 1972 are among the most visible images of intercultural tragedy and triumph. Sports has come to reflect globalization: the European Union has taken the integration of sports and migration seriously for some time (Gasparini & Cometti, 2010). Some sports have come to dominate and identify cultures (soccer in Brazil, for instance), but global expansion of sports has resulted in situations such as new soccer teams in China being populated by Brazilian stars bought up for the purpose (MacKenna, 2016). Mangan and Hong (2013) describes the ways in which the Beijing Olympics in 2008 set the stage for China's ascent to modern superpower status.

Sports is just one of many cultural events that draw spectators. Spectators may seem like a passive background to the event (except for their noise), but theories of spectatorship, mostly emerging from film and theatre studies but applicable to sports as well (Kennedy, 2001), postulate that sports spectators are deeply psychologically engaged with what they watch. Their often strident loyalty to particular sports and teams puts them on a par with opera fans and other high-culture partisans. Sports spectatorship has been a means of examining selective attention related to prejudice (Hastorf & Cantril, 1954). Recent studies have examined different motivations for sports spectatorship across cultures. While collectivist cultures might emphasize community, family bonding, and team attachment in distinction to individualist cultures' focus on individual performance and pleasure as motivations for attending sports events, there may be more sharing of these motivations than expected (Han, Mahony, & Greenwell, 2010). However, as evolutionary theories predict, there is a persistent sex difference across cultures in terms of who watches sports: men predominate (Bailish, Deaner, Rainham, & Blanchard, 2016).

Exposition, Confrontation, and Simulation

Access pre- and post-game interviews from different regions (for instance, interviews with cricketers from Pakistan) and compare across regions. Also compare the commentators at the Metropolitan Opera in New York, who also conduct play-by-play synopses and fan interviews at the intermissions. Sports, because of the diversity of its participants, especially in college settings, is a natural place for confronting issues of exclusion and privilege. Starting in the United States, construct a discussion around the acculturation issues raised in Anthony Kontos's (2009) contribution to the essential collection of studies of athletics and culture worldwide, *Cultural Sport Psychology* (Schinke & Hanrahan, 2009). Adopt a soccer or cricket team from another culture and follow its fortunes in the online standings (avoid betting!). Set up a test of sex discrimination as practiced by male fans hearing female sports announcers (Dicaro, 2017): see if this extends to commentary delivered in other languages. Examine the ways in which sports are globalizing, leading to crossing of new boundaries: view the video account of girls boxing in Pakistan (Popalzai, Shastri, & Thomas, 2017) and discuss.

REFERENCES AND SUGGESTED READINGS

Apostolou, M. (2015). The athlete and the spectator inside the man: A cross-cultural investigation of the evolutionary origins of athletic behavior. *Cross-Cultural Research, 49*(2), 151–173.

Bailish, S., Deaner, R. O., Rainham, D., & Blanchard, D. (2016). Sex differences in sport remain when accounting for countries' gender inequality. *Cross-Cultural Research, 50*(5), 395–414.

Crowther, N. (2007). *Sport in ancient times.* New York: Greenwood Publishing Company.

Dicaro, J. (2017, September 18). Safest bet in sports: Men complaining about a female announcer's voice. *The New York Times* (online newspaper). Retrieved from www.nytimes.com/2017/09/18/sports/nfl-beth-mowins-julie-dicaro.html [Accessed September 23, 2017].

Gasparini, W., & Cometti, A. (Eds.) (2010). *Sport facing the test of cultural diversity.* Strasbourg, France: Council of Europe Publishing (online). Retrieved from www.coe.int/t/DG4/EPAS/resources/6718%20Sport%2facing%20cultural%20diversity%20 assemble.pdf [Accessed September 23, 2017].

Green, C. D., & Benjamin, L. T. Jr. (2009). *Psychology gets in the game: Sport, mind, and behavior, 1880–1960.* Lincoln, NE: University of Nebraska Press.

Han, D., Mahony, D., & Greenwell, T. C. (2010). A cross-cultural approach for understanding motivation differences between Korean and American sports fans. *2010 North American Society for Sport Management Conference* (Marketing Abstract 2010–103) (online). Retrieved from www.nassm.org/files/conf_abstracts/2010-103.pdf [Accessed September 22, 2017].

Hastorf, A. H., & Cantril, H. (1954). They saw a game: A case study. *Journal of Abnormal Psychology, 49*(1), 129–134.

Kennedy, D. (2001). Sports and shows: Spectators in contemporary culture. *Theatre Research International, 26*(3), 277–284.

Kontos, A. (2009). Multicultural sport psychology in the United States. In R. Schinke & S. J. Hanrahan (Eds.), *Cultural sport psychology* (pp. 103–116). Champaign, IL: Human Kinetics.

MacKenna, E. (2016, February 1). China is latest destination for Brazilian stars. *The New York Times* (online newspaper). Retrieved from www.nytimes.com/2016/02/02/sports/soccer/in-the-brazilian-soccer-market-the-buyers-are-now-chinese.html?mcubz=3 [Accessed September 23, 2017].

Mangan, J. A., & Hong, F. (Eds.). *Post-Beijing 2008: Geopolitics, sport, and the Pacific Rim.* New York: Routledge.

Popalzai, S., Shastri, V., & Thomas, J. (2017). Punch with Pakistani girls at a Karachi boxing club. *The New York Times* (*Daily 360* video feature, online). Retrieved from www.nytimes.com/video/world/asia/100000005030850/pakistani-girls-at-a-karachi-boxing-club.html [Accessed September 23, 2017].

Schinke, R., & Hanrahan, S. J. (Eds.) (2009). *Cultural sport psychology*. Champaign, IL: Human Kinetics.

Cross-references: Physical Toughness, Endurance, and Resilience

TOURISM

Cross-cultural psychologists and students of culture generally are warned away from tourism. Tourism can exploit, expropriate, and damage both the physical and human aspects of the toured culture. Also, tourism, while it is a form of exploration, may lead rapidly to a focus on superficiality and the satisfaction of immediate needs and, in turn, the expectation of conditions similar to one's own culture in a new place. (Think of the passenger ensconced in the interior of a 12-story cruise ship, or, in more prosaic surroundings, the camper in a 38-foot fifth wheel parked at a rustic site.) International tourists are said to focus primarily on the following aspects of a new culture: housing, transportation, arts, language, food, media, currency, leisure activities, and, lastly, the indigenous population (Funk & Brun, 2007). But while these are essential elements of knowledge for understanding and adjusting to any culture, they are also just the aspects on which information can be most quickly garnered at a hotel kiosk. Indeed, one prevalent perspective of tourism is to view it in strongly commercial terms, an activity in which hosts accommodate to the national cultural characteristics of the visitor (Reisinger, 2011). Organized, marketed tours are commodified 'packages' that focus on profit and efficiency and demand a acquiescent and usually underpaid labor force on the part of the host culture. Even the best-intentioned tourism, similar to well-crafted exchange experiences, hardly can offer the kind of extended contact and intimate interaction with a host culture that long-term residence can afford. The word *afford* also leads to another objection to tourism: usually, tourism is a privilege of the monied elites of all cultures, and is a way to further increase social and cultural distance between the visitors and the visited. Even if international travel is out of the question (though it becomes more affordable and accessible all the time), the negative effects of 'being a tourist' can occur in local and regional settings as well. An opportunity for touring is also one of many short-term points of contact between cultures, and some of psychology's most eminent figures—most prominent among them Sigmund Freud—were also among its most enthusiastic tourists (Kennedy, 2007).

Exposition, Confrontation, and Simulation

Over the past several decades, much effort has gone into trying to establish the grounds for responsible, ethical tourism that respects and elevates indigenous cultures while also informing and reducing prejudices in the visitor. Suggestions for better practice range from basic and practical, like dressing similar to locals (see e.g., Walsh, n.d.), to the seriously spiritual and ethical (McCormick, 2004). Planning a responsible tourist's itinerary seems like a natural activity to focus attention both on the essentials of tourism as well as on mitigation of its ill effects. There are many sites devoted to sustainable and ethical tourism (e.g., the self-contained module from UNESCO; Fien, Calder, & White, n.d.). Taking cues from these, plan trips of varying durations, local, regional, and international, to provide maximum advantage for tourists and hosts. As a variation on this, design a manual for tour guides to use that will assist them in informing visitors about important aspects of the host culture that are visible only to the initiated.

REFERENCES AND SUGGESTED READINGS

Fien, J., Calder, M., & White, C. (n.d.). Sustainable tourism. *UNESCO TSLF (Teaching and Learning for a Sustainable Future) website* (online). Retrieved from www.unesco.org/education/tlsf/mods/theme_c/mod16.html [Accessed October 9, 2017].

Funk, D. C., & Brun, C. J. (2007). The role of socio-psychological and culture-education motives in marketing international sport tourism: A cross-cultural perspective. *Tourism Management, 28*(3), 806–819.

Kennedy, M. (2007, March 20). Dreaming of the seaside: Freud's travel letters tell of happy days in Blackpool. *The Guardian* (online newspaper). Retrieved from www.theguardian.com/news/2007/mar/21/topstories3.science [Accessed October 9, 2017].

McCormick, T. (2004). The good sojourner: Third World tourism and the call of hospitality. *Journal of the Society of Christian Ethics, 24*(1), 89–104.

Reisinger, Y. (2011). *International tourism: Cultures and behavior.* New York: Routledge.

Walsh, K. (n.d.). Differences between a tourist and a traveller. *USA Today Travel* (online newspaper). Retrieved from http://traveltips.usatoday.com/differences-between-tourist-traveller-103756.html [Accessed October 9, 2017].

Cross-references: Immigration and Refugees; Sustainability and Population; Fuel

INDEX